Leisure and Aging

Ulyssean Living in Later Life

Francis A. McGuire

Rosangela K. Boyd

Raymond E. Tedrick

Sagamore Publishing
Champaign, IL

Interior Design: Michelle Summers
Cover Design: Todd Lauer

ISBN: 1-57167-379-2
Library of Congress Card Number: 99-68907

www.sagamorepub.com

Printed in the United States

Contents

Acknowledgments

We are indebted to our students who have helped form and solidify many of the ideas in this book. We would also like to acknowledge the contributions of Dr. John Kelly and Dr. Kathleen Halberg, who were involved in earlier efforts to write this book. Dr. Joe Bannon refused to let us not finish this project and we thank him for that. Finally, we appreciate the efforts of Susan McKinney, production manager, who displayed just the right mix of patience and persistence necessary for bringing this project to fruition.

Introduction

We are in the midst of the graying of America. There are more people over the age of 65 than there have ever been, and this trend will continue well into the future. This cadre of older individuals is unlike any seen before. They are generally healthier, more financially secure, and more independent than previous cohorts. In addition, they are probably more visible and vocal than previous groups of older individuals. In fact, it is impossible to watch the news, walk into a grocery store, or board an airplane without coming into contact with older individuals.

However, the increasing presence of elderly people in our society has not necessarily resulted in a deeper understanding of this group. Certainly, the work of gerontologists has cleared up many misconceptions of older people and the aging process. We know more about the mechanisms of aging, physical as well as social, than at any time in history. Our knowledge base is expanding every year. Unfortunately, many have not received these messages. An archaic view of aging still is firmly entrenched in our society. It is viewed as a time of loss and decline with little hope for the future. In fact, to speak about the future and old age together will strike many as ludicrous. What is the future in aging within this perspective? At best, stability for as long as possible at worst, death after confinement to a long-term care facility. Unfortunately, our misguided images often interfere with our ability to effectively work with this population.

Several years ago, there was a popular book entitled *All I Really Need to Know I Learned in Kindergarten,* which purported to identify life's most important lessons. The author's thesis was that many of these lessons were learned early in life. A similar compartmentalizing of life into periods of appropriateness appears to extend into other areas. There is a time to learn and a time to earn, a time to grow and a time to fade away. The result of this perspective has been the placing of limits on the later years. Individuals who break out of this mold are viewed as media marvels meriting special attention. For example, June inevitably brings stories of septuagenarians graduating from college, December stories typically include pieces on extremely active older volunteers, and in April the media celebrates individuals who have achieved athletic milestones later in life. The focus of these stories is the remarkable ability to accomplish these things in spite of being old. We view this perspective as inappropriate. People do not do things in spite of being old. Rather, they achieve success because of who they are. Being old should not be viewed as a handicap to accomplishing anything. In fact, the most difficult thing many people face in reaching their goals is a resistant society that places obstacles in the way of many older people and prohibits them from reaching their potential.

A major concern of gerontologists is the quality of life of older individuals. The role of activities in enhancing later life is often examined as part of this concern. The use of leisure, simply defined as freely chosen activities, to fill time and replace what has been lost through retirement appears to be an important element in the quality of life. However, this perspective on activities fails to acknowledge the powerful force they can be. Rather than being merely a substitute for what has been lost, leisure can provide new pathways to growth and development. People who select this approach are not unusual or overachievers. They are instead individuals dedicated to living. We have adopted the term "Ulyssean" from McLeish (1976) to describe this approach. The Ulyssean approach varies. It does not imply anything about the quantity of activities. It does, however, require a willingness to be open to new ideas and opportunities. The perspective is built upon the belief that each year of life provides occasions for renewal as well as growth. These opportunities can be enhanced by trained professionals who are able to assist older individuals in using leisure to contribute to the quality of life.

This book is designed to help identify ways leisure can contribute to later life. It links the aging process and leisure to Ulyssean living. This is accomplished in three ways. First, basic information about aging and the aging process is provided. The first five chapters are devoted to helping develop an understanding of what happens as people age. The focus is on social, biological, cognitive, and psychological factors related to aging. The relationship of these factors to Ulyssean living is explored throughout this section. The second part of the book explores leisure and its role in later life. Chapters 6 through 9 are designed to increase knowledge of the place of leisure in the later years, with particular attention paid to the Ulyssean approach. The final section of the book examines the environments where aging occurs. Community as well as institutional settings are discussed as we detail the relationship of the environment to the quality of life.

One caution is needed at this point. The assumption in many parks and recreation curricula seems to be that aging is the purview of therapeutic recreation programs. Students who are interested in working with older individuals are seen as needing a therapeutic recreation emphasis to be effective professionals. That perspective is not shared by the authors of this book. Certainly, there are subgroups within the aging population who do need therapeutic intervention. There are older adults with mental health problems, developmental disabilities, and cognitive and physical impairments. Although this book includes material related to these groups, the focus is not on these special populations. Rather, the intent is to provide an overview of the aging process and its relationship to leisure. Further study is clearly needed if the reader's interest is in working with subgroups of elderly.

Chapter 1

◆

The Aging Journey

This book is about two misunderstood concepts: aging and leisure. Aging is typically viewed as a largely undesirable period of life during which a series of physical, cognitive, social, and emotional declines occur. Leisure is often seen as somewhat frivolous and certainly secondary to the more serious business of life. The authors of this book disagree with both perspectives. In fact, we view aging as a natural part of the life cycle, accompanied by advantages as well as losses. Leisure is a primary realm of behavior during which great personal growth and development can occur. This book is about the joining of these two forces.

As a culture, we have tended to perceive old age as a time set apart from the rest of life. To many it has been seen as a problem, and older individuals are sometimes viewed as part of the problem. They may be viewed as individuals whose time has come and gone and who have now moved to the fringe of society.

This perception of social uselessness has frequently been accompanied by personal hopelessness. Decisions are made for people solely on the basis of age. Some believe that the life of the individual ends at 65, when a period of less than full life begins. This attitude is manifested in recreation programs that are designed to help the elderly fill their empty hours and keep them busy until death. Time is viewed as the enemy, and activities are viewed as a weapon to fight it. Fortunately, this outdated perception is changing.

As a result of the growth of gerontology, the study of old age, and an increased awareness of aging, we have come to realize that old age is not a period of problems, unhappiness, and decline. In fact, we now know there is really no such thing as a well-defined period of life that is appropriately labeled "old age." The reality is that later life is a time of opportunity, growth, and happiness for many. Therefore, individuals involved in service delivery to this group must understand aging, the aging process, and leisure from a broad, non-stereotypic perspective. As in all cases of ignorance and prejudice, education is the tool of the informed. There is a responsibility to learn to help older individuals be all they can be.

Most older individuals are not daring or heroic. Rather, they lead simple lives marked by success and failure, continuity and change. There is no such thing as the typical older person. As you read this book, look around you. You may be surrounded by other students. You share at least one characteristic with them: you are all students. Nevertheless, you would probably be unhappy if someone you did not know came along and claimed to know everything she needed to know about you because you are a student. You would even be more unhappy if this person then produced a list of the recreation activities you could participate in and identified them as "appropriate" student activities.

Of course, this would never occur, since we all know students are unique. Similarly, it is not right to label certain activities "senior citizen activities" and base an activity program on them. The purpose of this book is to provide you with accurate information about aging and the aging process. This information should start with the conviction that all individuals, regardless of age, are unique. Increasing age does not eliminate that uniqueness. In fact, it magnifies it.

We are gradually coming to view the advantages of aging as being as real as the disadvantages. One of the advantages that has received little attention is the increase in the amount of unobligated time many individuals have. The authors of this text have conducted many pre-retirement seminars for individuals facing retirement. Inevitably, these programs include sessions on financial planning, health, retirement benefits, and leisure. Just as inevitably, leisure is given the shortest length of time on the program. While each of the other areas may consume a half day or even several days, the session on leisure receives one or two hours on the agenda. This occurs for at least two reasons.

The first is that leisure is not seen as that important. People need fiscal and physical well-being in retirement. Leisure is viewed as secondary to these twin pillars of happiness. The second reason is a perception that leisure will take care of itself. How hard can it be to find something to do with that additional 30 hours per week?

This attitude also appears to pervade the gerontology literature. Relatively little appears in journals such as *The Gerontologist* and *The Journal of Gerontology* pertaining to leisure. In fact, Alexander Comfort's (1976) view of leisure would probably find many supporters today. He wrote, "Leisure is a con." He continued that people "don't need the Coney Island-Retirement Village package which makes them into permanent children; this is good for an afternoon, not for a life-style" (p. 124).

Unfortunately, many leisure professionals have provided unwitting support for Comfort's uncomfortable perspective on leisure. This has resulted from an acceptance of an outdated perspective of old age as a time of loss and decline and a stereotypic view of leisure programs for older people. This text will approach aging from a different perspective and use that perspective to show that leisure is not a con perpetrated upon the elderly, but rather is a potentially powerful force in helping make the later years positive and exhilarating.

A POSITIVE PERSPECTIVE ON AGING

Rowe and Kahn's (1998) groundbreaking book, *Successful Aging*, discusses the failure of gerontologists to incorporate a new, positive view of aging. They wrote, "The progress of gerontology began to stall in the mid-1980s . . . There was a persistent preoccupation with disability, disease, and chronological age, rather than the positive aspects of aging" (p. xi). They believed a conceptual foundation was required to understand aging and all its components. We agree and have provided such a foundation, or unifying concept. <u>Old age is viewed throughout this text as a stage in the lifecourse.</u> It does not stand alone, apart from all that has come before. It is a time of continued growth and development marked by continuity with the past. The model followed in this book views aging as a journey, or series of journeys, rather than as an arrival at a terminal point in the life span. Within this perspective, the increased unobligated time that many individuals experience is not considered a problem but an opportunity. It is an instrument for growth and development.

John McLeish (1976) coined the term "Ulyssean Adult" to identify individuals who continue to seek new adventures and opportunities in their later years. The prototype for such an individual comes from Ulysses, who was over 50 years of age when the adventures described in the Odyssey began and close to 70 when he began his last voyage.

According to McLeish, only death can end the journeys of such an individual. The Ulyssean lifestyle should not be limited to the select few blessed with an extraordinary personality. McLeish wrote, "The Ulyssean life is on some term, in small or large arenas, potentially accessible to all men and women" (p. 31). Indeed, MacLeish stated:

> To gain entry to the country and company of the Ulyssean people no passport is required. No restrictions exist as to race, class, religion, political ideology, or education—just the reverse. The Ulyssean country is an open commonwealth of older adults of every racial group under the sun; its membership includes every degree of wealth and non-wealth, every level of education, every form of belief and non-belief. Membership has nothing to do with whether one is physically well or dogged by ill-health, whether one is personable or plain, well-travelled or confined to a limited area . . . . It is a process, not a state; a process of *becoming,* and great practitioners of the Ulyssean way would certainly describe themselves as voyagers, not inhabitants. (p. 285)

Although MacLeish was using the Ulyssean concept to explain creativity in later life, it also provides a conceptual framework for understanding the potential of leisure in late adulthood. To be Ulyssean is to seek out opportunities for growth. Leisure can provide the arena for development. It can also provide a mechanism for developing the skills needed to approach life with the zest and confidence necessary to Ulyssean living.

A Ulyssean life is possible not only in the later years but may be easier to achieve during that period than at any other point in life. MacLeish believes a "Ulyssean life is possible, and the Ulyssean way is accessible and free, because in many ways the conditions required for the creative life are *more available* in the later years of adulthood than earlier in life (p. 246). Many older Americans have the time, experience, and freedom needed to enter the Ulyssean world. They are released from many roles, such as work and family related, which restrict behavior and limit the opportunity to enter new worlds. Concurrently, many years of experiences provide a plethora of potential paths for Ulyssean journeys.

Dangott and Kalish (1979) supported this belief in the potential for Ulyssean living in the later years. They wrote "the old concept of aging was a downhill path, beginning at age 60 or 50 or even 40 or 30; it implied slow deterioration, accelerating with time. The new concept of aging dispels these grim inaccuracies. Instead of a single downhill path, there can be a network of paths, many going uphill; instead of accelerating deterioration, there can be opportunity for extensive personal growth" (p. 1). Their words are as true today as when they were written. Unfortunately, they have not yet become part of the "conventional wisdom" guiding the delivery of leisure services. Although Dangott and Kalish's belief that aging should be viewed as an opportunity for growth rather than as a period of deterioration was stated approximately 20 years ago, the "old concept" of aging prevails. Rowe and Kahn (1998), directors of the MacArthur Foundation Study of Successful Aging, indicate that the aged are viewed as "sick, demented, frail, weak, disabled, powerless, sexless, passive, alone, unhappy, and unable to learn—in short, a rapidly growing mass of irreversibly ill, irretrievable old Americans" (p. 12).

Calls for a new perspective on aging have been part of the gerontological literature for many years. For example, Prado (1986) called for a perspective change in how aging is viewed. Prado's central thesis is that we retain a view of aging from the era when few people lived past their fifties. This antiquated view of aging sees "the aged as a homogeneous group marked by above-average dependency on others, special economic needs, health problems, and a general decline of competency and productivity" (p. 3).

Prado's new perspective is based on the belief that accumulating data on aging pointing toward the revelations it makes about the positive aspects of aging is not enough to change concepts of later life. A shift, or in Prado's words "a new conceptual matrix," in perspective may be needed to bring about a realization of the richness and diversity of aging. The change requires realization that "certain changes that seem real enough in aging are better thought of as a function of what we *do* than of what we *become*." Recent evidence indicates that much of what had been seen as part of aging is actually the result of disease, disability, inactivity, and lack of exercise.

An emphasis on old age as a time of decline will result in leisure programs based on stereotypic attitudes of what is appropriate for older people and will result in a limited approach to activity provision. Anything that will help pass the time will do.

Activities that are work-like in nature may be helpful, since they are more palatable to retirees than other activities. Nothing too challenging, strenuous, or new should be attempted, and those individuals who break the mold are seen as media marvels. However, if the positive nature of aging and the role leisure can play in personal growth and development are recognized, programs cannot be constricted by ageistic notions of "appropriate" leisure.

Leisure activities are vehicles. They can be ships upon which individuals embark on Ulyssean journeys. Rather than deciding what activities are best suited for people who share a chronological age, leisure service providers must realize that any activity is a useful vehicle for the journey if the participant so decides. The emphasis shifts from the activity to the individual. As a result, the function of the leisure service provider shifts from activity provider to enabler, guide, facilitator. The individual involved in providing leisure services to older people becomes a member of the crew on the Ulyssean journey. The older individual is in control of the ship. Such a perspective is necessary if leisure is to become one of the uphill paths conceptualized by Dangott and Kalish and not a con foisted upon the elderly.

It is important to look at aging realistically. There are losses, primarily physiological, that are concomitants of the aging process. These declines (see Chapter 3) are a natural part of the aging process. However, they are not the entire story. There are many positive aspects that are necessary to understand if aging is to be realistically perceived. It is necessary to separate the myth of aging from the reality. Much of what we "know" about old age is based on long-standing myths and stereotypes. Two aspects of aging, social and demographic, provide an excellent starting point for what will come later in this book. They provide basic information for a context for viewing aging.

SOCIAL ASPECTS OF AGING

When examining the aging process, it is important to consider both individual and environmental factors, since behavior is a consequence of the interaction of a person with his or her physical and social environment. The following sections will address social factors influencing successful aging. Initially, the changes in social roles will be addressed. Secondly, societal responses to aging will be covered. The focus will be on how professionals working with older adults can assist them in coping with negative changes and maintain a sense of well-being during their Ulyssean journey.

CHANGES IN SOCIAL ROLES

In order to understand social roles, it is necessary to recognize that every individual lives in a social context that influences his or her behavior. The process of "socialization," that is, the process through which we absorb values, beliefs, and knowledge that guide our behavior as a member of a social group, is a lifelong one. From a very young age, we are directly or indirectly instructed to behave in ways that conform to the norms created within our social group. We learn to conform as a result of reinforcement or punishment encountered as we interact with other members of the group.

This process also teaches us to assume certain roles. We may carry out a variety of roles, each related to a particular position we occupy in society. For instance, in a family context, we may be parents, siblings, or partners; at work we may be the employee, employer, or co-worker; in the community, we may be a civic leader, a neighbor, or a volunteer. The list varies according to the tasks we carry out. The roles we play are filled with social expectations; it is through a general consistency in behaviors associated with such roles that we are able to establish relationship patterns with one another.

How do social norms and roles change as we age? After conducting a review of literature, MacNeil and Teague (1992) concluded that "there are few norms pertaining to specific behaviors of the elderly, and that the few norms that do exist are primarily extensions of middle adulthood norms" (p. 53). Given the fact that there are no specific norms associated with old age, individuals have more flexibility to choose to behave in ways that have been successful for them in the past. Having no set norms may be perceived as negative if norms are directly associated with having social value; however, when norms are seen as constraints to creativity and choice, their absence may be interpreted as a reward for those individuals who spent much of their life conforming to social demands.

Cox (1998) paints a positive picture of the opportunities future cohorts of older individuals will have. The post-industrial society will see the emergence of recreation, leisure, and education as "legitimate means of enriching the quality of one's life" (p. 54). As a result, old age will be marked by an expanded range of socially acceptable roles. An increased focus of quality of life, concomitant with a decreased focus on the importance of productivity, will place leisure, and leisure service providers, in the forefront of meeting the needs of individuals in later life.

SOCIAL RESPONSES TO AGING

The examination of social responses of younger generations toward the elderly is especially relevant if we consider that the percentage of older people in the U.S. population is growing steadily, leaving today's younger cohorts with the responsibility of caring for the welfare of the elderly in the near future. Many of these young individuals will be expected to perform some role that will directly or indirectly affect the well-being of older adults; examples of such roles are: caregivers, service providers, volunteers, and policy makers. Besides the potential to affect service delivery, attitudes may also affect opportunities for social interaction and active involvement available to the older individual. Another rationale presented for the study of social responses toward the elderly is that self-image and consequent behaviors are affected by conceptions of the elderly currently held by society members.

Some authors stress the existence of negative stereotypes about old age (Birchenall & Streight, 1993). Other researchers, like Schonfield (1982), blame methodological inaccuracies for the general assumption that such stereotypes exist, concluding that society has a stereotypic view regarding the elderly. Reviewing the body of research, we may be led to believe that both positions have some merit but cannot stand alone.

After many years researching the topic of social responses toward the elderly, Palmore (1990) summarized the stereotypes, attitudes, and types of discriminant behavior uncovered by his and other investigators' studies. He classifies each concept as negative or positive.

NEGATIVE STEREOTYPES

1. Most older persons are sick or disabled.
2. Most older persons have no sexual activity or desire.
3. Old persons are ugly.
4. Mental abilities start to decline after middle age.
5. Most old persons are "senile."
6. Old workers are not as effective as younger ones.
7. The majority of older persons are socially isolated and lonely.
8. Most older persons live in poverty.
9. Older persons feel miserable (cranky, depressed).

POSITIVE STEREOTYPES

1. Older persons are kind and warm.
2. Most older persons have great wisdom.
3. Older persons are more dependable.
4. Older persons are well off financially.
5. Older persons are a powerful political force.
6. Older persons are free to do whatever they want.
7. It is possible to halt the aging process.
8. Old age is full of peace and serenity.

Rowe and Kahn (1998) reviewed myths about aging and were able to identify the six most common. They were able to debunk each based on the scientific literature in the gerontological field. The myths included:

1. *To be old is to be sick.* The evidence clearly contradicts this belief. People are living longer and healthier than ever. The number of older individuals with disabilities is declining, fewer older individuals are experiencing severe limitations in activities of daily living, and there is agreement that aging and disease are not synonymous. Chapter 3 provides strong evidence for the fallacy of the belief that old is the equivalent of sick.
2. *You can't teach an old dog new tricks.* The evidence (see Chapter 4) indicates learning is a lifelong process. There is no chronological age at which individuals are no longer able to learn.

3. *The horse is out of the barn.* This myth is based on the belief that a lifetime of bad habits cannot be reversed. Smoking, high blood pressure, being overweight, and poor physical fitness all have deleterious effects on the body. However, the belief that there is a point in life at which changes in these behaviors would not be beneficial is untrue. Evidence strongly supports the value of making positive lifestyle changes in old age.

4. *The secret to successful aging is to choose your parents wisely.* Although heredity is related to longevity, there is ample evidence that various environmental factors contribute to physical aging (see Chapter 3 for further details). People are not prisoners of their genes. Lifestyle choices impact the aging process more dramatically than heredity.

5. *The lights may be on but the voltage is low.* This myth relates primarily to sexual activity in later life. While there may be a decrease in sexual activity by some older individuals, many continue to be sexually active. In fact, "many older people enjoy an active sex life that often is better than their sex life in early adulthood. The idea that your sexual drive dissolves sometime after middle age is nonsense" (Mayo Clinic Health Letter, 1998).

6. *The elderly don't pull their own weight.* Most older individuals are not burdens to society. About 12% were in the labor force in 1997, many more are contributing to society through volunteer efforts, and most are vital members of their communities.

NEGATIVE ATTITUDES

1. Very few people perceive the sixties or seventies as the best years of one's life.
2. Most people choose the sixties and seventies as the worst years of a person's life.
3. The older years are the worst because of bad health or physical decline, loneliness, and financial problems.
4. Children prefer being with younger adults than older adults.
5. Most people have a mixture of negative and positive attitudes toward the elderly, but few have predominantly positive attitudes.

POSITIVE ATTITUDES

1. Some people look forward to retirement as the "golden years."
2. Society holds pseudopositive attitudes about the elderly, offering compliments even when performance does not meet standards held for younger members of society.

NEGATIVE DISCRIMINATION

1. Employment practices are still discriminatory (e.g., early retirement packages).
2. Governmental agencies providing services to the elderly are found to discriminate, particularly against the oldest age groups.

3. Families discriminate by deferential treatment of the elderly.
4. Housing segregation occurs, with the elderly becoming concentrated in certain areas.
5. Health care practices are still inadequate to cover the needs of older persons.

POSITIVE DISCRIMINATION

1. Tax benefits, discounts, and employment benefits are available.
2. In the political arena, the elderly fare better as candidates for office and enjoy legislative benefits.
3. Medicare is available only for the elderly.
4. Some families see the elderly as matriarchs or patriarchs.
5. Governmental programs support public housing for the elderly and retirement communities cater exclusively to them.

In addition to stereotypes, some individuals are guilty of ageism, the "biased conception of someone based on his or her chronological age" (Cox, 1993, p. 18). This negative view of aging is typified by statements beginning with "he is too old to . . . " or "at her age she should . . . . " This misinformed perspective on aging can only be combated by information and interaction.

An effective way of reducing negative perceptions about the elderly is through programs bringing old and young individuals together. The benefits of intergenerational programs have been widely noted (Scannell and Roberts, 1994; Newman, Ward, Smith, Wilsson, McCrea, Calhoun & Kingson, 1997; McGuire & Hawkins, 1999) and should therefore be encouraged in most recreation centers as a means to foster changes in perceptions and create increased opportunities for social interaction and exchange. Not only should younger adults be put in the positions of helpers to the elderly, but they should also have the opportunity to learn from the elderly. Contact is not enough to change attitudes; the quality of the interaction is crucial.

Another factor observed in the literature is that experience working with older adults becomes more effective when combined with instruction. Therefore, a combination of intellectual and affective components should be included when developing intergenerational experiences. We only value what we appreciate; if we want older persons to be valued, we need to create avenues for them to present themselves in a positive light and for younger generations to learn to appreciate them as individuals, not simply members of a stereotypical group.

The importance of having an accurate knowledge of aging cannot be overstated. The leisure service provider lacking such knowledge risks treating the individuals served in such a way that stereotypical beliefs are supported. Forgetfulness will be interpreted as senility, any interest in sexuality will support a "dirty old person" image, conservative opinions will signify rigidity, time spent alone will be viewed as a time of isolation and loneliness, a decision to not become involved in activities will be blamed on depression and fear, and automobile accidents will prove it is time to revoke the driver's license.

If older individuals are to be viewed as the unique, varied individuals they are, it is necessary to erase the false pictures that have developed in many of us. Whether our function is to facilitate leisure involvement or deal with aging parents, the first step is to gather factual, accurate knowledge of the aging process and the forces experienced by the aging person.

DEMOGRAPHY OF AGING

Prior to examining the forces shaping leisure in later life, it is important to understand the general characteristics of the aging population in America. Demographics provide a composite picture of this group. However, demographics do not provide information about any given individual. Knowing the percentage of individuals residing in urban areas or the proportion of people who are college graduates does not increase knowledge about the individuals behind the statistics. Nevertheless, demographics provide a necessary starting point to understand the forces resulting in the social phenomenon of aging.

LIFE EXPECTANCY

More people are living longer than ever before. Life expectancy at birth in 1900 was 47.3 years, and in 1996 it was 76.1 years. Recent increases in life expectancy are increasingly due to decreases in mortality among individuals who are middle aged or above. This is in contrast to earlier in the century when increases in life expectancy were attributable primarily to decreased death rates in the young. As a result, life expectancy at age 65 has increased dramatically. Since it is unaffected by infant mortality rates, life expectancy once individuals reach age 65 is a more accurate indicator of later life longevity. In 1900 an individual who was 65 could expect to live an additional 11.9 years. By 1996 this had increased to 17.7 years (Administration on Aging, 1997).

However, life expectancy varies based on gender and race. There has been a gender gap in life expectancy, with women experiencing greater increases in life expectancy than men. A female born in 1995 had a life expectancy of 79.3 years, whereas a male had a life expectancy of 72.5 years. A women reaching age 65 in 1996 had a life expectancy of an additional 19.2 years, whereas a similarly aged man could expect to live an additional 15.5 years. In addition to gender differences in life expectancy, there are racial differences. White males born in 1995 had a life expectancy of 73.6 years compared to 64.8 for black males and 74.9 for Hispanic males. The comparable figures for females were 80.1 years, 74.5 years, and 82.2 years. Similar racial differences exist once people reach their 65th birthday. White females have an average life expectancy of 19.4 years after age 65. Black females have a life expectancy of 17.6 years at age 65, and Hispanic females have an average of 21.8 additional years. The 15.7 years of additional life expectancy at age 65 experienced by white males compares to the 13.6 years for black males and 18.5 years for Hispanic males (Administration on Aging, 1997b).

Projections for the year 2010 indicate that 65-year-old men will have a life expectancy of 16.2 years and women can expect 21 additional years of life at age 65. Obviously, life does not end at 65 or some other arbitrarily defined benchmark. Many more years are available for growth, developments, and change.

AGE COMPOSITION

The American population is growing older. In 1900, fewer than 4% of the population was 65 or over. By 1996 this had increased to 12.8%. This represents approximately 34 million individuals. Every day approximately 5,570 individuals celebrate their 65th birthday and approximately 4,680 persons over 65 die. The net increase in the 65 and over population is 890 every day! The projections for the future indicate this aging trend will continue. The Census Bureau's "middle series" projections have the over 65 population doubling by the year 2050 to 80 million. The aging of the baby boom could result in one in five Americans over the age of 65 by 2050 (U.S. Census Bureau, 1997).

The increase in the population of individuals 85 years of age or over, frequently labeled "the oldest old," has been dramatic. In fact, they are the fastest growing age group. There was a 274% increase in the number of people 85 or over between 1960 and 1994, and they now compose 10% of the entire elderly population. By the year 2050 the oldest old will make up 24% of the 65 and over population and 5% of the total population of this country (U.S. Census Bureau, 1997).

RACE AND ETHNICITY

The proportion of the white population over the age of 65 is greater than the proportion of either the black or Hispanic population. Approximately 15% of the white population is 65 or over. This compares to 8% of the non-Hispanic black population, 6% of the Hispanic population, and 7% of the population of other races (Native Americans and Asian/Pacific Islanders) (Administration on Aging, 1997).

The proportion of the older population composed of minorities is increasing. According to the Administration on Aging (1997) 15% of the elderly population in the United States is other than non-Hispanic white. This will increase to approximately 33% by 2050.

RESIDENTIAL DISTRIBUTION

Fifty-two percent of all individuals 65 years of age or over resided in nine states: California, Florida, New York, Pennsylvania, Texas, Illinois, Ohio, Michigan, and New Jersey. Each of these states had over 1 million residents aged at least 65. In 1996 Florida had the highest proportion of residents 65 or over, 18.5%. It was followed by Pennsylvania (15.9%), Rhode Island (15.8), West Virginia (15.2), and Iowa (15.2). The states with the smallest proportion of older residents were Alaska (5.2%), Utah (8.8), Georgia (9.9), Colorado (10.1), and Texas (10.2). Every state experienced an increase in the percentage of residents aged 65 and over between 1990 and 1996. The states with the greatest increase were Nevada (44.9%), Alaska (41.5), Hawaii (23.3), Arizona (23.1), Utah (17.3), Colorado (17.1), New Mexico (16.8), Delaware (15.2), and Wyoming (15.0) (Administration on Aging, 1997).

In 1995, most older people (67%) lived in family settings. The most common living arrangement was with one's spouse. Seventy-seven percent of all males and 48% of females aged 65 or above lived with their spouse (Administration on Aging, 1997). On the other hand, 13% of men and 32% of women aged 65 to 74 lived alone. The number of elderly living alone increases with advancing age. Over half (57%) of all women and 32% of men over 85 live alone (U. S. Census Bureau, 1997).

Few older individuals reside in nursing homes. Only 4% of the over 65 population is in a long-term care facility. However, 15% of those 85 or over are living in this setting.

GENDER

Women outlive men and as a result there are more women than men in the elderly population. For every two males aged 65 or over there are approximately three females. With increasing age there is an increasing disparity in the number of men and women. The ratio of women to men in the 65 to 69 population is 6 to 5. However, the discrepancy between the number of women and the number of men increases to five women for every two men in the 85 and over population (U. S. Census Bureau, 1997).

MARITAL STATUS

One result of the longer life expectancy of women is a likelihood they will outlive their husbands. In fact, 75% of noninstitutionalized older men were married and living with their spouse in 1993, while only 41% of the older women were living with their spouse. Approximately 48% of all older women were widows compared to 14% of older males (U. S. Census Bureau, 1997).

ECONOMIC CHARACTERISTICS

The older population is poorer than the general population. However, there is great variation in the financial status of the elderly. The Administration on Aging (1997) reports that in 1996 the median income of households headed by individuals 65 years of age or over was $28,983. However, 23% of households with heads 65 or over had incomes of $50,000 or above, and 16% had incomes below $15,000. Families where the head was white had a median income of $29,470, whereas the median income for blacks was $21,328 and for Hispanics was $21,068 (Administration on Aging, 1997).

The poverty rate for older individuals is slightly below that of the general population. Approximately 10.8% of the elderly population were below the poverty level in 1996 compared to 11.4% of the 18–64 age population. However, an additional 7.6% of all individuals 65 and over were classified as "near-poor." These people had incomes within 125% of the poverty level. The poverty rate was higher among blacks (25.3%), Hispanics (24.4%), older women (13.6%), and older persons living alone or with nonrelatives (20.8%) than among the general population of elderly (Administration on Aging, 1997).

The meaning of limited income is dramatic in the later years. According to Harris (1978), "income is the crucial determinant of how the aged live. The level, adequacy and maintenance of income directly affect other aspects of the lives of the elderly" (p. 36).

CONCLUSION

The data reported above provide a macro-level perspective of the aging population in the United States. They form a starting point from which to build an understanding of this age group. However, the reader should not lose sight of the individuals making up the statistics. As people age, they become increasingly unique. Therefore, it is impossible to make predictions about the behavior of older people based on the above information. According to Kalish (1975):

> Highly accurate predictions can be made about newborns based only on knowing their ages and that they are basically normal. As people become older, our ability to predict behavior simply from knowing a person's chronological age diminishes . . . In brief, older adults vary more in biological and behavioral functioning than do younger adults (p. 4).

As Myers (1990) indicated, "traditionally we have distinguished between aging as an individual phenomenon and aging as an aggregative process through which population structure is modified" (p. 21). Generally, individuals providing leisure services will be more concerned with aging at the individual level rather than at the structural level. Services should be based on the needs of each individual. Nevertheless, an understanding of aging in the aggregate is significant for the development of policy related to leisure services.

An equally important approach is to examine subgroups of the aging population. For example, the oldest old, those 85 years of age and over, are receiving increased attention. They can be defined by their specialized needs and by the level of services needed. Later chapters of this book will examine several subpopulations of the elderly.

The perspective we take toward aging will influence the services we provide. If the later years are viewed as a time of decline, lost hope, and ultimately death, services will be based on maintaining functioning to as great a degree as possible while placing minimal demands and expectations on the individual.

An alternative perspective, and the one to be pursued in this book, is what Kalish identified as a Personal Growth Model of Aging over 15 years ago (1979). As a result of role loss (viewed as an opportunity, not a problem), the reduced need to be constrained by social convention, increased discretionary time, and motivation growing out of knowledge that time is finite, older individuals have the opportunity to enter a new stage of development marked by growth and expansion. The Ulyssean lifestyle described in this chapter is harmonious with the personal growth model.

Although there are losses that accompany the aging process—some biological and necessary but many social and contrived—these do not negate the opportunity for growth. All periods of the life cycle are marked by events and situations that are potentially confining. The high school student without money, the individual committed to caring for children and unable to attend law school, the 48-year-old executive unable to quit her job and become an artist because she fears an uncertain future—all are operating under constraints. They are no less burdened than the 70-year-old with arthritis.

These individuals have the potential to change their situations, or at least accept them and begin a Ulyssean journey. The help of a trained professional may be needed. This book is the start of your Ulyssean journey toward becoming a trained professional prepared to deliver leisure services. As you examine the information to be presented, remember the later years can be one of the freest, most fulfilling periods of life. Many individuals will have more unobligated time than ever. Older people are people first and only incidentally "old" as a result of the labeling process experienced by all groups. It does not mean infirm, disabled, or used up. It identifies an individual who has successfully negotiated at least 65 years of life, nothing more and nothing less.

Chapter 2

◆

Theoretical Perspectives on Aging

By Bryan McCormick

Approaches to studying aging face some difficulty, as there is disagreement over what is meant by the very term "aging." After all, the process of aging in its most comprehensive sense begins at birth and ends with death. We are all currently in the process of aging. An improvement might be to substitute the term "old age" in order to specify a particular period in a lifetime of aging. Yet even the term "old age" presents some ambiguity. When does one become "old"? While I may be considered "old" by my elementary school–aged children, I am still considered "young" by my 80-year-old grandparents. Much effort has gone into attempting to understand the aging process, often at the theoretical level. This chapter explores these attempts to address the particular experiences of people in later life and to identify how it is qualitatively different from younger age periods.

THEORETICAL PERSPECTIVES ON AGING

Early approaches to theories of aging examined the experience of aging from one of two perspectives. Either they focused on the personal experience of aging as related to change and adaptation in later life, or they focused on social factors that shape the experiences of later life. More recently, theories of aging have tried to incorporate both individual experience and social factors into explanations of later life experience. This chapter presents an overview of eight major theories related to aging and later life. These theories were selected to be representative of general perspectives on the experience of aging. However, readers should be aware that a number of other theories of aging have been proposed.

Personal Experience of Later Life

Theories such as disengagement theory (Cumming & Henry, 1961), activity theory (Lemon, Bengston, & Peterson, 1972; Longino & Kart, 1982), and continuity theory (Atchley, 1977; Neugarten, Havighurst, & Tobin, 1968), have all presented ideas about the experience of becoming older. In particular, these theories have tended to use the concept of "successful aging" as an indication of personal experience in later life. While the three theories share a focus on aging successfully, they are based on different general social-psychological theories and, as a result, characterize the process and outcomes of aging differently. A brief presentation of each of these theories, in terms of characteristic processes and outcomes, follows.

Disengagement Theory

Disengagement theory was one of the first theories on aging to be explicitly stated. The theory was developed by Cumming and Henry (1961) based on data collected from 279 white adults between the ages of 50 and 80 years old, residing in Kansas City. According to disengagement theory, aging in later life is a process characterized by gradual social disconnection (Cumming & Henry, 1961). This disconnection takes place through the severing of relationships and through a change in the nature of remaining relationships. Further, according to disengagement theory, this process of social disconnection is beneficial both to the individual and society.

Process of Disengagement

The first aspect of disengagement theory is that there is a severing of relationships. According to the theory, the process of disconnection can be seen in the reduction in individuals' role counts (the number and variety of interactions with others), interactions (the density or amount of time spent in interaction with others), and social life space (the number of interactions engaged in during the past month). Overall, "the aging person sees fewer kinds of people, less often, and for decreasing periods of time as he grows older" (Cumming & Henry, 1961, p. 51). However, not all relationships are disengaged from equally. Kin relationships, particularly relationships with children, tend to be the most enduring.

In addition, disengagement theory argues that not only are social ties severed, but those relationships that are retained change in nature. These changes entail a shift in the quality and goal orientation of remaining relationships. As people age and disengage, they are less likely to seek love and approval from those with whom they retain social ties. The implication of this aspect of disengagement theory is that as people age they become less concerned with others' approval and more likely to act on egocentric interest. That is, not only does aging include a disengagement from social relations in terms of the number of social ties, it also entails a disengagement from social expectations of relationships.

OUTCOMES OF DISENGAGEMENT

One of the basic beliefs of disengagement theory is that this process of disengagement is one of mutual satisfaction between the individual and society. In the view of disengagement theory, older people want to gradually separate themselves from society in anticipation of final disengagement (death), and society needs them to disengage in order to make room for younger generations.

While Cumming and Henry (1961) identified this process as one of mutual satisfaction for both the individual and society, they also note that there are a number of variants in terms of general disengagement. Cumming and Henry (1961) noted the following variants:

> When both the individual and society are ready for disengagement, completed disengagement results. When neither is ready, continuing engagement results. When the individual is ready and society is not, a disjunction between the expectations of the individual and of the members of his social systems results, but usually engagement continues. When society is ready and the individual is not, the result of the disjunction is usually disengagement (p. 214).

They further noted that in the last case, lowered morale can follow. That is, people who are socially pressured to disengage when they are not ready for disengagement would demonstrate patterns of "unsuccessful aging."

However, while disengagement theory characterized most disconnection from society as mutually satisfying for the individual and society, it did identify some difficulties related to disengagement. "Because the abandonment of life's central roles—work for men, marriage and family for women—results in a dramatically reduced social life space, it will result in a crisis and loss of morale unless different roles, appropriate to the disengaged state are available" (Cumming & Henry, 1961, p. 215).

According to the authors, these losses entail for men a lack of instrumental tasks and the loss of status identity. In addition, they noted that resolution to these problems comes through changes in the ego that lead to a preoccupation with inner states. For women, upon death of spouse, losses entail the loss of an emotional social relationship, loss of status derived from their spouse's occupation, and a shift from obligatory (based on husband's social obligations) to voluntary relationships (based on personal interests).

Overall, the characteristic process of aging according to disengagement theory is one of gradual separation of social ties, changes in the character of remaining social ties, increasing constriction of life space, and increasing egocentricity. The outcomes of disengagement are satisfactory to both the individual and society in that there are fewer demands placed on the energies of older people, they can begin to prepare for final disengagement, and through disengagement they "make room" in society for younger generations.

CRITIQUE OF DISENGAGEMENT THEORY

While evidence does suggest that some disengagement occurs in involvements in later life (e.g., Gordon & Gaitz, 1976; McGuire & Dottavio, 1986), these disengagements tend to be most prevalent among the oldest segments of society who reduce involvement in physically demanding engagements. Another consideration is that the sample from which disengagement theory was principally derived was an urban sample. One theory of aging that is presented later argues that in societies based on industrial systems of production, the status of older people declines. The findings of disengagement may be more a function of an urban setting that affords fewer opportunities for meaningful engagement than the results of a "natural" process.

ACTIVITY THEORY

While disengagement theory was one of the first explicitly stated theories of aging, much of the work in social gerontology prior to the 1960s was implicitly based on what was later to be identified as activity theory (Breystpraak, 1984; Lemon, Bengston, & Peterson, 1972; Longino & Kart, 1982). In addition, the formal statement of disengagement theory by Cumming and Henry (1961) gave impetus to the development of a formal statement of activity theory (Breystpraak, 1984). While Havighurst and Albrecht (1953) first identified the principle on which activity theory is based, it was not until 1972 that Lemon et al. (1972) presented a formal statement of activity theory.

PROCESSES OF ACTIVITY

In almost direct opposition to disengagement theory, activity theory maintained that successful aging depended on one's ability to maintain social activity, not disengage from it.

Activity theory has taken much of its foundation from a sociological perspective termed "role theory." Role theory argues that people's identities are largely created through the roles they assume in their lives. People play a number of different roles over their lives. One may assume such roles as "mother or father," "son or daughter," "college student," "professor," or "business executive" just to name a few. We create these roles in our lives through action. However, over the course of our lives, opportunities for acting out certain roles are lost or change significantly.

Activity theory argued that successful aging was dependent on maintenance and enactment of roles through participation in activity. From the perspective of activity theory, the severing of relationships without the creation of new relationships would result in diminished opportunities for role performance.

OUTCOMES OF ACTIVITY

According to activity theory, one's sense of self (self-concept) is strongly dependent on role occupancy. The self-concept is dependent on role occupancy because through the occupation of a role and the interaction with others associated with the role, one's identity is validated by others' responses. This validation of one's self-concept by others is termed "role support."

Activity theory stated that intimate interpersonal activities elicit the greatest role supports, followed by relatively impersonal formal activities, and solitary activities elicit the weakest role supports since others can only provide imagined role support (Lemon et al., 1972). Studies of older people have found that informal social activity is positively related to life satisfaction. (Lemon et al., 1972; Longino & Kart, 1982). Older people who reported the greatest frequencies of social activity also demonstrated the highest levels of life satisfaction. In addition, research has found that solitary activity has little relationship, positive or negative, to life satisfaction (Longino & Kart, 1982).

The loss of roles results in the loss of arenas of role performance and hence a loss of role supports. The loss of role supports equates to a loss of identity, or sense of who one is. At the heart of activity theory is the belief that the loss of activity, without replacing those activities, results in a decrease in life satisfaction (Lemon et al., 1972). That is, according to activity theory, disengagement would constitute unsuccessful aging.

CRITIQUE OF ACTIVITY THEORY

While activity theory has been explicitly stated and empirically tested with some consistency in the findings, there are a number of grounds on which it can be criticized. First, while it has been applied in the area of social gerontology, the principles of the theory are based in role theory. In the formal statements of activity theory, there are no reasons why it is a theory of aging as opposed to a general theory of adaptation and life satisfaction. It is only truly a theory of aging if the underlying belief is that old age is characterized by role loss and/or role change more so than younger ages. To the extent that old age is characterized by role loss, activity theory would come close to disengagement theory.

Another difficulty with activity theory is that the direction of causality is difficult to determine. Are high activity levels cause for high levels of life satisfaction, or are high levels of life satisfaction cause for high levels of activity? Finally, Longino and Kart (1982) note one of the difficulties of this theory. That is, activities provide a context for role performance, and it is the relationship between the actor and the audience that would appear to be more determinative of role support, positive self-concept, and higher life satisfaction than the activity itself.

CONTINUITY THEORY

A third perspective on aging that developed in gerontological literature was that of continuity theory (Neugarten, Havighurst, & Tobin, 1968; Atchley, 1977). The initial orientation of continuity theory was to link adaptation and adjustment to personality types (Breystpraak, 1984).

Continuity theory held that neither society (in the form of social expectations of disengagement) nor personal action (in the form of high levels of activity) were determinative of successful aging. Instead, the relative degree of success in aging was a function of personal style of adaptation and adjustment that had been developed over the course of one's life.

Neugarten et al. (1968) argued that while there may be older people who disengage and are satisfied with their lives, it is also possible that some people who maintain high activity involvement in later life are also satisfied with their lives. In addition, they also noted that some people may be dissatisfied with disengagement, while others may be dissatisfied with continued high levels of activity involvement.

One basic difference between continuity theory and the other personal experience theories of aging is that while activity and continuity theories sought to characterize the experience of aging as a single pattern, continuity theory sought to identify a variety of patterns of aging.

PROCESS OF CONTINUITY

Atchley (1991) identified that continuity theory was not to be considered as psychologically determinative. That is, while life styles are predispositions to continuity, continuity itself is a function of predispositions and situational opportunities. While people may develop characteristic styles of adaptation, these styles can only be enacted if their life situations permit. In terms of life styles, Neugarten, Havighurst, and Tobin (1968) identified eight patterns of aging. These patterns were developed based on (a) personality styles, (b) level of role activity, and (c) life satisfaction.

The first three patterns are grouped under the "integrated" personality type. People with an integrated personality are those who have a complex mental life, intact cognitive abilities, and a positive self-concept.

The pattern for those of the "re-organizer" type is one in which lost opportunities for role activity are substituted with new role activity. These people maintain high levels of role activity.

The second pattern is termed "focused." People exhibiting this pattern of aging demonstrate a narrowing in the variety of roles they play but expansion in the amount of time devoted to those roles.

The third pattern of aging is termed "disengaged." This pattern is representative of disengagement theory. Neugarten et al. (1968) noted that these people disengage as a result of personal preference, not as a result of losses in social opportunities or physical abilities.

The second group of patterns of aging are grouped under the "armored-defended" personality type. People with this personality type are achievement oriented and exhibit high defenses against anxiety. In addition, these people demonstrate a need to "maintain tight control over impulse life" (Neugarten et al., 1968, pp. 175-176).

One pattern of aging exhibited among people with this personality type is that of "holding on." People with this pattern show a need to maintain roles of middle age well into later life. For these people, aging constitutes a threat (Neugarten et al., 1968). The second pattern within the armored-defended personality type are people who exhibit a pattern of "constricted" aging. For this pattern, there is a preoccupation with losses and deficits associated with aging. People demonstrating the "constricted" pattern of aging deal with these threats and losses through limiting their social interactions and expenditure of energies.

The third group of patterns are representative of people demonstrating a "passive-dependent" personality type. People with this personality type show little initiative or energy, and tend to rely heavily on others. One pattern within this personality type is that of "succorance-seeking." These people have high needs for responsiveness from others and adapt to aging through reliance on one or two other people. They seek people from whom they can receive assistance in meeting both material and emotional needs.

The second pattern within the passive-dependent personality type is the "apathetic" pattern. For these people, passivity is "a striking feature of their personality" (Neugarten et al. 1968, p. 176). They exhibit a pattern in which losses resulting from aging tend to reinforce lifelong patterns of apathy and passivity.

The final personality type has only one pattern of aging. Within the "unintegrated" personality type is the pattern of "disorganized" aging. People exhibiting this personality type demonstrate defects in psychological functioning, poor emotional control, and deteriorated cognitive processes. People presenting a "disorganized" pattern show only limited role activity.

OUTCOMES OF CONTINUITY

The outcomes of continuity are dependent on the personal styles of adaptation that older people have developed and used over the course of their lives.

For people with an integrated personality, outcomes of continuity are positive. Essentially, for these people, the degree of role activity has little impact on life satisfaction or successful aging.

For those patterns characteristic of people with armored-defended personality types, life satisfaction tends to be high to medium. For people with this personality type, successful aging is related to their abilities to maintain either high numbers of roles, or maintain a few important roles.

The outcomes of aging for people with passive-dependent personality styles tend to be less positive than the previous two personality styles. Aging among people with a passive-dependent personality style tends to involve both medium to low role activity and life satisfaction.

Finally, people with an unintegrated personality style show poor overall functioning, and, as a result, the experience of aging tends to result in low life satisfaction.

In summary, continuity theory posits that aging in old age is a function of one's adaptational style developed over one's life. Implicit in continuity theory is a view of the individual as seeking to maintain continuity. Thus, continuity is to some extent negotiated based on personal style and situational opportunities.

CRITIQUE OF CONTINUITY THEORY

In general, the personal experience of "successful aging" according to continuity theory is dependent upon people's competence in adapting to change, which has been developed over their lives. However, as it is presented, there is no particular reason that continuity theory pertains to the personal experience of later life. To state that people develop styles of adaptation over their lifetimes and that these styles continue into later life says nothing about the qualities of later life. For example, if the theory is truly one of continuity, one would assume that people demonstrating a "constricted" pattern of aging have always had few role activities and medium to low life satisfaction. However, continuity theory does make implicit statements about the quality of aging.

As noted above, activity theory pertains particularly to later life. One assumption is that later life is characterized by role loss more than previous age periods. Continuity theory makes a similar assumption in that unless later life is more characterized by adaptation than earlier periods of life, it ceases to be a theory particularly pertaining to later life.

SUMMARY OF PERSONAL EXPERIENCE THEORIES OF LATER LIFE

Personal experience theories of aging locate the meanings of aging within aging people. Through the severing of social ties, the maintenance of activity, or continuous patterns of adaptation, negotiation of later life is seen. All of the above theories make certain assumptions about later life if they are to be considered characteristic of this part of life. These assumptions are that later life is characterized by severing of social ties, loss of social opportunities, or greater demands for adaptation.

SOCIAL FACTORS SHAPING THE EXPERIENCE OF LATER LIFE

While the above theories of later life have focused on personal experiences, other theories have presented later life in terms of its social context. These theories consider processes of socialization, processes of stratification, and social system-level change as influential on the experience of later life. This section will present factors of socialization, stratification, and systemic social change in terms of their actions and outcomes on the context of later life.

The three theories considered in this section share a common basis in that they consider aging as being influenced by the characteristic processes and structures existing in societies. The processes and structures considered include how people enter and exit various roles how certain roles are distributed based on age, and finally, the process of "modernization" is considered as a number of interacting changes occurring within a society, which create changes in the status of "old age."

SOCIALIZATION TO OLD AGE

Irving Rosow (1975) argued that later life implies a social position. That is, later life is qualitatively different from earlier age periods because the position people in later life occupy in society is different from social positions occupied by people in younger age periods. In order to understand the social position of later life one has to grasp the transition from one social position to another and the alterations in social identity and relationships that accompany such transitions.

Rosow uses a life-stage approach characterized by successive stages with associated, normatively guided age-sex roles. These stages and their defining roles have distinctive patterns of activity, responsibility, authority, and privilege. Rosow characterized the transition from one stage to the next as "status sequences" and noted that these changes frequently entail rites of passage, social gains, and role continuity.

PROCESS OF SOCIALIZATION TO OLD AGE

As with activity theory, the theory of socialization to old age draws from role theory. However, while activity theory considered the relationship between role occupation and successful aging, socialization to old age considers how people learn and adopt the social role of "old age." Learning and adopting social roles is the process known as socialization. Through the process of socialization novices in social roles learn new norms, behavior patterns, and self-images and, as a result, are integrated into society. Implicitly, Rosow identified that social integration is the basis for a high quality of life.

Rosow identified three basic conditions for socialization. First, the actor must have knowledge of expected actions based on norms of the new role. Second, the actor must have the ability to perform these actions adequately. Finally, the actor must have sufficient motivation to adopt the new role and associated behaviors.

One difficulty in terms of socialization for older people is the implicitness of the norms applicable to old age roles. Rosow argued that the only consistently identified norms for older people deal with intergenerational family ties. These norms essentially proscribe forms of relation with family (independence as long as possible, and maintenance of family relations). This absence of norms regarding old age results in a lack of expectations to effectively structure an older person's activities and general life outside of the realm of familial relationships. Rosow (1974) noted "in this sense, an old person's life is basically 'roleless,' unstructured by the society, and conspicuously lacking in norms, especially for nonfamilial relationships" (p. 69).

The second condition for socialization is that the actor must have the ability to perform role-associated actions with some degree of proficiency. What this means is that when engaged in the actions of a particular role, the individual must receive some form of positive feedback that the performance is in keeping with the norms of the role. As noted above, there are few norms to structure old age roles. In the absence of clear norms, or socialization criteria, role performance cannot be defined as either conformist or deviant. Performance, hence, is not available for reward or punishment.

The third condition for effective socialization is that the individual must have sufficient motivation to adopt the new role. That is, the person to be socialized into new roles must want to adopt this new role. According to Rosow (1975)this is problematic for older people in an industrialized society. A number of institutional forces operate in American society to limit and curtail the status of old age.

One change is that rapid developments in science and technology have created a society in which "strategic knowledge" (knowledge that is socially valued) is rapidly replaced. As a result, socially valued knowledge is no longer located in older people but in formal education.

Changes have also occurred in the workforce, such that the greatest labor demands exist in high-technology jobs. Unless older people can keep pace with rapid changes in technical knowledge, their abilities to compete for these jobs is limited. Another factor in the limitation on the status of old age has been the increasing individuation and self-sufficiency associated with industrialization. That is, interdependence has increasingly given way to independence, such that the extent to which younger generations rely on older generations has diminished.

Finally, in a society dedicated to progress, the heritage carried on by present generations is relatively small, and hence, older people as symbols of continuity and tradition have limited social power. Given the effect of these institutional forces, there is little motivation to adopt old age roles due to their relatively low social status.

OUTCOMES OF SOCIALIZATION TO OLD AGE

People in transition to old age face a different form of change from passages experienced earlier in life stages. While they possess the necessary ability for socialization to old age, they lack the knowledge (since norms and roles are vague) and motivation for this socialization, given the socially devalued status of old age. Given that the outcome of socialization is social integration, the question for older people becomes how effectively they are socially integrated through old age roles.

Rosow noted that three factors are relevant in analyzing the social integration of older individuals. First, in terms of social values, older individuals show no significant differences from younger people in social values as a function of aging. As a result, at least in terms of social values, the elderly are essentially integrated in society. Second, social roles, particularly central life roles such as employee and spouse, are lost as a function of aging, resulting in reduced integration. Third, social integration involves group memberships. Given the loss of social roles, Rosow argued that group memberships decline with increasing age resulting in reduced integration.

In summary, becoming old presents a devalued position with ambiguous norms and role losses. In addition, there is little motivation to be socialized into these roles. As a result, old age becomes a "roleless role," and older people are poorly integrated into society.

AGE STRATIFICATION THEORY

Another social factor in later life concerns the nature and process of one's location and change in the age structure of society. This perspective has been identified as "age stratification theory" (Riley, 1971, 1985). Basic to this perspective is the view that society is conceived of as "an age stratification system within which important roles are age-graded and particular individuals and successive cohorts of individuals are continually aging" (Riley, 1985, p. 370).

Streib (1985) noted that stratification generally is considered the "process dealing with the distribution of valued things" (p. 339). As with socialization approaches to "old age," the distribution of roles according to age is of particular relevance to age stratification theory. Riley (1985) argued that changes in the age structures of a society and associated age-graded roles influence individual aging.

PROCESSES OF AGE STRATIFICATION

The boundaries of age strata are socially defined and vary from societies in which there may be few age strata to those in which there may be many (Riley, 1985). Age strata are groupings, based on age, that are recognized within a society. For example, in U.S. society, we tend to recognize age strata of childhood, adolescence, young adulthood, middle age, and old age. The age strata within a society vary in terms of size and composition. In addition, age-related characteristics and capacities are related to various age strata in a society. That is, age strata differ in the "contributions they can make to the activities and processes of the groups and the society to which they belong" (Riley, 1985, p. 378).

Roles, on the other hand, are stratified through criteria that open or close certain roles to certain age strata. For example, roles can be tied formally to chronological age such as voting rights. However, criteria are just as likely to be age-related physical concomitants (the role of "parenthood" is limited by development of secondary sex characteristics) or social norms (the role of "retiree" is only available to adult strata). Finally, age affects how people are expected to perform in roles and the rewards and sanctions related to role performance.

Riley (1985) argued that at the heart of age stratification theory is an attempt to understand both how changes in the age structure of society and the process of individual aging come about. Riley (1985) noted that aging of the individual is biological, physical, and social, and that as a cohort ages, its members "move forward across time and upward through age strata" (p. 371). Tied to this movement through age strata are movements through a sequence of age-structured roles.

OUTCOMES OF AGE STRATIFICATION

While successive cohorts are born and move upward through the succession of age-graded roles together, society can be seen as made up of people occupying a variety of age strata. The particular makeup of the society, in terms of age strata, is constantly changing. Riley (1985) noted that "each cohort experiences a unique era of history" (p. 371).

Overall, age stratification theory is based on a view of society in which aging individuals are constantly changing as they age, and the society within which they are aging is changing over time as well. Riley (1985) states that "because of social change, different cohorts cannot grow up and grow old in precisely the same way . . . . Persons in the older age strata today are very different from older persons in the past or in the future" (p. 371).

MODERNIZATION THEORY

The third theory of aging that considers social factors influencing later life is that of modernization theory (Cowgill, 1974). Modernization theory largely grew out of a comparative perspective on aging across cultures (Cowgill, 1974). The premise of modernization theory, simply stated, is that the status of older people declines with increasing modernization. However, this begs the question, just what constitutes modernization?

PROCESS OF MODERNIZATION

Cowgill (1974) stated the following definition of modernization:

> Modernization is the transformation of a total society from a relatively rural way of life based on animate power, limited technology, relatively undifferentiated institutions, parochial and traditional outlook and values, toward a predominantly urban way of life based on inanimate sources of power, highly developed scientific technology, highly differ-

entiated institutions matched by segmented individual roles, and a cosmopolitan outlook that emphasizes efficiency and progress (p. 127).

Cowgill (1974) noted two key elements in this process. First, modernization is the transformation of a total society; there are no aspects or pockets of the society left untouched. Second, the process is unidirectional. It always moves from predominantly rural to predominantly urban.

Cowgill (1974) specified four general changes accompanying modernization that impact on the status of older people. These four changes are (a) technological advances in health, (b) the application of scientific technology to economic production and distribution, (c) urbanization, and (d) literacy and mass education.

The effects of technological advances in health (including public health, nutritional, and medical advances) on social change tend to change the age structure of societies (Cowgill, 1974). Initially, the change is such that they tend to reduce infant mortality rates, thus bringing about a "younging" of the society. In addition, these changes tend to extend longevity among the population. Cowgill (1974) identifies, however, that the long-run effects of the changes in health technologies is a reduction of birth rates, which, coupled with extended longevity, leads to an aging of the society.

The second area of modernization change associated with a changing status for older people is that of economic modernization. While the changes associated with modernization in economic production are pervasive, Cowgill (1974) cited the emergence of new and specialized occupations as most relevant to changes in the status of the old people of a society. As the means of economic production for a society are increasingly modernized, changes occur in the knowledge and skills required for participation in many areas of the labor force. Since these occupations are new and specialized, the knowledge and skills needed tend to be acquired more through education than through experience. As a result, younger workers tend to have an advantage over older workers.

Urbanization presents another major aspect of modernization that affects aging. Cowgill (1974) noted that while urbanization is closely related to changes in economic production, it has significance to facets beyond those of changes in economic production. Two principal effects of urbanization were noted by Cowgill (1974). First, urbanization is associated with an increasing separation of work from the home. Second, urbanization tends to produce a separation of "youthful urban migrants from their parental home" (Cowgill, 1974, p. 132).

The fourth aspect of modernization that is salient to aging is literacy and mass education. Pre-modern societies were dependent on an oral tradition for knowledge beyond that of personal experience. In this type of society, older people held a valued status since their personal experiences were more extensive than those of younger people.

In a society without written language or with few literate members, knowledge is inherently tied to people. Cowgill (1974) identified that efforts to promote literacy are usually undertaken early in the process of modernization. Along with efforts to promote literacy are programs to improve the educational level of the members of a society. According to Cowgill (1974), these efforts and programs are particularly targeted to the young.

OUTCOMES OF MODERNIZATION

Cowgill (1974) asserted that with changes in modernization of a society, the long-term effects are the creation of an aging society. This aging of a society, in turn, leads to an increased competition between generations for jobs or roles as a result of a greater proportion of older generations living longer. Cowgill (1974) argued that out of this competition, in a modernizing society with changing occupations (due to science in economic production) and valuing youth, the old will be "eventually pushed out of the labor market" (Cowgill, 1974, p. 130).

The second outcome of the process of modernization results from the development of new and specialized occupations. The emergence of these new occupations are relevant because they tend to develop in urban areas, tend to accrue greater monetary rewards, and they tend to be assumed by younger, more mobile members of the society. Cowgill (1974) argued that this adoption of higher status roles by younger members of the society creates a status inversion in which children achieve higher status than their parents, as opposed to moving up to the status of their parents. Interestingly enough, this very phenomenon is one conceptualization of "progress" in modern societies, that is, to want one's children to "do better" in life than oneself. In addition, the emergence of new professions tends to deprive older people of the traditional role of vocational tutor.

The third outcome of modernization is a result of changes in patterns of residence associated with urbanization. As noted above, urbanization tends to separate work from the home and younger generations from older ones. According to Cowgill (1974), the result of these two effects of urbanization is to weaken the bonds of the extended family, increase the spatial separation between generations, and to establish the nuclear family as the norm.

All of these effect tend to create a social ethic of independence among generations, replacing an ethic of interdependence. However, given the potential for status inversions and devalued status in the labor market noted above, independence tends to translate to dependence for older people whose children have achieved greater social status and rewards.

The final outcome of modernization is a result of increased literacy and mass education, which are primarily targeted toward younger generations. The effect is that "once a society is launched into the process of modernization, no matter what its stage of development, adult children are always more highly educated than their parents" (Cowgill, 1974, p. 135).

Additionally, once the process of modernization begins, the rate of social change continually accelerates (Cowgill, 1974). With rapid social change, the young are increasingly socialized for a future that is unknown. When knowledge is independent of people, and the past and present experiences of the old are not thought to be relevant to the future of the young, the status of old people in the society declines.

Summary of Social Factors Affecting Later Life

The three theories presented above have characterized later life as related to social roles that are both age and status stratified. In addition, the process through which these roles are created, distributed, and entered into is influenced by the degree of differentiation and specialization of roles within the society. In general, the above theories characterize later life in industrialized societies as ambiguous and normless, with available roles that hold relatively low social status, and the experience of aging is ever changing such that it tends to be cohort specific. With the exception of age stratification theory, the presentation of later life according to these theories is relatively bleak.

The Negotiation of Later Life

Increasingly in the study of aging, there has been a shift from research methods that attempt to describe the nature of aging to the description of the process of aging. This can be seen in calls for the use of longitudinal research methods, in which people are studied over many years (or even a lifetime!). The theories that have grown out of this change are relatively recent (mid 1980s–present) and approach aging as neither solely personal experience nor socially determined. Instead, theories of this sort have recognized that the personal experience of aging both influences, and is influenced by, social expectations and opportunities. As a result, these theories attempt to explain how people negotiate the process of aging.

Life Course Perspective

Although the life course perspective is included in this chapter, there is some debate whether or not it constitutes a "theory" (Bengston, Burgess, & Parrott, 1997). However, there appears to be some consistency in the way gerontologists employ the concept. In essence, the life course perspective assumes that people's histories influence personality and attitudes, that the modern life course has been institutionalized with "accepted" stages (school, work, marriage, child-rearing, retirement, etc.), and that the outcomes of earlier life experiences can persist and influence later life experience (George, 1996).

PRINCIPLES OF LIFE COURSE PERSPECTIVES

The first principle is that the life course perspective examines how social and historical factors interact with individual experience. Along these lines, life course perspectives typically examine socially recognized sequences, differentiated by age, that characterize the life of the individual. According to George (1996), a key assumption of this interaction of history and biography is that heterogeneity exists. In other words, within a single cohort, the pattern of life course transitions and the impact of these transitions is not assumed to be singular. Instead, variability is assumed to exist both within and across cohorts (Dannefer, 1988).

A second principle is that the life course can be understood by examination of transitions and trajectories (Elder, 1985). George (1996) stated that "transitions refer to changes in status (most often role transitions) that are discrete and relatively bounded in duration, although their consequences may be observed over long time periods" (p. 250). In comparison, the concept of trajectory implies that over the long term, patterns of stability and change can be seen in the lives of aging people. Along this line, some theorists have used the metaphor of a "career" (e.g., Elder, 1985; Marshall, 1979) to explain later life trajectories.

IMPLICATIONS OF LIFE COURSE PERSPECTIVES

Unlike other theories of aging, life course perspectives on aging tend not to offer descriptions of the experience of later life. Instead, the perspective offered is that the experience of later life can only be understood in terms of what has gone before. The nature and sequence of transitions individuals experience over their lives may continue into later life, or changes in the trajectories may occur. In a sense, the life course perspective has certain similarities to continuity theory. However, unlike continuity theory, life course perspectives also include the possibility for fairly radical changes in trajectories at any stage in life, including later life. In addition, the negotiation of later life is not unidimensional. There are multiple trajectories, and later life is just as heterogeneous in its patterns as earlier life stages. Although life course perspectives have attempted to explain the interaction of the individual and society, they have also been criticized as being deterministic. Marshall (1995) argued that life course perspectives that have cited the agent of change as culture or one's social system, have minimized the agency of the individual. In other words, life course analyses that simply focus on the impact of transitions into and out of highly socialized roles on aging individuals do not give adequate attention to the power of the individual to negotiate these transitions.

GERODYNAMICS

Another theoretical perspective that has been proposed to explain the experience of aging is that of gerodynamics (Schroots, 1995a, 1995b). As noted above in the life course perspective, one of the challenges of theories of aging is the issue of heterogeneity or variability with age. The premise of gerodynamics is that with increasing age comes increasing variability. Schroots (1995b) termed this "differential aging." The theory of gerodynamics was proposed as the process that drives differential aging and, hence, the increasing variability seen as people age.

PRINCIPLES OF GERODYNAMICS

Based on laws of physics related to systems, Schroots (1996) proposed that the increasing variability of life experience could be explained through two concepts. First, one characteristic of systems is that over time, they tend to move from energetic and orderly to dissipating and disorderly. This physical law (the second law of thermodynamics) is referred to in physics as "entropy." For the human system this process ultimately results in the death.

However, entropy alone seems inadequate to explain living systems. According to Schroots (1995b), this is due to assumptions of equilibrium in the second law of thermodynamics. According to laws of physics, systems work to restore equilibrium or a steady state. However, living systems continue to function in far-from-equilibrium states and may redefine what constitutes "equilibrium." In other words, living systems, including individuals, may reorganize in order to adapt to increasing disorder. For example, as was seen in the theory of gerotranscendence, people may redefine their existence in the face of increasing physical decline (disorder). As a result, the second main concept of gerodynamics drew from "chaos" theory. In general, chaos theory proposed that entropy was not inherently related to decline. Instead "under nonequilibrium conditions certain systems run down, while other systems simultaneously evolve and grow more coherent at a higher level of organization" (Schroots, 1995b, p. 57).

Overall, Schroots (1995b) defined the process as follows, "in terms of non-linear dynamics (chaos theory) aging can now be defined as the process of increasing entropy with age in individuals, from which disorder and order emerge" (p. 57). The result is a "branching" of the life course in which fluctuations and challenges may cause the individual to respond in higher- or lower-order structures. Higher-order structures correspond to more integrated functioning, whereas lower-order structures correspond to declines in functioning (Schroots, 1995a; 1995b). However, living systems are constrained by biological factors. Inevitably, there is an increasing trend toward disorder (entropy) over time, ultimately resulting in the death of the individual.

IMPLICATIONS OF GERODYNAMICS

According to the theory of gerodynamics, the outcomes of aging are difficult to specify. Schroots (1996) stated that "there is a wide range of individual differences in the rate and manner of aging at all levels of analysis—biological, psychological, and social" (p. 748). Thus gerodyamics is more descriptive of the process of aging than its outcomes. However, the theory does propose that over time, there is a preponderance of branches in one's life experiences in which lower-order structures occur. Ultimately the individual experiences overwhelming disorder that results in his or her death. Yet one of the important implications of this theory is that events that exist at branching points are not necessarily negative. For example, although it would seem that the death of a spouse would be a negative experience, for some people this experience may in fact be liberating. Another important concept brought to light by this theory is that the process of aging is not unidimensional. In other words, although at the biological level an individual may experience a branching point that results in a lower-order structure, or functioning, this same branching point may not affect other aspects (e.g., social, psychological, cognitive) of functioning. Finally, as noted at the beginning of this section, the process of gerodynamics assumes variability in the process of aging. As a result, there is no assumption that the experience of aging is identical for everyone.

SUMMARY OF THE NEGOTIATION OF LATER LIFE

Both of the theories presented in this section make two assumptions. First, in order to understand aging one must follow aging individuals over time. Both the life course perspective and gerodynamics make the assumption that in order to understand how people experience later life, one must understand their history. In other words, both of these theories imply a need to use longitudinal methods for studying aging. To an extent, earlier theories, such as continuity theory, made a similar assumption that aging in later life was often consistent with patterns in earlier life stages. A second major assumption that differentiates the gerodynamic and life course approaches from either the personal experience or social forces theories is the explicit assumption that aging is a heterogeneous process. One of the major reasons for this heterogeneity is that later life is seen as a process of negotiating challenges and experiences. This differs considerably from theories such as disengagement theory, which makes a broad assumption about the experience of later life. Overall, the theories presented in this section are, historically, the most recent. They have developed, to some extent, as a response to earlier theory that has not adequately captured the variety of experience in later life.

CONCLUSION

This chapter has presented eight theoretical perspectives on aging. These perspectives are not the only existing theories. However, they were chosen to provide an overview of the attempts to explain the experience of growing old. The theories view aging as a life period in which one is faced with potential changes. These changes may result from changing personal expectations and abilities, from changes in social structure and social expectations, or a combination of both. The quality of late life is defined by how effectively the individual manages these changes.

As noted in the beginning of the chapter, the term "aging" presents difficulty in definition. However, when one considers the experience of old age, two factors should be examined. First, aging is a process, and each individual experiences it differently. Second, society also structures the experience of aging. There are social norms, expectations, and systemic forces that impact the experience of aging. Ulyssean adults successfully develop their own style to negotiate the social factors that shape the aging experience.

Chapter 3

◆

Biological Processes

When Butch Cassidy told the Sundance Kid, "Every day you grow older, that is the law," he addressed two important realities of life. The first reality is that growing older is an inevitable part of living; it is a law common to all species. Related to this same concept, there is the assumption that aging is a progressive process that does not occur suddenly. Contrary to what some seem to believe, individuals do not wake up on their 65th birthday to realize they have become old overnight. Biological growth and development last for approximately the first three decades of human life. After that, the slow degenerative process associated with aging begins (Cox, 1993).

Although the process of biological aging is an unavoidable "law," it allows for both variability and generalization. The great variability in aging is one of the main reasons why a definition of old age based on chronological age is inappropriate. Aging is a highly variable process that occurs at different rates for different individuals and at different rates within an individual.

While some will experience the effects of biological changes in their 60s, others will not feel their impact until the age of 80 or older. In addition to differences in rate of decline, variability is also observed in the types of changes that happen to each person. For example, although some hearing loss is considered a quite common aspect of old age, many older people do not have significant problems with their hearing.

Such variability may be explained by at least three reasons. Although members of the same species share some genetic characteristics, individual genetic makeup may account for differences among human beings. Also, the path of aging is expected to be altered by environmental and lifestyle factors, such as pollution, diet, and amount of exercise. Another explanation to consider is the interaction between biological aging and social and psychological aging in determining the makeup of the aging individual; therefore, changes in biological functions may be aggravated or minimized by such factors as social support, personal attitudes, and opportunities to exercise control.

Certain aspects of senescence, however, may be generalized because they are shared by all. Timiras and Hudson (1993) identify these shared characteristics as:

universality, intrinsical irreversibility, deleteriousness, and progressiveness. The potential limitations imposed by biological aging must be recognized if effective preventive and/or rehabilitation programs are to be developed.

Organ reserve capacity may be defined as "the level of excess energy stored in various bodily organs beyond what is required for immediate functional needs" (MacNeil & Teague, 1992, p. 74). All individuals are born with excess organ reserve that is used to restore "homeostasis"—balance and regulation of all bodily functions—anytime the body is placed under physiological stress. As individuals age, reserve capacity decreases and, consequently, so does the body's ability to restore equilibrium. Therefore, one of the effects of biological aging is the general slowdown in the ability of all bodily systems to return to pre-stress levels. As stated by Timiras and Hudson (1993), "Decrements become apparent only in response to increased demands and stress. When the aging organism is challenged by environmental changes, the efficiency of maintaining homeostasis is decreased compared with younger ages" (p. 32).

In studying the aging process, there is a risk of either seeing it with rose-colored glasses or with pessimistic eyes; both of these positions represent extremes that may prevent older adults from receiving the adequate support needed to maintain a Ulyssean approach to later life.

The potential role of physical decline in later life should not be overestimated. The gradual nature of the aging process allows most individuals ample opportunity to cope and adapt to the changes their bodies undergo. Senescence is not synonymous with illness and disability. Most older adults are able to lead full, unencumbered lives until well into old age. Many individuals are able to adapt and compensate for losses (Crandall, 1980; Hooyman and Kiyak, 1993).

Nevertheless, such declines cannot be ignored. Over 80% of individuals over 65 years old have some type of chronic condition with approximately 19% experiencing total limitations in activities of daily living and 3.5% categorized as severely disabled (U.S. Senate Special Committee on Aging et al., 1991; Administration on Aging, 1997b). By being able to realistically appraise the impact of changes in biological processes, service providers will be better prepared to identify techniques that will assist in keeping functional losses minimal. The role of service providers may be better understood by examining the concepts of "primary aging" and "secondary aging."

PRIMARY AND SECONDARY AGING

Primary aging, or genotypical aging, is the deteriorative, degenerative process experienced by all species. It is universal, inevitable, naturally occurring, gradual, and variable. It cannot be reversed, retarded, or postponed. It could be conceptualized as "pure" biological aging, without the intervention of external forces. According to Helender (1978), this form of aging is theoretically optimal, since the only factor limiting further development is the biochemical structure of the genetic code.

Secondary aging, or phenotypical aging, however, goes beyond primary aging. It is the speeding up of the genetically determined aging process. It can be more clearly represented by those factors that accelerate natural decline, such as stress, poor nutrition, radiation, untreated disease, and unhealthy lifestyle habits like smoking and lack of physical activity. Many of these factors may be altered through intervention. In fact, the likelihood that a Ulyssean lifestyle will be maintained in later years will be enhanced to the degree the older individuals and service providers take an active role in cleaning the path of primary aging from as much secondary aging debris as possible.

The figure below (Figure 3.1) summarizes the goal of service providers working with individuals growing old. Line A traces the path of primary aging by showing the gradual decline in functioning experienced with increasing age. It is what Helender (1978) referred to as "optimal aging." If no environmental influences interfered with the aging process, this line would suffice to depict the path of aging. Yet no individual leads a life totally devoid of environmental influences; that is why line B, representing secondary aging, is also needed. As the graphical representation indicates, the line for secondary aging shows a faster decline in functioning as age increases.

FIGURE 3.1

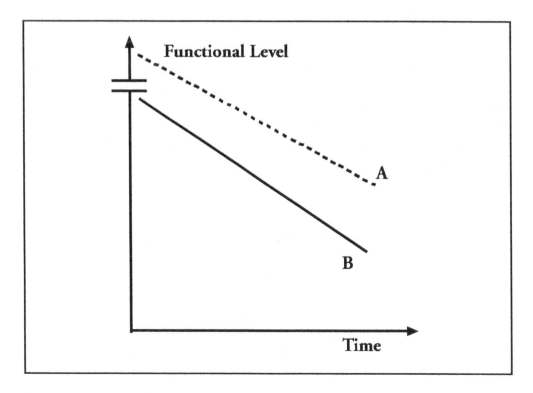

(J. HELENDER, 1978)

FIGURE 3.2

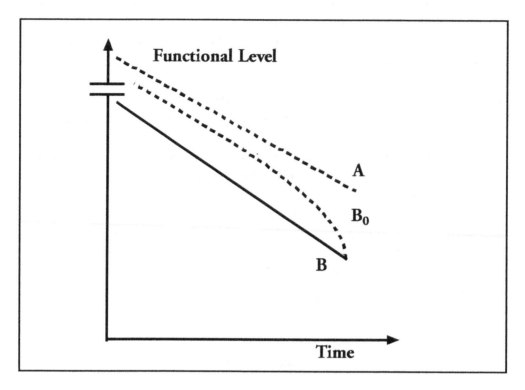

(J. HELENDER, 1978)

The gap between lines A and B can, thus, be viewed as the premature functional loss caused by environmental interference in the genetically determined aging path. At this point in history, there are no interventions known to alter genetic programs; consequently, primary aging does not seem amenable to change.

Although it may be naive to expect that deleterious environmental factors can be eradicated, it is realistic to believe that the gap between the two lines may be narrowed through appropriate interventions. This position is illustrated in Figure 3.2 by the dotted line (B_0), falling between lines A and B. This new line represents the desired path of aging, one in which the negative effects of secondary aging have been met with planned intervention. Line B_0 shows how service providers may help shape everyday existence in such a way that the path of secondary aging is brought closer to that of optimum or primary aging.

It is important to keep in mind, though, that all the above lines are imaginary ones. It is not possible yet to determine the exact extent to which both genetic and environmental influences shape the aging process.

Scientists have been successful in identifying many of the factors responsible for accelerating the aging process. As a result, they have been able to identify several strategies for enhancing later life. For example, there is ample evidence that exercise "can prevent or reverse about half of the physical decline normally associated with aging" (CIGNA HealthCare of Colorado, 1995). The benefits of strength training in reversing or slowing the loss of muscle strength have also been well established. Other factors such as nutrition, stress reduction, and smoking cessation are also effective in maximizing the likelihood of a long and healthy life.

The MacArthur Foundation Study of Successful of Successful Aging has focused to a large extent on the issue of improving the physical and mental abilities of older Americans (Rowe & Kahn, 1998). The concept of successful aging, as defined in the study, is based on a belief that the absence of disease and disability is only part of successful aging. Low risk of disease and disease-related disability, high physical and mental functioning, and active engagement with life are the components of successful aging. They come together to provide optimum aging. Achieving successful aging, therefore, requires an active approach marked by awareness of risk factors and the motivation to address those factors. The good news from this research is that people can take responsibility for their own aging. It is not something that befalls an individual, rather it is something the individual has a role in creating. Lifestyle is more important than genetics in determining the path aging will take.

WHY DO WE AGE?

For years, scientists have been contemplating the question "why do people age and eventually die?"; the search for answers has led to the development of various theories of aging. According to Cox (1993) although a variety of theories exist to explain the biological aging process, none has "yet convinced the scientific community of its validity" (p. 85). Recent advances, however, have some researchers convinced we are on the right path to answer this question. A brief examination of the variety of explanations for physical aging follows.

Ryan (1993), based on Hayflick's (1985) work, indicated that the primary categories of aging theories are: "organ theories (immune system, neuroendocrine), physiological theories (free radical), and genome-based theories (genetic)" (p. 32). The multitude of theories precludes examining them all in this text. However, a brief description of some of the more common perspectives will provide a picture of historic and current beliefs. (For additional information, see Campanelli 1990; Ebersole & Hess, 1998; Timiras & Hudson, 1993; Wold, 1993; Bowles, 1998). Hooyman and Kiyak (1993) identify five theories helpful in understanding aging.

WEAR AND TEAR THEORY

Aging is viewed as a preprogrammed process that sets off a biological clock. Humans are viewed as gradually wearing out as age increases, and ultimately the wear and tear progresses to a point where the life span is "used up."

AUTOIMMUNE THEORY

Aging results from the body's immune system producing antibodies that attack itself, in addition to attacking foreign bodies, bacteria and viruses. According to Weiner, Brok, and Snadowsky (1987) this process leads to cell dysfunction and death.

CROSS-LINKAGE THEORY

Collagen, the connective tissue in most organ systems, changes with age and results in loss of elasticity in muscle tissue, skin, blood vessels, and other organs. The result is a decline in normal cell function.

FREE RADICAL THEORY

Free radicals are highly reactive chemical compounds possessing an unimpaired electron. Produced normally by the use of oxygen within the cell, they interact with other cell molecules and may cause DNA mutations, cross-linking of connective tissue, changes in protein behavior, and other damage (Hooyman and Kiyak, 1993, p. 90). Antioxidants, such as vitamin E and beta carotene, have been identified as potential inhibitors of damage from free radicals and are currently the focus of popular antiaging remedies.

CELLULAR AGING THEORY

This perspective views aging as resulting from the gradual decline in the cells' ability to replicate. According to Hooyman and Kiyak (1993) this is one of the most promising theories for explaining the causes and processes of aging.

This perspective views aging as resulting from the gradual decline in the cells' ability to replicate. According to Hooyman and Kiyak (1993) this is one of the most promising theories for explaining the causes and processes of aging. Cells can divide a limited number of times, a phenomenon referred to as the "Hayflick limit," and once this limit has been reached, cells no longer reproduce. One theory for why cells appear to have a clock which keeps track of cell divisions is the telomere hypothesis. Telomeres are responsible for maintaining the structure of DNA and genes. They shrink each time DNA replicates, it appears shortened telomeres may not be able to facilitate DNA replication, and at that point cells cease dividing (American Museum of Natural History, 1998; Johnson, Marciniak, and Guarente, 1998) This hypothesis holds great promise but awaits further research.

Despite significant strides in understanding the biological mechanism that triggers senescence, there is still no unified theory of aging. However, it is known that genetics clearly have a role in how we age. In fact, it is estimated that 7,000 genes are involved in the aging process (Columbia/ HCA, undated). It is also known that a variety of environmental and personal forces also shape physiological aging. Such a view seems to best fit the notion of primary and secondary aging examined in the last section. In order to align it with Ulyssean thinking, it would be helpful to add the idea of environmental impact not always constituting an insult to the individual, but rather contributing to the maintenance of optimal aging.

The following section will examine the biological aspects of aging as they relate not only to potential loss, but as they also represent opportunities for the older adult and service provider to develop creative approaches to maximize functioning.

Specific Changes in Biological Systems

The aging process, whatever its cause, results in specific, identifiable changes in bodily function. However, prior to examining these changes, it is important to put them in perspective. The declines, per se, are not as relevant as their meaning to the older adult and the degree to which they may be combated by intervention. According to Kalish (1982), the meaning of particular changes can be ascertained by focusing on the following questions:

1. Does it matter? Do these changes have an impact on the lives of the people affected?
2. Does it imply other changes of a more serious nature?
3. Will an intervention alter the path of decrement? Will a surgical procedure, or any health treatment, serve to lessen or eliminate the problem? Will improved social relationships, the re-establishment of feelings of personal meaningfulness, an in crease in sensory stimulation, or other interventions, make a difference?
4. Is there any mechanical device that can help? Eyeglasses, hearing aid, etc.?
5. How is the individual coping with his losses? How can she be helped to cope more effectively? (pp. 21–22)

By examining the losses of aging within this framework, it is possible to identify those which are inevitable and cannot be helped, those which cannot be altered but which may require supportive services to prevent them from becoming obstacles to growth, those which may be helped but do not require immediate attention, and those which may be altered and require prompt action.

The next section of this chapter will explore some specific changes which accompany the aging process in some of the major bodily systems and interventions which may ameliorate the losses experienced by individuals. The active approach required for Ulyssean living is embodied in these interventions. In addition to the references accompanying each section, a variety of resources provides extensive information on physical aspects of aging (Birchenall & Streight, 1993; Ebersole & Hess, 1998; Ferri & Fretwell, 1992; Lewis, 1990; Ryan, 1993; Schneider &

Rowe, 1990; Wold, 1993; National Institute on Aging Age Page, 1995a, 1995b, 1995c, 1995d, 1996a, 1996b, 1996c).

PHYSICAL APPEARANCE

If asked about how most older persons look, a large number of Americans would probably mention wrinkled or sagging skin and graying or receding hair. Changes in the layers of the skin combined with reduced activity of sebaceous glands account for dryer and less rigid skin. Although both baldness and gray hair are genetically determined, some loss of pigment and thinning of the hair are expected changes.

These changes, although variable among older adults, do occur to some degree to all human beings as they age. More than having a functional significance, they primarily have social implications. Depending on how individuals utilize social standards for self-evaluation, they may also have some impact on self-image and self-concept. Uneasiness about physical appearance may result in reluctance to participate in activities where these badges of aging are exposed. Aside from the mere cosmetic functions, the skin also is responsible for regulating body temperature and sensory perception (which will be discussed under "touch").

Of special importance to those individuals who are no longer ambulatory is the tendency of the skin to develop pressure sores (also known as decubitus ulcers) when under prolonged pressure on bony areas. Sitting or lying for long periods of time on rough seats or wet clothes as well as poor nutrition may precipitate skin breakdown.

One health factor commonly ignored, though, is nail care. With age, nails become rougher and, if not properly cared for, may cause infections. Discomfort brought about by nail problems may lead to locomotion problems, reducing independence (Saxon & Ettel, 1987).

Teeth are another area that have both cosmetic and functional meaning. Due to changes such as decrease of enamel and simple attrition caused by continued usage, older adults may have problems with their teeth. If proper care is not given, both teeth and gum will show decay. Not only are teeth important for social interaction (speech, smiles, social meals), but they also are needed for chewing food and reducing it to pieces manageable by the digestive process.

There are also changes in the shape and size of the body with increasing age. Lean body mass decreases and fat is increasingly deposited toward the center of the body. In addition, height decreases as a result of changes in joints, muscles, and bones. Changes in body size and shape may result in difficulties with balance, gait, and mobility.

ULYSSEAN APPROACHES

Concerns with physical appearance should be respected, although older adults should also be encouraged to discuss their options before they seek major interventions such as plastic surgery. Education programs that prepare individuals for age-related changes and society's reactions to them may decrease feelings of inadequacy, helping older adults decide what changes are acceptable and which they would like to "correct."

Such educational programs should also concentrate on changes that will more directly affect functioning. Discussion groups, led by wellness specialists, may be helpful in generating awareness regarding issues such as dental care and foot care. They may also assist older adults in identifying strategies to cope with losses and learn to live with "older equipment" in their Ulyssean journey.

For individuals who use wheelchairs or need prolonged periods of bedrest, it is important that either they or their caregivers are taught how to shift weight, adjust positions at regular intervals, avoid rough bedding or seats, watch their diet, and apply medication when even minor abrasions are detected.

MUSCULOSKELETAL SYSTEM CHANGES

Two specific age-related changes are loss of muscle mass and decrease in muscle elasticity. With muscle mass loss, individuals usually experience decreased strength and endurance. Muscle strength peaks between age 20 and 30 and gradually declines thereafter; however, significant decline does not occur until individuals reach their late 60s or 70s (MacNeil & Teague, 1992).

Decrease in the number and bulk of muscle fibers may eventually result in "atrophy." Muscular atrophy is closely related to physical inactivity. Deterioration in muscle mass may also contribute to muscular fatigue and difficulty in establishing prompt homeostasis after exposure to intense muscle activity. Reduced elasticity will often result in decreased flexibility which, when combined with skeletal changes, may result in stiffness and mobility problems (Saxon & Ettel, 1987; HealthAnswers, 1997a). Changes in muscle structure may also lead to coordination problems. Impaired muscular coordination may contribute to an increased accident rate in old age.

With increasing age, many people undergo a decrease in bone mass. A consequence of bone loss is increased porosity and brittleness. If bone degeneration is extreme, it is called "osteoporosis." Several factors have been identified as contributors to this condition; some of them are: (a) calcium deficiency, (b) deficiency in vitamin D, (c) lack of exercise, and (d) estrogen deficiency (Saxon & Ettel, 1987; National Institute on Aging Age Page, 1996c). It is estimated that osteoporosis-related fractures occur in 12.5% of older males and 50% of older females (National Institute on Aging Age Page, 1996c). One of the visible manifestations of osteoporosis is curvature of spine and consequent loss of height; as much as three inches, reduction in stature may be observed in old age (Atchley, 1991).

Spinal problems such as scoliosis are also potential complications of this condition. Lack of spinal alignment may create the need to adopt a new form of gait as an attempt to regain balance.

The joints, including the knee, elbow, and ankle, tend to stiffen with age; as a result, movement can often be painful and restricted. Although arthritis is a disease of all ages, it is prevalent in later years, affecting half of all individuals 65 or over (National Institute on Aging Age Page, 1996b). It is the leading chronic condition limiting general activities in this age group, second only to heart conditions when limitation in major activities is considered. There are over 100 different forms of arthritis. The two most common, osteoarthritis (non-inflammatory disorder characterized by degeneration of connecting cartilage) and rheumatoid arthritis (a disease of connective tissue marked by joint inflammation, redness, swelling, and tenderness), involve pain and may reduce activity. Arthritis may also limit functioning through its effect on the ability to grasp and manipulate objects. The degree of affliction varies throughout time, and a crisis may be precipitated by factors such as stress and extreme changes in temperature.

The poor posture, diminished height, and gait changes that often accompany changes in bones and joints may increase the likelihood of older adults having accidents. Persons 65 and over have the highest accidental death rate in the United States. Accidents are the seventh-leading cause of death in individuals 65 years of age and over (Brock, Guralink, & Brody, 1990).

The complications resulting from muscular and skeletal changes may block the path to Ulyssean journeys, as they reduce the older adults' ability to achieve desired goals. Several suggestions to address the challenges created by changes in the musculoskeletal system will be discussed below.

ULYSSEAN APPROACHES

The ideal form of Ulyssean intervention is prevention, followed by early detection. Health education programs focusing on proper nutrition will assist the older adult in selecting the types of food needed to avoid problems such as osteoporosis.

Educational programs may also create awareness regarding risk factors and warning signs for some conditions. For instance, arthritis sometimes goes undetected because stiffness is not uncommon to the elderly. If the older adult is educated about other symptoms, she or he will be more likely to seek medical assistance.

By learning what aggravates the condition, the individual may be able to avoid much of the discomfort that interferes with a Ulyssean lifestyle. The early identification of some of these conditions may also result in elimination or reduction of secondary effects, such as loss of independence and social interaction. If leisure service providers interpret their role as that of a facilitator who assists people in being all they can be, then the inclusion of health-related programs such as health screenings with other traditional recreation programs makes sense.

One programmatic intervention that seems appropriate for a variety of purposes, ranging from prevention to rehabilitation, is exercise.

Research indicates that vigorous physical conditioning brings about significant improvement in several areas including musculature and body composition, musculoskeletal flexibility, and increased bone mass (Goldberg and Hagberg, 1990; Lakatta, 1990: Dinsmoor, 1993; National Institute on Aging Age Page, 1995b). Thirty minutes of moderate activity every day is recommended. A complete exercise program will include aerobic or endurance activities, strength activities, and stretching activities. Such activities as walking, jogging, and swimming would be most beneficial. Swimming is also one of the recommended forms of exercise for individuals undergoing treatment for joint problems since it allows for range of motion training. Recently, more and more types of "water exercise" programs are catering to older adults. Weight training has become recognized as one of the most beneficial forms of exercise.

A word of caution about exercise: It must fit the needs and limitations of older persons. An overly enthusiastic recreation specialist, hearing about all the benefits of aerobic exercise, may decide to introduce aerobic classes into her program. Although aerobic activity is indeed very beneficial, some of the motions used in regular aerobic classes may not be appropriate for persons suffering from skeletal problems such as arthritis. In this case, exercise could do more harm than good. However, the fear of causing injury should not stop service providers from instituting exercise programs, since the dangers of not exercising outweigh those of exercising. A less experienced professional may want to rely on exercise programs that have been especially developed for use with older adults.

In programming for older adults, it is important to take physiological changes into consideration. For example, sitting activities should have stretch breaks, since prolonged periods of sitting may result in stiffness. Also, planned breaks are needed in physical activities. Because of the increased time it takes for homeostasis to be restored, older persons may need more frequent breaks to recuperate from exertion.

It is also a good practice to allow each individual to find an appropriate pace in order to avoid unnecessary stress. For those working with persons with arthritis, it is helpful to understand precipitating factors such as extreme temperature changes to prevent them from blocking the older adult's active lifestyle.

Diet and nutrition are also important interventions when seeking a Ulyssean lifestyle in the later years. For example, losing weight may reduce the stress on an individual's joints and therefore reduce the impact of arthritis. The importance of getting enough calcium in building strong bone has been well documented. Nutrition education programs are important tools in maximizing opportunities for healthy living.

Older individuals are at risk of falling and suffering injury as a result of predisposing risk factors and situational risk factors. Predisposing factors include the use of medication, disability to lower extremities, gait and balance difficulties, cognitive impairment, poor vision, foot problems, and sensory changes. Situational factors include stairs, snow, and unseen or loose objects on the floor or stairs (Simoneau and Leibowitz, 1996). Saxon and Ettel (1987) provide several suggestions for decreasing the likelihood of falls. The first concerns the type of furniture used; preferably, protruding legs on chair and tables should be avoided, and solid chairs with arms should be used to provide support and decrease the amount of strain put on joints when sitting. Other things to avoid are rugs, waxed floors, or any other type of slippery surfaces. Because accidents with older adults are also related to poor vision, other suggestions for safety will be discussed when "vision" is examined.

CARDIOVASCULAR SYSTEM

With increasing age, the following changes in the cardiovascular system occur (Rockstein & Sussman, 1979; Saxon & Ettel, 1987; Ryan, 1993; HealthAnswers, 1997b):

1. Heart valves increase in thickness and rigidity; this loss of elasticity decreases efficiency and may produce heart murmurs.
2. The heart muscle weakens and heart rate decreases; the heart becomes less effective as a pump, showing reduced cardiac output and resulting in decreased endurance.
3. The amount of fatty tissue in the heart increases, and deposits of fatty tissues are also present in the veins and artery walls.
4. Blood vessel walls, particularly arterial walls, become thicker and harder. It is estimated that maximum blood flow through the coronary artery is 35% lower at age 60 than at age 30.
5. Arterial walls lose elasticity; with increased arterial resistance, blood pressure also increases.
6. The heart muscle takes longer to recover after each beat; this may diminish the heart's capability to compensate for stress, when it is forced to beat faster.

Two conditions known to be associated with cardiovascular disease are arteriosclerosis and atherosclerosis. Arteriosclerosis refers to the thickening and loss of elasticity of arterial walls, popularly known as "hardening of the arteries." It results from calcification in the lining of vessels and from atherosclerosis. Atherosclerosis is the deposit of pasty, fatty materials in the arteries, eventually blocking blood flow.

Cardiovascular disease is the major cause of death in later years. After the age of 60, heart disease kills one in four (U.S. Senate Special Committee on Aging et al., 1991; Rowe & Kahn, 1998). Even when not fatal, it disrupts daily routines; heart conditions head the list of chronic conditions causing major disability in the elderly in the U.S. Among the three top causes of mortality among the elderly in the U.S., two pathological conditions associated with cardiopulmonary deficiencies appear. They are myocardial infarction (known as heart attack) and Cerebrovascular accidents (known as strokes). They result from shortage of oxygen to the heart muscle and to the brain, respectively. In both cases, the arteries through which blood is carried are either blocked by clots or burst.

The three major causes of interruption in oxygen supply are: thrombosis, embolisms, and hemorrhages. Thrombosis is the obstruction of the blood vessel by large clots (or thrombi); embolism is the occlusion of the vessel by a free-floating clot (or embolus) that was formed somewhere else in the body and traveled to the artery, blocking blood flow; hemorrhages occur when a weakened arterial wall ruptures, allowing the blood to flow to adjacent tissues, increasing pressure on them (MacNeil & Teague, 1992).

ULYSSEAN APPROACHES

Programs designed to increase cardiovascular fitness are particularly important, as are those designed to identify and eliminate risk factors. Diet, cigarette smoking, and exercise should be discussed. Stress has also been identified as a risk factor; therefore, training programs that teach individuals to handle stress may be beneficial as well. Programs such as meditation, yoga, Tai Chi, and biofeedback may be of interest to people seeking to reduce stress. Lifestyle management should be introduced in rehabilitation programs geared toward individuals who have already experienced heart attacks.

It seems clear at this point that a crucial part of these programs should be encouraging the older person to engage in physical activity. Research has consistently shown that vigorous physical conditioning brings about improvement in cardiovascular fitness, lowers blood pressure, increases ability to relax, and reduces body fat, thus lessening the impact of factors related to heart disease. Also, programs in cardiopulmonary resuscitation should be instituted in community centers and other places.

It is important to keep in mind that an older individual's endurance is lower than that of younger individuals. As with the muscular system, the cardiovascular system of older adults takes longer to return to equilibrium.

RESPIRATORY SYSTEM

The following are age-related changes specific to the respiratory system (Rockstein & Sussman, 1979; Saxon & Ettel, 1987; MacNeil & Teague, 1992):

1. Skeletal changes in the rib cage limit capacity for extension, which limits the amount of air that may be taken into the lungs.
2. Lungs lose elasticity and muscles may become weakened and atrophied; increased energy is needed to sustain adequate ventilation. It is estimated that voluntary breathing capacity at age 85 is only half of what it was at age 25.
3. The amount of air that can be expelled after each inspiration decreases and residual air volume increases within the lungs, limiting the amount of air available for oxygenation; residues not expelled by lungs may lead to viral and respiratory infection.

4. The total respiratory functional surface is reduced; the ability of the lungs to exchange air with the blood system decreases and each breath becomes less effective. The ability of the lungs to oxygenate blood decreases about 50% from age 20 to age 75.
5. With less oxygen being available to the cells, the respiratory system becomes limited in reserve capacity; feelings of fatigue and shortness of breath are not uncommon when the body is exposed to demanding physical activity.

Declines in the respiratory system rarely produce disability in older adults; however, when compounded with environmental factors, they may create problems for Ulyssean living. Rockstein and Sussman (1979) and Hooyman and Kiyak (1993) warn about the deleterious impact of environmental insults, such as pollution and smoking, on the respiratory system. Also, the cardiovascular and the pulmonary systems are closely related. Cardiovascular problems may lead to secondary pulmonary abnormalities.

ULYSSEAN APPROACHES

Most of the recommendations for the cardiovascular system also apply here. Again, education about environmental and lifestyle factors is desirable. Simple activities such as coughing to expel secretions and proper swallowing to prevent aspiration of foreign substances by the lungs may be crucial, considering that older adults may be more susceptible to contracting diseases such as pneumonia.

As mentioned above, major limitations due to age-related respiratory declines are expected in some older individuals. The most important point to remember about such changes is that physical exertion may be especially stressful on the lungs; consequently, pacing activities is important to allow the person proper air exchange and maintenance of homeostasis.

GASTROINTESTINAL SYSTEM

Old age is marked by a decreased efficiency in the gastrointestinal system. Some of the age-related changes are listed below (Rockstein & Sussman, 1979; Crandall, 1980; Saxon & Ettel, 1987; Ryan, 1993; Texas Agricultural Extension Service, 1995a):

1. Less saliva is secreted as a result of atrophy of the salivary glands, impacting not only chewing ability, but also producing dryness and proliferation of bacteria in the mouth.
2. The number of taste buds in the mouth decreases.
3. Loss of teeth occurs, affecting the ability to chew.
4. The peristaltic movements of the esophagus decline, increasing the time it takes for food to reach the stomach.

5. Loss of muscle tone in the stomach may result in reduced gastric motility; this combined with reduced secretion of digestive enzymes that break down food contents may delay digestion.
6. Shrinkage of intestine lining and decrease in the number of absorbing cell, diminish the efficiency of the small intestine to absorb nutrients.
7. Decreased muscle tone in the intestinal muscle may also limit peristalsis once food residues reach the large intestine.
8. Loss of elasticity in abdominal muscles makes constipation more likely to occur.
9. Inefficiency in the production of bile may increase the risk for gallbladder disease.

The aforementioned changes do not typically have a significant limiting impact on the lifestyles of older adults. It is possible that when associated with other lifestyle factors, gastrointestinal changes will affect proper nutrition. For example, loss of teeth and digestive problems may be accompanied by factors such as low income, lack of knowledge regarding nutritional diets, depression, medication aftertaste, physical restrictions affecting meal preparation and shopping, as well as the lack of motivation to cook and eat alone. A cycle may be formed since inadequate nutrition will also induce tooth decay and aggravate digestive problems and, possibly, constipation.

ULYSSEAN APPROACHES

There is a need for nutrition education programs. Such programs should be designed to increase knowledge of proper nutrition and encourage efforts to eat nutritious meals. Best food buys, both economically and nutritionally, as well as meal preparation, should be discussed. The availability of programs such as meals on wheels or nutrition sites funded through the Older American Act could be brought to the participant's attention. Pot luck suppers and similar efforts to share meals might be organized for those to whom eating has social meaning. According to Rosenberg (1993) there are 10 nutritional keys to a healthier life. They should be incorporated into a nutrition program. They include:

1. Establish and stick to good eating patterns as early as possible. Good nutrition should become a habit and include five servings of fruit and vegetables, complemented with grains and legumes.
2. The immune system will be strengthened by eating foods containing nutrients such as vitamin E and B6 as well as the mineral zinc. Rosenberg recommends foods such as whole grains, seafood, green leafy vegetables, lean meats, and margarine or vegetable oils.
3. Foods rich in vitamin D and calcium help prevent bones from becoming brittle and porous.

4. The digestive system requires at least 20 grams of fiber every day to stay healthy, regular, and active.
5. Vision is assisted through the intake of vitamins C, E, and beta carotene. These also help delay problems such as cataracts.
6. Cardiovascular disease is combated through limiting fats, cholesterol, and sodium while focusing on foods high in vitamins B6, B12, and folate. Soluble fiber, calcium, and potassium are also important.
7. Vitamins B6, B12, and folate help keep the nervous system and the mind functioning at a high level. Grains and leafy vegetables are key foods.
8. Staying active while choosing a diet low in fat and high in complex carbohydrates and fiber helps maintain ideal body weight.
9. A hearty appetite results from a mix of aerobic exercise and simple activities that strengthen muscles. The result of a good appetite is consumption of more nutrients.
10. Rosenberg's final recommendation is: "Exercise. Exercise. Exercise."

According to Rosenberg, "The bottom line: Our research shows, without a doubt, that good nutrition coupled with a regular program of aerobicizing exercises can have a beneficial effect on the health of almost all older people—*and is the best way we know to retard and even reverse the process of aging*" (p. 3 emphasis added).

URINARY SYSTEM

Although changes in this system have very little impact on functional ability for most people, they may interfere with continued involvement in certain activities. Some of changes to be considered are (Saxon & Ettel, 1987; Ryan, 1993):

1. Blood flow in the kidneys decreases; the amount of blood circulating through the kidneys at age 80 is about half of what it was at age 20. With less blood available to transport nutrients and waste products, the body becomes less efficient in its purification processes.
2. The numbers of nephrons (responsible for eliminating chemical waste products from the blood) drops as individuals age; consequently, filtration rate decreases (approximately 50% from age 30 to 75), and the body has increased difficulty in absorbing filtered substances and expelling toxic ones.
3. Loss of muscle tone and elasticity in the urinary structures leads to inability to completely empty the bladder; residues not excreted may produce renal infections.
4. Bladder capacity (the amount of urine the bladder is able to hold) decreases about 50% individuals reach old age. This, combined with the inability of the bladder to eliminate all its contents, makes for a need to urinate more frequently. With age, the signal given by one's body indicating it's time to

urinate may be delayed until the bladder is almost full; this may intensify feelings of urgency.

A problem experienced by at least 10% of individuals 65 years of age or over is urinary incontinence. Ranging from mild leakage to uncontrolled wetting, it can be a major cause of activity curtailment. However, most cases can be either cured or controlled when proper treatment is received. Urinary incontinence is not caused by aging. Rather, it results from factors such as disease or drugs (National Institute on Aging Age Page, 1996a). Whatever the cause, social interactions and self-esteem may be affected by inability to control one's body fully.

ULYSSEAN APPROACHES

For those persons experiencing problems with bladder control, physical exercise focusing on muscle tone may be helpful. Sensitivity to the need to urinate more frequently is an important aspect in providing pleasant experiences to older adults. Making frequent stops during longer community trips or asking a nursing home resident if he or she needs to use the restroom before being taken to a particularly lengthy activity may reduce the chances of humiliation and allow the person to relax and enjoy the activity more completely.

ENDOCRINE SYSTEM

Although some structural changes may be observed in different glands, they rarely have any impact on normal functioning in old age. Perhaps the most relevant change in this system is related to the pancreas. A decrease in insulin secretion is noted with advancing age; this may account for a reduced glucose tolerance in some older adults. Although diabetes mellitus (the adult form of diabetes) is known to manifest itself as early as 40 years old and is not considered an age-related disease, it is impossible to disregard the fact that it occurs about seven times as often among those 65 years of age or older (National Institute on Aging Age Page, 1991).

Diabetes is among the 10 top chronic conditions affecting major activities of older adults (U.S. Senate Special Committee on Aging et al., 1991), and is one of the 10 leading causes of death in the United States (Saxon & Ettel, 1987). In addition, it may have secondary complications, such as blindness, heart disease, and kidney disease, and may cause difficulty in healing infections, leading to amputations.

ULYSSEAN APPROACHES

In dealing with older adults in health education programs, it may be helpful to discuss the symptoms associated with diabetes (thirst, constant urination, unexplained fatigue, visual difficulties, ulceration, etc.). Early detection may prevent further complications. Also, discussing dietary needs and suggesting flavor full alternatives to prohibited food items may heighten the older person's sense of control and increase compliance.

In dealing with individuals already exhibiting diabetes, service providers should be attentive to possible indications of insulin insufficiency, be aware of possible medication secondary effects, and be ready to adapt activities to accommodate some of the classic symptoms listed above.

REPRODUCTIVE SYSTEM

Changes in both the male and female reproductive system occur with age. The basic changes for both sexes are described below (Saxon & Ettel, 1987; National Institute on Aging Age Page, 1995d):

FEMALES

1. As women reach menopause, fertility terminates.
2. The vagina wall contracts and loses elasticity.
3. The Barthlin gland, which lubricates the vagina, becomes less effective; a longer period of stimulation is required before appropriate lubrication occurs.
4. As a result of reduced circulating hormones, the vulva becomes more susceptible to infection and inflammation.
5. As a result of the loss of subcutaneous fat and elasticity, external genitalia, such as the clitoris slightly shrink.
6. A combination of muscle tone loss, replacement of glandular tissue by fat, and reduction in skin elasticity produces less firm breasts.

MALES

1. The number of sperm decreases.
2. The level of testosterone drops; testes diminish in size.
3. The prostate, bulbo-urethal glans and seminal vesicles show regressive changes resulting in a reduction in volume of seminal fluid; ejaculatory force diminishes.
4. Enlargement of the prostate may put pressure on the urethra, interfering with the flow of urine.
5. Changes in the veins and arteries and the erectile tissue of the penis may increase the time required to achieve erection; erection is lost faster after ejaculation; however, erection may be sustained for a longer period of time before ejaculation occurs.
6. The refractory period (time between ejaculation and ability to respond again to sexual stimulation) is longer.

The important question to be asked about the above changes is "do they matter?" In spite of structural and functional changes, older adults remain capable of experiencing sexuality. The reason why some may not is most likely related to factors such as social pressure, lack of information, lack of suitable partners, or other physical reasons.

ULYSSEAN APPROACHES

Sexuality and sensuality are important aspects of everyone's life; they are filled with emotional components. Sexual identity is part of an individual's overall identity. To increase the opportunities for a comprehensive style of Ulyssean living, it is important to facilitate sexual satisfaction in later years if so desired by the older person. Facilitation may include discussing society's taboos, recommending counseling or medical services when problems are present, and respecting privacy needs (particularly when communal living is the case).

NERVOUS SYSTEM

Even though some structural changes do occur in the aging brain, they do not appear to greatly impact the ability of most individuals to function. The most significant change in the brain is related to the slowdown of the central nervous system. Reaction time, that is, that time elapsed from stimulus to response, increases with advancing age. Such changes in reaction time are proportional to the level of task complexity and may be affected by factors such as previous experience with the given task and motivation to perform it.

Because the central nervous system regulates the overall level of functioning of the human organism, it is natural to expect that this slower pattern of response will be common to many activities performed by the older person; nevertheless, the slowdown is usually minimal, having little impact on the ability of the individual to lead a Ulyssean lifestyle.

ULYSSEAN APPROACHES

In a society that thrives on its fast pace, any indication of slowness may be devalued. Allowing older adults enough time to respond may be the best way to assist them in maintaining their Ulyssean pattern of growth. By believing in the ability of older adults to learn and perform different tasks, service providers are responsible for creating optimum opportunities for learning. They also need to become aware of making activities meaningful in order to build up motivational levels. Last, they must develop tolerance for individual differences and learn that "the good things in life are worth waiting for."

SENSES

The senses provide individuals with a window through which the world is perceived. Vision, hearing, touch, smell, and taste permit contact with the environment and awareness of the world. As with other physiological systems, the senses decline with age.

Because losses are gradual, the individual usually has enough time to adjust, sometimes not even realizing that changes have occurred. It is not unusual for older persons to compensate for losses in one sense modality by making more efficient use of other unimpaired sense organs. This does not mean that the other senses improve to make up for impaired ones; it simply means that the individual is maximizing the use of certain senses to adjust to losses in others. Changes in each sense modality will be discussed next (Rockstein & Sussman, 1979; Atchley, 1991; Saxon & Ettel, 1987; Schneider & Rowe, 1990; Ryan, 1993; Braus, 1995; National Institute on Aging Age Page, 1995a, 1995c; Texas Agricultural Extension Service, 1995a, 1995b, 1995c; HealthAnswers, 1997c).

VISION

One of most certain concomitants of aging is decreased visual acuity. In fact, nearly everyone over the age of 60 needs glasses at least part of the time, and visual impairments are third on the list of chronic conditions limiting activities in old age. However, fewer than 20% of the elderly have vision poor enough to impair driving, only 5% become unable to read, and many elderly people will retain good vision into their ninth decade of life. The following are age-related changes in sight:

1 . Loss of transparency in the lenses, accompanied by reduction in pupil size, results in decreased acuity, the ability to see small objects clearly. The decline begins at age 40; by age 65, about 60% of the women and 40% of the men will have less than 20/70 vision and will need corrective aids such as magnifying glasses to counter acuity loss.
2. As the lenses of the eyes become more rigid and eye muscles lose tone, the ability to shift from far to near vision (accommodation) declines; a visual deficiency known as presbyopia (*presby* = old, *opia* = sight), characterized by decreased ability to see close images sharply, is not uncommon. One sign of presbyopia is the need to hold reading materials away from the eyes in order to focus. It is usually first noted between ages 40–55, when the greater declines take place.
3. Changes in the retina result in a decrease in dark and light adaptation and vice versa; in other words, as people age, they take longer adapting to changes in light intensity. Difficulty in adjusting to the glare may create reluctance about driving at night when oncoming headlights may seem too bright. Also, waking up at night to use the restroom may require turning on

a night light since it will take some time to adjust to the darkness in the room.

4. Visual threshold (the minimum amount of light needed to stimulate the visual receptors and allow the brain to recognize visual information) increases with age; greater illumination is needed to register information.

5. The lens in the eye gradually becomes more yellow, affecting color discrimination. By age 70, older adults have great difficulty in discriminating shorter light waves of the color spectrum (colors in the blue-green-violet range). They are better able to discriminate longer light waves, thus differentiating reds, yellows, and oranges more effectively.

6. Changes in the fluid in the eyes may cause "floaters" or small particles in one's vision. They may be noticed on bright days or in well-lit rooms. They are normal and do not typically reduce vision.

7. Many older individuals experience dry eyes as a result of the decreased production of tears. Dry eyes may result in itching, burning, and possibly loss of vision. Special eyedrops can relieve the condition.

8. There may be a reduction in peripheral vision with increasing age. The visual field may therefore be reduced.

Although not common to all older persons, cataracts, glaucoma, macular degeneration, and diabetic retinopathy are related to aging. These diseases can permanently damage the eyes if medical attention is not sought.

Cataracts. Cataracts result from a change in chemical makeup of the lens, which produces a clouding effect. They usually develop gradually, and the most common symptoms are: (a) blurred vision, (b) excessive tearing or discharge, (c) double vision, (d) halos around lights, and (e) changes in the color of the normally black pupil.

Cataracts are present in about half of the population in their 80s. However, cataracts can be treated successfully by surgery in many cases (Braus, 1995).

Glaucoma. Glaucoma is a consequence of increased pressure in the eyes due to an inefficient drainage of eye fluids. The fluid pressure damages the optic nerve and causes vision loss. It occurs more frequently after age 30 and is difficult to detect because there are hardly any symptoms until irreversible damage occurs and vision loss is felt. Some may experience nausea or headaches but misinterpret them as sinus infections. Checkups with an ophthalmologist may prevent more serious consequences. Treatment usually includes eyedrops, pills, laser treatments, and surgery.

Macular degeneration. Macular degeneration develops more frequently among persons 65 or older, representing the leading cause of severe visual loss in the elderly. It is caused by damage to the macula, a small portion in the retina, which is responsible for fine, acute, straight-ahead vision. Loss of central vision will interfere with tasks such as reading and driving. There is no known cure for this condition.

In some cases, if detected early, laser treatments may help. Peripheral vision is left intact, allowing individuals to rely on partial vision to function.

Diabetic retinopathy. Diabetic retinopathy results from damage to the small blood vessels. Sometimes the weakened blood vessels swell, leak into the retina, causing blurred vision. Newly formed vessels may burst and bleed into the center of the eye and form scar tissue, producing severe vision loss. Approximately 40 % of all diabetics have some degree of this disease. As with macular degeneration, this condition is best detected through eye examination. If diagnosed early, laser treatment may be used to lower risks of losing sight.

HEARING

Hearing impairment is one of the most chronic conditions among the elderly (fourth on the list of conditions affecting general activities); however, it does not always translate into restriction of major activities (tenth on the list). Among Americans with hearing impairments, 60% are 55 years or older, although it only occurs in 15% of those 55-64 years old, 24% of those 65-74 years old, and 39% of those 75 years old or older.

Certain behaviors are good indicators of decreased hearing ability. For instance, when an individual constantly accuses others of mumbling, he or she may be showing difficulty in distinguishing sounds. Other signs are the need to turn up the volume on radio or television, having to roll up the window when in heavy traffic to be able to hear someone else's voice, failing to hear the doorbell or the phone, or having to keep the ear close to the phone to follow the conversation.

The medical term used to describe age-related hearing loss is presbycusis. It is caused by nerve cell degeneration; therefore, it is permanent. It is more common among men, affects both ears, and progressively worsens with advancing age. The use of a hearing aid can help the individual partially increase hearing ability.

One of the common problems experienced due to presbycusis is difficulty in understanding high-frequency and pitch sounds such as higher-pitched voices of children and females, high-frequency consonants such as s, z, f, g, and t, or other sounds such as whistles and bells.

Other functional abnormalities in hearing include impaired sound localization, diminished sound sensitivity, and reduced loudness perception. The effects of aging on hearing may be compounded by prolonged exposure to environmental sound pollution throughout life.

A common hearing problem in older individuals in tinnitus, roaring, ringing, or other sounds heard inside the ear. Ear wax, ear infection, nerve disorder, or excessive use of aspirin or other antibiotics may cause tinnitus. Other causes for hearing problems are conductive hearing loss and sensorineural hearing loss. Conductive hearing loss occurs when sounds from the eardrum to the inner ear are blocked. Ear wax, infection, fluid, or abnormal bone growth are possible causes. Damage to the inner ear or auditory nerve can cause sensorineural loss (National Institute on Aging Age Page, 1995a).

TOUCH

There appear to be several changes in the sense of touch with increasing age, although it is uncertain whether they are age related or the result of disease and disorders. Three areas show functional changes. The first, touch sensitivity, the ability to perceive objects brought in contact with the hands, seems to decline with age. Also, pain sensitivity appears to decline; older individuals seem less sensitive to both the sensations of pain and pressure. Pain is usually a natural sign given by the body to alert individuals that something is wrong; therefore, losses in this adaptive device may result in unnecessary harm to the person.

With aging, people also show a lessened ability to resist cold and heat, to adjust to temperature changes, and to maintain homeostasis even in unchanging environments. Cold and heat sensitivity are also important because they affect the level of comfort experienced by an individual.

Although not considered part of the sense of touch, balance will be included since it is related to sensitivity. Proprioception, or the perception of one's position in and relatedness to time and space, is impaired with increasing age. Dizziness also becomes an increasing problem with advancing age. With gradual losses occurring in the vestibular senses, balance and equilibrium become impaired.

TASTE

The data on age-related changes in taste are conflicting. Age itself may not be related to losses in taste. Rather, environmental factors may be responsible. Nevertheless, there is a decrease in the number of taste buds with age. Sweet and salty tastes are typically lost first, followed by bitter and sour tastes. Losses in taste may be related to a decrease in the number of taste buds, and they may be affected by eating habits, medication intake, or cigarette smoking. It is not uncommon to hear older persons complain about tasteless food or to see them putting extra salt in the food, which is unhealthy, since it may lead to hypertension. Increased intake of sugar may also be observed. In addition, declines in taste may be accompanied by a decreased interest in food and eating. The result may be poor nutrition and excessive weight loss.

SMELL

Recent studies have confirmed the belief that smell decreases with age. Odor identification abilities diminish, and odor thresholds increase. The reduction in odor sensations may be associated with what is interpreted as decreases in taste, since both senses are so closely related. Changes in smell become significant if the notion of safety is raised; both the odor of smoke and rotten food, when not detected, may become hazardous to the older person.

As previously stated, changes in the senses usually occur gradually and can often be compensated for. Decrements in sensorial sharpness may interfere with Ulyssean living if they prevent the individual from enjoying pleasurable experiences or limit social exchange. Individuals may place self-imposed limits on their behavior, as in the example presented below:

> Irma, with great reluctance, began to talk about her failing eyesight. Because of her pride and fear of becoming dependent on others, she decided to stay home in familiar surroundings and not come to the center any longer. She confessed she was afraid of crossing streets alone, yet was reluctant to ask someone to help her. She was embarrassed to eat meals with friends because occasionally she spilled food or knocked over cups of coffee. She could not see the numbers on the playing cards so she had to give up bridge. These were just a few of the problems Irma described that were forcing her into isolation and depression (Robertson & Welcher, 1978, p. 19).

When losses are coupled with environmental dullness, sensory deprivation may occur. Individuals undergoing physical and mental deterioration are particularly vulnerable to sensory deprivation. With lack of appropriate stimulation, the person may become confused, have difficulty focusing on a given topic, and lose parameters for reality orientation. When deprivation is extreme, hallucinations and delusions may occur (MacKenzie, 1980). This may generate a destructive cycle for psychological well-being, since individuals labeled as "disoriented" may experience little social contact and stimulation.

ULYSSEAN APPROACHES

With many of the problems associated with sensory changes, early detection can either correct them or offer devices to minimize their negative effects. It is important that symptoms of visual and hearing impairment are recognized by both the older individual and practitioners, so that fast action may be taken to battle them.

Sensory retraining programs are useful in reversing or compensating for sensory decline. Practice at using the senses may increase their effectiveness. Sensory retraining programs, designed to provide older individuals with differentiated stimuli to improve perception of and response to physical and human environments, can result in an increased ability to adapt to sensory losses. In such programs, individuals are given the opportunity to exercise their senses. Stimuli useful in this process include mirrors and colorful objects (sight); sharp and acrid substances compared with other sweet, pleasant-smelling ones (smell); music, records of sounds, humming (hearing); soft, smooth, and rough items (touch); candy, pickles, spices (taste). Further information on sensory stimulation is provided in Chapter 11.

Other suggestions to maximize the ability of older adults to use their senses and are listed below. They apply to those designing environments for the elderly and also to those who teach older individuals how to make their own homes more conducive to Ulyssean living (Shore, 1976; Saxon & Ettel, 1987; Texas Agricultural

Extension Service, 1995b, 1995c; HealthAnswers, 1997c; National Institute on Aging Age Page, 1995a).

VISION

Regarding lighting

1. Allow for an even distribution of light in the room. Instead of one 200-watt bulb, use four 60-watt bulbs in different points of the room.
2. Use dimmer switches or three-way lamps to control degree of light in the room.
3. Use blinds or shades on windows to reduce brightness during the day, and keep a ceiling light on to balance incoming light.
4. If bright light is needed, use fluorescent light or ceiling fixtures.
5. Keep night light on all night to help adjust to dark/light changes.
6. For watching television, use floor lamps to avoid glare.
7. Use gooseneck lamps or battery-lighted magnifiers when there is a need to focus on small objects.
8. Have lamps and light switches in places where they can be easily accessed when entering the room.

Regarding color contrast

1. Contrast the color of food, kitchen utensils, dishes, and tablecloths; avoid transparent glass cups and dishes that seem to disappear against the background.
2. Draw a colored line on measuring cups or pans if it is hard to see water level;
3. Paint walls a light color and hang light-colored drapes if the room seems too dark.
4. Paint cupboards or cover with contact paper to help see doors.
5. Make use of yellow, orange, and red as background color; avoid blue, green, and violet.
6. To help identify different keys, stick different colored tape around the top of each one.
7. Use contrasting colors of yellow, orange, and red to identify areas and objects.
8. Avoid using subtle color contrasts such as pink on red or light brown and dark brown. The easiest contrast to see is black on white. In addition, leave white space on documents rather than filling pages with print (Braus, 1995).

Regarding safety

1. Increase lighting on steps or stairways.
2. Avoid waxed floors (to avoid glare) or cover them with non-slippery cover-

ings.

3. Paint doorsills a bright color to avoid tripping over them.
4. To help see borders of tub, drape dark bathmat over its side.
5. Use different colors for bottom and top steps; paint handrail with bright color.
6. To avoid leaving stove on, paint a small colored dot on the "off" point of stove knobs.
7. Use different textures to indicate changes.
8. Emergency numbers should be written in large print and kept close to the phone.
9. Low objects such as footstools or magazine racks should be kept out of the way to prevent tripping.
10. Be aware of fast-moving beings such as cats and children.
11. Use a color-coded system to distinguish among different medications.
12. Provide transportation to evening programs.
13. Keep windows and mirrors in vehicles clean.

Other tips

1. Order talking books from the National Library Service for the Blind for those individuals having trouble reading print; have magnifying lenses available for those who require enlargement.
2. Use or provide adaptive devices such as telescopic glasses, lenses that filter light, magnifying glasses, software that enlarges text on computer screens, large-print clocks/watches, large-print telephones, large-print playing cards, bingo cards, or other games available though special catalogs.
3. In making signs, use large print and big surfaces; contrast colors to enhance discrimination; avoid using unnecessary words that only take up space.
4. In developing printed materials, use large, well-spaced lettering; use comfortable line lengths, from five to six inches.
5. Make use of symbols to mark areas such as restrooms, dangerous places, or individual rooms in community residences.
6. If visual presentations are given (or films shown), arrange chairs to accommodate constriction of peripheral or central vision.
7. Position objects consistently.
8. Position objects in a person's visual field.
9. Use auditory as well as visual cues.

Hearing

1. Do not shout; instead, enunciate words clearly and speak in well-paced manner; avoid high pitches in voice tone.

2. Look directly at the person when talking to him or her.
3. In a group situation, to attract someone's attention, call the person by name before addressing any questions or comments to them; if near the person, touching may also be appropriate.
4. Use gestures and signs and facial expressions as cues.
5. Be objective and organize information well; give most relevant information first; elaborate on details later.
6. Check for understanding. Stay patient. Repeat information if necessary; be ready to ask question in a different way when you suspect a person is reluctant to admit to not hearing it.
7. Do not cover mouth or chew while speaking.
8. Avoid background noise and distractions.
9. If communication through speech seems inefficient, write message down.
10. Avoid microphones when speaking to persons with hearing aids.
11. Make use of special devices designed for persons with hearing impairment, such as lights connected to doorbells or TTY telephones.
12. Use short sentences.

Touch and balance

1. Avoid uneven or slippery floor surfaces that may cause falls; fasten rugs firmly to the floor.
2. Keep floor clean of debris.
3. Avoid pedestal tables that tip easily; use four-legged tables instead.
4. Encourage people to make use of supportive devices, such as canes, railings on walls, and arms of sturdy chairs to keep balance or to come to standing position.
5. Warn individuals about the risk of dizziness with abrupt movements such as getting out of bed too fast.
6. For individuals lacking stimulation, enhance touch sensations through rubbing different textured objects against the skin.
7. Carefully monitor and adjust hot water temperature.

Taste and smell

1. Create awareness of the risks of not recognizing certain odors; teach individuals to be careful about foods that have been stored for longer periods of time and to check if gas has been properly turned off.
2. Teach about different spices and how to make foods more flavorful without the need to add salt or sugar.
3. Enhance environmental smells, and encourage people to take time to smell different aromas.

One general rule in using the senses to their fullest is to adopt a multisensorial approach. To maximize the capacity to compensate, make use of as many sources of stimulation as possible; when communicating, use both verbal and visual cues; combine taste and smell for more pleasurable experiences. By understanding changes are seeking creative alternatives to help individuals adjust to them, service providers enable them to maintain independence and self-respect as they proceed in their Ulyssean journey.

CONCLUSIONS

As people grow older they will face inevitable declines in physiological functioning. However, the evidence clearly indicates that the rate of decline is influenced by a variety of lifestyle factors, such as exercise and nutrition. The realization that biological aging is amenable to intervention has resulted in increased programmatic efforts to slow the aging process. The results of these effort are being seen in the daily lives of older people. A recent report from the National Institutes on Health (1997) cited data from the National Long Term Care Surveys indicating that disability rates among older Americans are falling dramatically and the rate of reduction is accelerating. The result of increased well-being and higher functional levels is increased opportunities for Ulyssean living.

It is helpful to examine the physical losses of aging by placing them in the context of the groups of individuals that service providers encounter in their daily practices. Because of the immense variability among older individuals, it should be expected that different levels of ability and disability will be seen. In a recent position paper (undated) Kelly calls attention to the fact that aging may be viewed as a continuum, a path along which different types of individuals travel. Not all older adults maybe classified as either healthy and active or disabled and dependent. In fact, the space between these two extreme cases is often filled by "in-betweeners," as Kelly indicates. This perspective is also illustrated by Atchley's (1991) health continuum, which ranges from a holistic sense of well-being to death (see Table 3.1).

Depending on the setting in which older adults are served, different stages of the above model will be encountered more frequently. For instance, in an age-integrated recreation center, consumers may fall within the two first stages, while in a senior center, they may range from stages three to six. Adult day care agencies and nursing homes, however, will probably see larger number of individuals in the last stages of the continuum. It becomes clear that the meaning of losses to individuals and the types of interventions needed to foster Ulyssean living patterns will depend heavily on each person's overall status concerning the aging process. While prevention will still be realistic for some, for others the major goal may be to minimize the secondary effects of particular conditions already present. Therefore, while some services may be supportive in nature, others may assume a more clinical character.

TABLE 3.1

STAGES OF THE HEALTH CONTINUUM

Good Health						Poor Health	
Absence of disease or impairment	Presence of a condition	Seeks treatment	Restricted activity	Restricted in major activity	Unable to engage in major activity	Institu-tionalized	Death

(ATCHLEY, 1991. REPRINTED BY PERMISSION OF WADSWORTH PUBLISHING.)

This chapter has provided an extensive description of the biological processes accompanying aging. Although many of the changes described in this chapter are inevitable, they need not be obstacles to Ulyssean living if trained professionals are able to effectively intervene.

Chapter 4

◆

Cognitive Processes

Wold (1993) indicated that "cognitive perceptual health pattern deals with the ways people gain information from the environment and the way they interpret and use this information" (p. 251). Perception involves collecting, interpreting, and recognizing stimuli, whereas cognition involves memory, intelligence, language, and decision making. Willis (1992) viewed cognition, along with physical health, as having a major role in maintaining independence in later life, particularly as it relates to everyday competencies. These include: managing finances, taking medication, shopping, using the phone, carrying out housekeeping chores, transporting oneself, and preparing meals (p. 80). Clearly, these factors relate to Ulyssean living.

In this chapter, the focus will be on the areas of intelligence, learning, memory, and creativity as they relate to the aging process. As with the previous chapter, the emphasis will not be on the magnitude of losses, but on the factors that may inhibit or contribute to Ulyssean living.

Rowe and Kahn (1998) address the question of whether cognitive losses are an inevitable part of aging. The answer, as with many such questions, is yes and no. There are losses in some mental processes but not all. Many of the losses, although real, are exaggerated. Other losses are still not sufficiently researched to be completely understood. It is important to keep in mind that the patterns of age-related changes detected in human cognition do not imply a deficit in functioning. As with the biological processes, losses are gradual and variable among different individuals; most are not noted until late old age. Furthermore, research has indicated that some of the changes observed may be delayed or even ameliorated with proper interventions. Even when losses are experienced, individuals have the capacity to cope with them by optimizing performance and relying on environmental support.

Once again, the questions raised in the previous chapter regarding the meaning of the losses to the individual are pertinent. Except for pathological conditions, which affect only a small percentage of older adults, losses typically are too minimal to have any significant impact on quality of life.

Specific Changes

Intelligence

The concept of intelligence is not an easy one to define. A construct used in psychology, it has been the topic of much debate because of its complex nature. Since it cannot be directly observed, intellectual abilities are inferred from actions and behaviors exhibited by individuals; in other words, competence is evaluated through performance.

A common procedure used in the measurement of intelligence is the administration of standardized tests, such as the WAIS (Wechsler Adult Intelligence Scale). The WAIS is divided into two domains: verbal and performance. Categories under the verbal domain include categories such as vocabulary, comprehension, and arithmetic, while performance encompasses picture completion, block design, and digit symbol.

Studies have shown that when this instrument is used to compare older adults to younger adults, differences are much more evident in the performance section of the test than on the verbal one, with verbal scores showing much stability over time (Botwinick, 1967).

Such differences in performance may be explained by viewing verbal tasks as related to crystallized intelligence (intelligence reflecting acculturation and general knowledge; Birren and Fisher, 1991) whereas performance tasks rely more heavily on fluid intelligence (the ability to reason, categorize, and sort information; Birren and Fisher, 1991). Fluid intelligence declines with age, whereas crystallized intelligence grows with age. Also, responses to performance tasks may involve speed; considering the discussion regarding slower reaction times among the elderly, it is understandable that they may be at a disadvantage in relation to such tasks.

Intelligence tests such as the WAIS have been the focus of much criticism. Ebersole and Hess (1990) have identified a variety of reasons why older people's performance may be unfairly represented by such tests. These include:

1. test content may not be relevant to older people;
2. older people may not be in the habit of being tested;
3. older individuals may not have developed test wisdom;
4. text anxiety may make concentration difficult;
5. factors such as nutrition may influence test scores;
6. older people may respond more slowly than their younger counterparts;
7. older individuals may be less likely to guess at answers than younger individuals.

Schaie (1996) reviewed results from the Seattle Longitudinal Study, a project measuring age changes and age differences in primary mental abilities. The study examined several abilities including: verbal meaning, space, reasoning, and number and word fluency. In addition, measures of inductive reasoning, spatial orientation, perceptual speed, numeric and verbal ability, and verbal memory were also taken. The results indicated there is generally a gain in these areas until the late 30s or early 40s followed by stability until the mid-50s to early to late 60s. At that point decrements are noted, although they are small, until the mid-70s. While all individuals experienced declines in at least one of the five areas of mental abilities, none of the study participants had declines in all five and fewer than half had significant declines in more than two areas. Furthermore, changes were more likely to occur in areas less central to an individual's daily life. The losses that occurred were more significant in situations that were highly challenging, stressful, or complex. Normal, familiar, practiced behaviors were less likely to be impacted by these losses.

An interesting concept has been receiving attention lately, that is, practical intelligence (Stemberg & Wagner, 1986). It holds promise as a more useful way of examining intelligence than the traditional testing methods. According to Schaie (1990), "There is an aspect of intelligence that is not measured by conventional processing or psychometric approaches because it involves the pragmatics of applying intellectual skills to everyday activities, and further, that the activities involved therein may differ across the life course" (pp. 300–301). Willis (1996) discussed this movement away from measuring cognitive aging in the laboratory and toward measuring it within the context of problem solving in everyday life. This approach provides a more realistic appraisal of the ability to think when presented with typical situations. While Willis indicated there are age-related differences in approaches to problem solving, factors other than age may be responsible. Further examination of this concept should cast new light onto the significance of intellectual decline to the routine demands faced by older adults.

Cross sectional and longitudinal studies. In measuring age-related changes in intelligence, different types of methodology have been employed. Cross-sectional studies compare different cohorts at one point in time in attempting to uncover differences in intelligence between younger and older adults. Cross-sectional studies usually show that intelligence increases until early adulthood, remains on a plateau until the fourth decade, and declines from the fifth decade on.

Such declines, however, may or may not be due to age, since generational effects may confound the results. Because of the experiences typical to different cohorts, it is possible that differences found reflect changes in the educational system or cultural values rather than actual losses in intellectual ability by older adults.

Longitudinal studies follow a group of individuals over a period of time, measuring them at different time intervals. These studies show only slight declines in some areas of intelligence, accompanied by improvements in other areas; they also indicate that such declines occur much later in life than was previously thought (MacNeil & Teague, 1987).

Like cross-sectional studies, longitudinal ones have drawbacks regarding internal validity. Repeated testing and survival of the most fit may contribute to more favorable findings associated with such studies. The combination of both methods through sequential developmental techniques seems to be a better alternative. Studies utilizing this type of methodology seem to indicate the existence of age-related declines in intellectual functioning; however, they clearly show that such changes are not pervasive and that they are not noticeable until relatively late in the life course.

The optimization of cognitive functioning. According to Schaie (1990), individuals tend to preserve levels of performance achieved at earlier ages by optimizing their intellectual functioning in adjusting to biological declines and environmental insults. This statement is based on a number of sequential studies of adult intelligence conducted by Schaie and associates (Schaie & Hertzog, 1986; Schaie, 1996).

Their findings seem to confirm the ability of older adults to maintain intellectual functioning levels by optimizing their abilities. The fact that declines were not consistent across all areas and that different areas showed decrements for different individuals also points to the need to look for factors that may explain the selectivity in maintenance or decline by different individuals throughout life.

Baltes, Smith, and Staudinger (1991) view this selective optimization with compensation model (see Chapter 5 for a more thorough discussion) as a "strategy of mastery that permits effective management of one's aging, despite age-associated losses in mental and physical reserves" (p. 152). This coping strategy requires individuals to focus on their strengths, practice and use remaining abilities, and find compensatory mechanisms when necessary. This model suggests that the impact of intellectual declines will be minimized through careful selection of the arenas for intellectual challenge as well as through practice in intellectual endeavors.

By reviewing the literature, Schaie (1990, 1996) has pointed to the following as possible variables mediating the maintenance of cognitive functioning: (a) absence of pathological health conditions, particularly cardiovascular disease, (b) speed of performance, (c) demographic characteristics such as education and occupational status, (d) stimulating environments, (e) flexibility in personality, and (f) self-efficacy.

MacKenzie (1980) has also suggested that social conditions may play an important role in maintaining mental abilities. "Older people who remain in the mainstream of life, who continue to pursue and initiate normal social contacts, and who remain personally involved with others are far less likely to experience intellectual decline than are elderly individuals who are cut off from others and endure long periods of social isolation" (pp. 66–67).

ULYSSEAN APPROACHES

From examining the information presented above, it seems clear that significant deficits are more the exception than the norm among older adults. For the most part, declines are not noted until later in life and are small and not specific enough to constitute major barriers to Ulyssean living. Furthermore, a number of studies have shown that cognitive training results in gains for older adults (Willis, 1987). This trend has been observed even for those who had already shown declines, with gains sometimes returning subjects to levels of functioning demonstrated over a decade ago (Willis & Schaie, 1986). Intellectual abilities such as concept formation, figural relations, and inductive reasoning are some of the examples cited in literature (Schooler, 1990).

If the factors mediating cognitive functioning are taken into consideration, some logical conclusions can be drawn. If speed of performance seems to interfere with effective functioning, individuals should be allowed enough time to consider their options in problem solving and decision making. Also the prevention of damaging health conditions such as cardiovascular disease should prove helpful in ensuring continued cognitive effectiveness. Considering the negative self-evaluations that may result in self-fulfilling prophesies, it is important to eradicate myths regarding age-related declines in intelligence. It is also important to manipulate the environment to eliminate threatening characteristics and to make it increasingly supportive.

Part of this task lies in providing positive stimulation. Continuous involvement in stimulating activities does to the mind what exercise does to the body. Environmental support should not be limited to the physical aspect, though. Human conditions such as social interaction should also be facilitated to enhance the Ulyssean experience.

LEARNING AND MEMORY

One of the greatest fears of many older individuals is Alzheimer's disease and the concomitant loss of independence. As a result, memory lapses are accompanied by anxiety and dread. It is crucial that service providers be aware of the normal changes in memory with age and be prepared to address issues relating to memory. In addition, service providers must base their programs on a realistic perspective of memory and learning in the later years. The old adage "You can't teach an old dog new tricks" seems to reflect society's views regarding learning and old age. As a result, a number of the programs offered for older adults are based on set routines. A belief in the ability of the old to learn new activities would demand the incorporation of more challenging and thought-provoking activities in programs.

Learning and memory are closely related. Memory involves the ability to retrieve information stored in the brain. Learning is the process of encoding information into memory. Both are crucial to Ulyssean living.

Hooyman and Kiyak (1993) indicated there are three types of memory, sensory, primary, and secondary. Sensory memory involves receiving information and briefly holding it. Sensory memory includes visual information such as colors, signs or words (iconic memory) and auditory input such as sounds. This information is quickly lost if it is not processed at a deeper level. For example, as you read this page, you are being bombarded with visual and auditory input. The sights and sounds around you are part of your sensory memory. However, most of this information will have been forgotten by the time you reach the end of this sentence.

However, some of the information is passed to primary memory. At this stage, the information has been processed, labeled, and prepared to be sent to secondary memory. Usually, it remains stored in short-term memory for only a short period of time, until capacity is reached with the input of new stimuli. If the information is not used or given further meaning, it is most likely to be displaced. If rehearsal takes place, the information may be retained longer under conscious attention. For example, if asked, you might be able to repeat what you just read in this paragraph. However, this memory will soon fade unless you actively seek to retain it.

To store information more permanently some form of encoding must occur. Through encoding, information is manipulated as to be given meaning and is organized in a conceptual way that allows for prolonged retention under secondary memory. When needed, information stored in long-term memory is sent back to short-term memory to be activated in the form of a verbal or motor response. This retrieval process is not always successful; when information previously stored is not accessible for retrieval, it is considered to be forgotten. Your secondary memory for this material, for example, may be tested during an examination. You will be required to retrieve stored information and display this knowledge on demand.

Research on age-related changes in memory shows that age differences in primary memory are negligible, provided that the individual has fully perceived the items to be remembered and that reorganization is not required. The data indicate, however, that older individuals do not perform as well as younger ones when secondary memory is involved. Even when primary memory is intact, declines in secondary memory are observable (Hooyman and Kiyak, 1993).

Another component of memory, known as remote memory (also called old memory or tertiary memory), is related to the ability to recall events from a distant past. Traditionally, it was thought that this type of memory remained quite stable with age. Anecdotal evidence of this belief is often provided from the number of war stories and family histories told by older adults. However, data obtained from laboratory tests show that older adults' performance at recalling events from the past is poorer than that of younger people.

Findings related to age-related differences in memory may be associated with what has been identified as implicit and explicit memory. Explicit memory involves intention to remember and is related to specific instructions given to the individual. It involves the conscious recollection of facts acquired through learning. For example, explicit memory is involved in the recollection of names, numbers, or directions. Implicit memory occurs without conscious recollection of remembering and is not preceded by instructions to remember. Implicit memory impacts learned skills and behaviors not relying on specific recollection of information.

Recent evidence suggests that age-related differences in explicit memory are more frequent and profound than in implicit memory (Hultsch & Dixon, 1990; Howard, 1992). Could it be that older adults are able to use remote memory when naturally and unconsciously stimulated by their environment, but when instructed to remember, their capacity to recall is less evident?

Another aspect of memory that has been examined is working memory, which is related the ability to do two things at once. For example, trying to subtract two large numbers in your head involves retaining the numbers in your memory while also performing the actual subtraction. Focusing on the subtraction may result in forgetting the original numbers. There is evidence that working memory declines in later life (Women and Aging Newsletter, 1996; West, Wincour, Ergis & Saint-Cyr, 1998).

Age-associated memory impairment (AAMI) is viewed as a normal part of aging. It involves subjective complaints of memory loss and mild deficiencies in memory performance. There is an absence of dementia or other medical conditions that could produce cognitive disfunctioning (Small, LaRue, Komo, & Kaplan, 1997). Estimates indicate that AAMI incidence ranges from 40% of all individuals in their 50s to 85% of individuals aged 80 and older. Memory decline in some individuals may be attributed to AAMI. However, a number of factors have been identified as interfering with memory in old age. For instance, when a variety of stimuli are presented at the same time, memory losses are intensified. This is not surprising since there is decline in working memory with increasing age. Difficulty is also apparent when background stimuli interfere with the task at hand.

Tasks of a complex nature also seem to pose more problems for recall, particularly when information to be retrieved needs to be modified in some way (Kalish, 1982); an example might be recalling the name of the five last presidents and listing them in alphabetical order. Also, when information is shown in a quick sequence or displayed only briefly, memory ability seems to be affected.

Rate of presentation of information and number of study trials have also been shown to affect memory performance. When task pacing is allowed and more opportunities for studying the materials are given, older adults seem to show improvement in recall (Backman, Mantayla, & Herlitz, 1990).

Differences in memory efficiency are also verified between recognition and recall (MacNeil & Teague, 1992). When the older person is given a list of names and asked to indicate which ones correspond to names of United States presidents, the likelihood of successful responses is greater than when the same person is asked to name as many presidents as possible.

Age-related differences in memory may also be explained by retrieval difficulty. The fact that recognition is possible points to the efficient acquisition of information. Nevertheless, difficulties in recall seem to indicate that older adults' ability to search for stored information is deficient. This deficit maybe associated with initial difficulties in encoding information in such a way that allows for ready retrieval.

It has been hypothesized that older adults may experience problems in processing information semantically or in utilizing the mnemonic devices needed to activate processed information (Cook, 1983). Age-related differences are almost nonexistent when support is offered at the stages of encoding and retrieval through semantic associations or category cues. When explicit instructions are offered regarding how to organize materials or how to use imagery or verbal mediators prior to presentation of information, differences are also attenuated (Backman, Mantayla & Herlitz, 1990).

Meaningfulness of material presented may affect not only learning, but also memory. This seems to be confirmed by the fact that experience in a certain area appears to be positively related to high levels of performance in that area (Backman, Mantayla, & Herlitz, 1990; Hultsch & Dixon, 1990). Information that is not considered relevant to the individual may not be adequately encoded. When relationships can be drawn from previous experiences and novel ones, the likelihood of later recall may be higher.

Research has indicated that the nature of materials to be remembered strongly impacts performance. Higher levels of recall are observed when stimuli are presented in a multisensorial way, when they are rich and varied in features, and when they are contextually organized (Backman, Mantayla, & Herlitz, 1990).

There is also evidence that medication impacts memory. According to the Women and Aging Newsletter (1996), a variety of medications are commonly associated with memory problems. These include: Aldomet, Ascendin, Dalmane, Elavil, Equanil, Haldol, Inderal, Mellaril, Miltown, Pamelor, Pepcid, Seraz, Symmetrel, Tagamet, Valium, and Xantac.

Although there are cognitive declines in the later years, most older individuals will not be seriously impacted by these losses. Rowe and Kahn (1998) provide hope for those who fear old age as an intellectual wasteland. They found that few specific cognitive losses are the result of the aging process itself and even in these losses there is great variability among the elderly. In addition, cognitive ability is composed of many functions, and these age at different rates. As a result, declines in some areas of functioning do not interfere with the ability to remain independent and function effectively.

ULYSSEAN INTERVENTIONS

Most of the factors associated with age-related learning and memory differences are amenable to intervention. A number of strategies to facilitate learning and recall will be identified below.

Ebersole and Hess (1998) provided an extensive list of special learning needs of some older adults. They can be effective in developing teaching strategies to use in programs and include:

1. Face the individuals with whom you are communicating so they can see your lips and facial movements.

2. Speak slowly and keep the tone of your voice low.
3. Present one idea at a time.
4. Whenever possible, focus on concrete rather than abstract material.
5. Provide sufficient time for individuals to respond.
6. Keep distractions to a minimum.
7. Use a variety of cues, auditory, visual, and tactile, to enhance learning.
8. Connect new learning to things learned in the past.
9. Use creative teaching strategies.

In addition to the above guidelines, the American Association of Retired Persons (1990) suggests the following:

1. Establish a comfortable environment for learning.
2. Assess the older person's expectations and take advantage of the older adult's interests, attitudes and motivation.
3. Emphasize the older person's abilities and experiences.
4. Establish the connection between new information and old knowledge.
5. Use reassurance, but do not talk down to the older person.
6. Try to retain attention by minimizing distracting background noises or other stimuli.
7. Repeat information when needed and emphasize important pieces of material.
8. Learn to interpret nonverbal signs, such as fatigue; take short breaks to allow for relaxation.

Many of the suggestions presented above apply to both learning and memory. The key words appear to be environmental support. In the area of memory improvement, Harris (1984) has detailed several approaches that may be utilized by programmatic interventions. He divided these approaches into four categories: (a) internal strategies, (b) external aids, (c) repetitive practice, and (d) physical treatments.

Internal strategies include the use of mnemonics. He suggests techniques such as creating a story linking a series of words to assist remembering these words, using the first letter of a series of words to be remembered to create a more easily remembered phrase, or associating a person's name with an unusual feature of that person to help remember that person later on.

External aids are objects used to store information externally or to help trigger a memory. Examples of the former are agendas, grocery lists, calendars, written medication schedules, and computer databases. A typical illustration of a triggering mechanism is the string around the finger; another might be leaving a medicine bottle next to the coffee pot to remember to take medication in the early morning.

Repetitive practice means repeating or rehearsing important pieces of information. This may be particularly helpful for information such as telephone numbers that need to be maintained in conscious awareness until the individual has a chance to write them down. It may also be helpful in memorizing lists or other types of information for which internal strategies may be difficult to find.

Physical treatments refer to the manipulation of chemical and biological processes on which memory depends. Some drugs, including those listed above, result in memory decline. Conversely, other drugs, such as Piracetam, may aid in memory.

There are several programs designed specifically to improve memory in the elderly. The notion of instituting "memory clinics" in community centers and long-term care facilities is an exciting one.

Such clinics could design strategies and programs to assist older individuals in focusing on their strengths in order to compensate for cognitive losses. Rowe and Kahn (1998) indicate that older individuals can significantly improve cognitive functioning through training and practice. For example, they describe a study which focused on the number of words individuals were able to recall after being shown a long list of words. Older individuals were able, on the average, to recall fewer than five words, while younger participants were able to recall more words. Five training sessions were held during which recall techniques were taught. Participants were taught to group words in clusters rather than attempt to remember specific words. In addition, they were taught to link words to locations or sequences already known. For example, remembering groceries was linked to walking through the kitchen. After the five sessions the older respondents' performance tripled compared to pre-training levels. In fact, the number of words older people remembered after training was higher than the number recalled by untrained young people. According to Rowe and Kahn, "people were amazed to learn that elderly men and women who have experienced some cognitive decline can, with appropriate training, improve enough to offset approximately two decades of memory loss" (p. 137). Clearly, opportunities for Ulyssean living can be enhanced through formal memory training programs.

A program of memory improvement was detailed in the Women and Aging Newsletter (1996) and includes several steps. First, individuals should focus on their strengths. These can be used to compensate for losses in other areas. Some people are good at remembering names, others at faces, others at directions, and others at small details. Organizing skills can be used to replace some aspects of memory. In addition, wisdom accumulated through experience is a useful tool in dealing with memory loss.

The second component of the memory improvement process is to identify reasons for forgetfulness and address those reasons. Research indicates that common reasons identified for forgetting include: distractions, sensory losses such as hearing limiting input, fatigue, anxiety, depression, medications, viewing things as not important, and an overload of things to remember. If an individual is able to isolate the reasons for forgetting, then interventions to address them can be initiated. For example, distractions can be overcome by learning to focus, medications can be altered, and sensory losses can be decreased through prosthetic devices.

The third approach to improving memory is to be attentive. People can learn to concentrate on the matter at hand and not be distracted by other input. Specifically focusing on where you are placing the car keys, rather than haphazardly throwing them down, will help remember where they are at a later time. Consciously thinking about events as they occur, for example, where you are parking your car, will be helpful in remembering its location.

The fourth approach is to use triggers when necessary to assist memory. Writing things down, putting objects such a keys in the same place all the time, repeating important information over and over again, making associations between items, and reviewing photo albums when seeing people who haven't been seen in a long time will all compensate for some memory loss. An example of using associational triggers recently occurred with one of the authors of this book. He was on an Internet site devoted to puzzles and memory games. One of the games involved looking at nine words arranged in three columns and three rows with one word in each square of the 3 x 3 matrix. The player was allowed to look at the words as long as desired. Pressing the "play" button then resulted in the words disappearing and the 3 x 3 matrix remaining with blank spaces replacing the words. This was followed by a series of trivia questions. The object of the game was to answer each question, using one of the nine words, and then clicking on the space in the matrix where that word had been. For example, one question was "The unproduced stage play 'Everybody Comes to Rick's' was turned into what classic film?" To succeed at this puzzle you not only had to know the answer was Casablanca but also had to remember that Casablanca had been in square 4 in the matrix. The first time the author played, he knew all the trivia questions' answers but was able to correctly place only four of them. The second game was exactly like the first except there were different words and clues. The second matrix looked like this:

Mia Farrow	Enterprise	Ellen
Scapula	Davey Crockett	Godzilla
Baldric	Friends	Dracula

It was decided to use a different strategy to remember the location of these words. A sentence was constructed for each line. Line one became "Mia Farrow boarded the Enterprise with Ellen." Line two became "the scapular (sic) had pictures of Davey Crockett and Godzilla." And line three was transformed into "Baldric was friends with Dracula." Not only was the author able to answer the trivia questions correctly but also was able to place each answer into the correct square on the matrix!

West and Grafman (1998) provide a list of seven memory strategies. Their suggestions, similar to those above, provide a framework that can be used to develop a memory program. Their recommendations:

1. Pay attention—They suggest actively monitoring and examining one's own behavior. For example, when placing car keys in a pocket, person could say, "I am putting the keys in my jacket pocket."
2. Rehearse and repeat—Rehearsing information, repeating it to oneself, is one way to store it in long-term memory.
3. Chunk—This refers to the process of grouping items together to aid in memory. For example, it may be difficult to remember a 10-digit phone number (864-656-2183) but may be easier to remember three chunks (864, 656, 2183) separately.
4. Use cues—Suggestions for using cues such as imagery and triggers are discussed above. Creating a mental snapshot of what is to be remembered in also an effective cueing mechanism.
5. Get organized—Consistently placing object, such as keys and medications, in the same place reduces the frustration of struggling to remember where they are located.
6. Mind your P Q R S T—This describes a five-step memory and learning exercise to organize text material, such as the directions for a VCR. PREVIEW the material to identify main points, create QUESTIONS identifying the essentials points to learn, REREAD the material to answer the questions, STUDY and understand the answers, and then TEST yourself for understanding.
7. Increase use of external aids—Notes, appointment books, calendars, timers, and clock radios may all serve as external aids.

Social support also impacts cognitive functioning and can be used to contribute to Ulyssean living (Rowe & Kahn, 1998). Social support includes encouragement ("well done," "that's right"), and allowing individuals to do things for themselves rather than doing things for them. In addition, social support can assist in developing self-efficacy (Bandura, 1982) (see Chapter 7 for more on self-efficacy). Older individuals need accurate, positive feedback in order to be convinced that their cognitive functioning is strong. Rowe and Kahn (1998) found that convincing older individuals they retain ability in the area of memory results in more time and effort to memory tasks and therefore gains in actual performance as well as in self-esteem.

The notion that old age is a synonym for memory loss is another one of the many myths that needs to be eliminated, particularly if memory lapses are to be identified as a sign of cognitive deterioration. The following passage by Samuel Johnson was appropriately captured by Cole (1981):

> There is a wicked inclination in most people to suppose an old man decayed in his intellect. If a younger middle-aged man, when leaving a company, does not recollect where he laid his hat, it is nothing; but if the same inattention is discovered in an old man, people will shrug their shoulders and say, "His memory is going."

Much of what is viewed as a natural part of the aging process is, in fact, pathological. For instance, significant memory loss is partially associated with Alzheimer's disease or other cognitive disorders rather than related to aging, per se. Losses in learning and memory are not significant enough to seriously detour older adults from their Ulyssean journey. The role of practitioners is to post enough signs along the way as to guide travelers to follow the path.

CREATIVITY

Creativity can be defined as originality in thought and expression; it can also be described as the ability for problem solving when facing novel situations. This domain of cognition has not received as much attention by researchers as areas such as memory and intelligence. Lately, however, there seems be a resurgence of interest in the topic. Simonton (1988) attributes this renewed interest, in part, to demographic trends.

Throughout the 20th century, researchers have focused on three major topics: (a) the existence of an age curve for creative output, (b) the connection between precocity, longevity, and rate of output, and (c) the relationship between quantity and quality of output (Simonton, 1990).

One of the classical studies often cited in literature was conducted by Lehman (1953). The conclusion of this study was that creative output, as measured by high-quality works, reaches a peak around age 30 and declines rapidly thereafter, thus showing a curvilinear relationship to age. Having examined three areas of creativity, scholarship, and sciences and art, Lehman also pointed to the difference in patterns among these categories. While mathematics showed the earliest peaks, philosophy showed some of the latest ones.

Lehman's findings were disputed by Dennis (1966), who opposed the measurement of creativity by counting major contributions rather than total output. When creative productivity across the life span was examined, results indicated that although the decade of the '40s seemed to be the most productive, results differed among different fields and, most importantly, decline in output was much less dramatic than Lehman had proposed. The drop-off observed was gradual; in disciplines such as history and philosophy it was almost negligible since output had peaked in the sixth decade and remained high for the seventh.

Lehman's proposition of creative output as a curvilinear function of age seems to be confirmed through more recent studies; it seems appropriate to look at this relationship as an inverted backward J-curve, representing the fast rise of productivity to reach a clear peak and its decline at a more gradual rate to the point where it represents about half of the output observed at the peak mark (Simonton, 1988). The location of the peak along the life span varies across disciplines, as does the rate of decline thereafter. Areas associated with the sciences seem to show the earliest peaks (20s and early 30s) and the greatest drop-off, whereas scholarship domains tend to show the latest peaks (40s and 50s) and the most insignificant declines thereafter.

The relationship between quality and quantity seems to indicate a positive correlation. High quality appears to be a probabilistic result of large quantity of output. The more produced, the greater the likelihood for exceptional quality work; regardless of age period.

There is a strong connection between precocity, longevity, and output rate. Those who show high levels of production at an early age also seem to be the ones who will remain productive until later years; both precocity and longevity are associated with high output rate throughout the life span.

In spite of the findings of research in the area of creativity and aging, examples of exceptional creativity in old age challenge the belief that creativity universally declines with age. Individuals such as Picasso, Tolstoy, Freud, and Sophocles exemplify great achievement after the seventh decade of life. What may explain these and other renowned cases of creative excellence?

In reviewing the literature, Abra (1989) gathered a number of potential contributors to creativity that may be affected as individuals age. Some of them will be discussed next. Flexibility of thinking is one area; rigidity in thinking and deficits in fluid intelligence may explain a drop in originality, one of the criteria used to judge creativity. When an individual's work relies heavily on originality, it may suffer with aging. This may explain why scientists show greater declines than philosophers. While the former are constantly seeking new directions, the latter often devote their time to perfecting a body of ideas. It seems obvious that the criteria for creativity largely affects conclusions regarding age-related changes.

Related to originality is the notion of enthusiasm. As individuals age, spontaneity and enthusiasm are gradually replaced by experience and sophistication. While enthusiasm leads to great originality, experience calls for more critical eyes and a focus on wisdom. According to Beard (1974), these two forces reach a balance around age 40, which might explain why productivity seems to reach its peak at this stage. It also explains why different disciplines peak at different ages; those relying on energetic pursuits of new forms of expression may peak at early stages, while those emphasizing experience would show high output during the later decades of life.

Another interesting issue is that of persistence. It was previously stated that quality depends on quantity. To generate high-quality work, one needs to be willing to produce in great quantities. Younger persons may be more receptive to the idea of trial and error and constant production, with less critical eyes. Older adults, on the other hand, tend to value accuracy in their work; they may spend more time looking for the perfect output, thus producing lesser quantities. Also, energy levels may interfere with the constant drive to produce.

The need for accuracy may also be associated with self-confidence and expectations. Average people are not expected to be exceptionally creative in old age; society sees individuals such as Grandma Moses as the exception rather than the rule. Older adults do not receive much support to express creativity and may therefore feel they have little to contribute. If the individual is already considered talented and has a history of achievement, old age may be accompanied by the fear of losing it, which may lead to high expectations and a need to outdo previous works.

One intriguing conclusion drawn by Abra (1989) is that "creativity may simply change rather than decline with age, with different stylistic and thematic concerns gaining priority" (p. 105). This would explain why playwrights focus more on spiritual matters as they age. One important factor to consider is that older adults constantly make use of creative abilities to adjust to a continuously changing world. Adapting to physical changes and to social losses may represent the ultimate challenge to creativity, one that wins no prizes because it is done gradually and surreptitiously.

Another issue to consider is the need to study average older adults who show patterns of lifelong creativity. A qualitative study led by Fergunson (1989) examined a variety of topics related to creativity in 20 elderly persons residing in the community or long-term care facilities. One of the findings relates to the fact that for some subjects, retirement opened doors for creative behavior. One subject indicated that "creativity comes after the creative person finds that he can free himself of outside interferences and then he can become more of himself" (p. 136).

Participants also disputed the notion that health hindered creativity. Neither acute nor chronic illness seemed to stop the creative process; on the contrary, some temporary illnesses even allowed them more time to pursue their interests. These two findings seem to point to potential opportunities rather than limitations in old age.

The above study also confirmed one of the reasons why people engage in creative work. According to Fergunson (1989):

> When an individual is able to do something for someone who has helped him/her and is able to give something to that helper, he/she is able to feel as if he/she has reciprocated that help. In turn such actions help him/her remain or feel less dependent; if not allowing him/her to be independent (p. 137).

The need to feel independent and feel that life has purpose cannot be underscored enough when Ulyssean living is the aim.

ULYSSEAN APPROACHES

Encouragement may be the major need of older persons in this domain. The need to feel useful guides most individuals' motivations. In a recent qualitative study of the role of leisure in the lives of older black women (Tedrick & Boyd, 1992), one of the participants, an energetic 91-year-old woman, mentioned that she used to make hats, of which she was quite proud. When asked why she no longer engaged in such activity, she responded, "I have no one to make them for." This woman's talent was not being capitalized on by the senior center she frequented.

A suggestion that applies to all settings serving older adults is to assess individuals' past skills and to foster a sense of autonomy and pride by making use of such gifts to keep the individuals connected with their families and communities. Gifts do not need to be confined to the artistic vein. One nursing home made use of the sales skills of one of the residents who had suffered from a stroke. Knowing that the woman had a history of exceptional performance as a salesperson, the staff provided her with a telephone so she could call community members and sell paintings produced by other residents. A good sales speech is definitely a sign of a creative mind; this woman had not only the opportunity to remain mentally active, but also to feel that her work was a contribution to her facility and to the community in general.

McLeish (1976) recommends gathering individuals in small groups and challenging them to awaken their creativity through a series of exercises. Some of the creativity-stimulating activities he suggested were:

1. Make a parody of a nursery rhyme.
2. Name five practical inventions which have not yet been invented.
3. List 10 new ways to use Scotch tape.
4. Take two objects as different as possible—a sock and a lawn mower for example—and identify how they might be paired in creative ways.
5. Suggest three or four historic people and describe how their meeting would create a bizarre, ludicrous, or comical conversation.
6. Describe three new uses for a computer.

The result of participating in exercises of this type will be revitalized creativity and a Ulyssean perspective.

CONCLUSION

This brief examination of cognitive processes in the later years provides an overview of intelligence, learning, memory, and creativity. The message is the same as that in Chapter 3: Declines occur; intervention is effective; Ulyssean living is possible.

A few lines of the poem "Ulysses" apply here:

How dull is to pause, to make an end,
To rust unburnished, not to shine in use!
And this grey spirit yearning in desire
To follow knowledge like a sinking star.

Death closes all; but something ere the end,
Some work of noble note, may yet be done
. . . but strong in will
To strive, to seek, to find and not to yield.

The potential for Ulyssean living in the later years is greatly increased in individuals with high levels of cognitive functioning. Learning, memory, and creativity are powerful tools for enhancing the quality of life. Although there are some declines in these areas in the later years, the good news is that in most cases the losses are neither overwhelming nor intractable. Indeed, the mind and things of the mind will "shine in use."

Chapter 5

◆

Psychological Aging

The examination of psychological changes that accompany the aging process deals with a variety of topics, such as personality, tasks associated with older adulthood as a developmental stage, adaptation to old age, and mental health of the elderly. The sections below will approach some of the major issues associated with these topics and also include recommendations to foster psychological well-being in older adults.

PERSONALITY

Overall, there seems to be little change in personality as a result of old age. As Kogan (1990) noted, "interindividual stability of specific traits across extended time periods is quite substantial" (p. 341). This continuity of personality structures over the life span is a consistent finding of most studies on aging and personality (Cook, 1983; Heckheimer, 1989; Ruth & Coleman, 1996). Older individuals have spent a lifetime developing strategies for coping and adapting. The evidence indicates these strategies endure as people age. Older individuals are active participants in their lives and most have developed the personal resources needed to survive. Entering old age does not diminish these resources. Such stability does not exclude, however, the possibility of some general personality alterations.

In one of the few longitudinal studies conducted with older adults reported in the literature, Neugarten (1964, 1977) and (Atchley, 1991) uncovered a global trend that begins in middle age and becomes more evident in old age. Such a trend, referred to as "interiority," is defined as a growing introspection, a change in focus from the external environment to the person's interior world. Neugarten's subjects also seemed to adopt a "passive mastery" of the environment, showing accommodation rather than spending their energies trying to change a world that seemed increasingly dangerous and complex.

Another characteristic generally discussed in the aging literature (Haight, 1991) is the tendency for men and women to move in different directions as they age, eventually showing signs of androgyny. That is, while males show more signs of nurturance and affiliation (traditionally considered female traits), females demonstrate more aggressiveness and independence (traditionally seen as male traits). Sex role differentiation thus seems to decrease in old age (Cook, 1983).

Some of the above findings may lead readers to believe that old age is a time of passivity and surrender. It is important to view such results in light of previous discussions regarding motivation and social context. In an earlier chapter, it was shown that the resistance to learn new information could be attributed to the older person's realization of what was meaningful to him or her. Motivation to learn is, then, associated with an evaluation of worth. After years of experimentation, the older person may come to adopt the same approach regarding where to invest his or her energies. Instead of reacting aggressively towards the outside environment, the individual may pick battles selectively, reserving more energy to spend in other important inner-world processes, such as life review. Such a view is consistent with the components of the selective optimization with compensation to be reviewed later in this chapter.

In terms of social context, it is important to look at the changes in the older population since 1960. Some of the findings of Neugarten's study may have been due to cohort effects, rather than universal, unchangeable characteristics of aging. Although her study used a longitudinal methodology, it surveyed individuals born in the beginning of the twentieth century.

An obvious question may be: "Will the next generation of older adults, particularly those in the baby-boomers cohort, exhibit these same traits?" These individuals, men and women, are known for their active involvement in society. They are expected to be healthier, more physically active, more engaged in self-advocacy, and more demanding of high-quality services.

Women are more engaged in the workforce than ever; they share many of the males' stresses that they were previously spared due to their traditional home-maker roles. Men, on the other hand, seem to be sharing the responsibility involved in caring for the family and the household. It will be interesting to see if this group will resemble the subjects in earlier studies.

DEVELOPMENTAL TASKS

One paradigm of age-related change in personality is based on developmental stage models. These models view later adulthood as a time of continued development and as qualitatively different from earlier stages.

For example, Kogan (1990) identifies the work of Erikson (1950), Loevinger (1976), and Levinson (1986) as representative of this approach. According to Erikson's (1950) psychosocial stages, individuals move from middle adulthood's tasks of "generativity vs. stagnation" to late adulthood's tasks of "integrity vs. despair." While middle-aged adults are concerned with leaving a legacy to their descendants, viewing their job and civic responsibilities as their major channels of productivity, older adults strive to find a sense of integrity, a feeling of closure related to the acceptance of life as lived.

One interesting approach to development is the notion of "maturity," a state of being that is needed to meet the psychological tasks of adulthood, beginning in young adulthood and reaching its full potential in the 50s and 60s (MacNeil & Teague, 1987). The characteristics of maturity, as proposed by Allport (1961) are:

1. Extended sense of self: having concern for others, actively participating in different dimensions of the surrounding environment.
2. Ability to relate warmly to others: developing bonds of intimacy and treating others with sensitivity.
3. Acceptance of self and sense of emotional security: accepting self and being able to express self, showing increased tolerance to frustration.
4. Accurate perception of reality: being able to perceive reality and act accordingly.
5. Capability for self-objectification: being aware of personal skills and limitations, possessing self-insights and ability to derive humor from shortcomings.
6. Establishment of a unifying philosophy of life: developing meaningful goals and working towards them.

Developmental tasks define the things an individual needs to accomplish, adjustments to be made, and problems to solve (Birchenall & Streight, 1993; p. 11). Although a variety of taxonomies of these developmental tasks exist, the Havighurst and Duvall model identified by Birchenall and Streight (1993) (see Figure 5.1) and the system developed by Ebersole and Hess (1998) (Figure 5.2) provide clear evidence of the foci needed in later life.

Examination of these three models yields intriguing possibilities for fostering continued development in the later years. There are clearly two opposite tasks the elderly must address. The first is adjusting to the physical losses which are a concomitant of aging. The body declines, health diminishes, and death approaches. An inner peace and acceptance are important in later life. Erikson's ego integrity is a noble goal. However, true development, Ulyssean aging, requires more than acknowledgment and acceptance of loss. It also demands searching for continued meaning in life. As Ebersole and Hess' model shows, there is a need to share wisdom, develop new activities, maintain relationships and become an active member of the community. Acceptance and growth are the twin developmental tasks in the later years. Adaptation is a crucial factor in achieving these tasks.

ADAPTATION

Adaptation has been viewed as resulting from both personal characteristics and environmental conditions and the interaction between the two (Hooyman & Kiyak, 1993). Ruth and Coleman (1996) define it as a "range of behaviors to meet demands, from developing habits to meeting problems and frustrations through managing intense anxiety" (p. 309).

Carp's (1972) components of adult life adjustment remain relevant to most individuals' adaptation to old age: (a) fairly stable personality and behavior, (b) positive attitude toward others, (c) favorable assessment of others, (d) active involvement in life, (e) satisfaction with past and present, (f) positive appraisal of general health, (g) intellectual competence, and (h) ego strength. Some of the resources for coping identified by Ruth and Coleman (1996) should be added to this list: an easy-going or optimistic disposition, internal locus of control, self-efficacy, and social support. Individuals who positively adapt to old age are those capable of dealing with crises without resorting to self-destructive measures, certainly a task that involves the ability to integrate the confronted situations with an overall positive perspective toward life, striving for resolution through the activation of one's internal and external resources. Older adults, in general, seem to adapt to the challenges and stresses old age brings, preserving their self-concept and self-esteem.

Even in the face of environmental forces that threaten their perceptions of self, older adults seem to draw on the notions established in younger years, adjusting such external forces to fit into their internal reality.

FIGURE 5.1

HAVIGHURST AND DUVALL'S DEVELOPMENTAL TASKS OF AGING

Adjusting to decreasing health and physical strength
Adjusting to retirement and reduced income
Finding meaning in life
Maintaining satisfactory living arrangements
Finding satisfaction within the family
Adjusting to the reality of death
Accepting oneself as an aging person

ERIKSON'S DEVELOPMENTAL TASKS OF AGING

EGO INTEGRITY VERSUS	DESPAIR
Person accepts that life has been what it had to be	Person develops dread of dying
Feeling that life has been good and meaningful	Disgust with oneself and one's failures
One has acted responsibly and led a successful life	Bitter because it is too late to start over and do it better

---

(BIRCHENALL AND STREIGHT, 1993)

FIGURE 5.2

DEVELOPMENTAL TASKS OF LATE LIFE IN HIERARCHIC ORDER

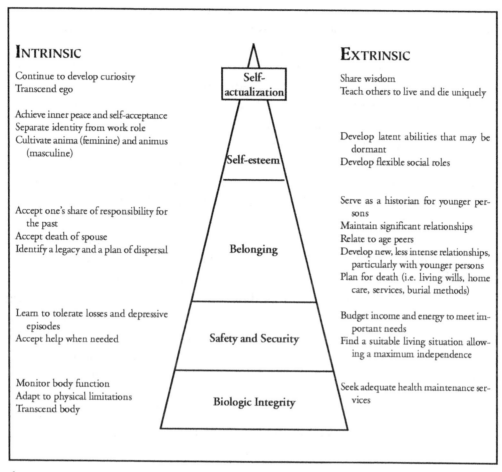

INTRINSIC

Continue to develop curiosity
Transcend ego

Achieve inner peace and self-acceptance
Separate identity from work role
Cultivate anima (feminine) and animus
    (masculine)

Accept one's share of responsibility for
    the past
Accept death of spouse
Identify a legacy and a plan of dispersal

Learn to tolerate losses and depressive
    episodes
Accept help when needed

Monitor body function
Adapt to physical limitations
Transcend body

EXTRINSIC

Share wisdom
Teach others to live and die uniquely

Develop latent abilities that may be
    dormant
Develop flexible social roles

Serve as a historian for younger per-
    sons
Maintain significant relationships
Relate to age peers
Develop new, less intense relationships,
    particularly with younger persons
Plan for death (i.e. living wills, home
    care, services, burial methods)

Budget income and energy to meet im-
    portant needs
Find a suitable living situation allow-
    ing a maximum independence

Seek adequate health maintenance ser-
    vices

Pyramid levels (top to bottom): Self-actualization, Self-esteem, Belonging, Safety and Security, Biologic Integrity

(EBERSOLE AND HESS, 1998) REPRINTED WITH PERMISSION OF MOSBY YEARBOOK COMPANY.

LIFE SATISFACTION

Individuals who adjust positively to old age are expected to show high life satisfaction. A number of variables have been found to correlate with life satisfaction. Indicators of positive psychological well-being suggested by Neugarten (1964) are: (a) pleasure taken in everyday life activities, (b) evaluation of one's life as meaningful and acceptable, (c) feeling of success from achieving life goals, (d) positive self-image, and (e) happy and optimistic moods and attitudes.

Research on factors associated with happiness pointed to variables such as: perceived health, physical ability, emotional bonding and social support, social participation, lost purpose in life, choice and control, institutionalization, and social support.

In a report to the President's Commission on Outdoors, McNeil, McGuire and O'Leary (1987) stated two conclusions regarding the life satisfaction of older adults: (a) positive experiences in leisure relate to positive adjustment to later adulthood, and (b) along with health, social economic status, and social interaction, leisure participation contributes to positive life satisfaction among older Americans.

Beck and Pagej (1988) found that for retired men in poor health, the number of activities engaged in were better predictors of psychological well-being than for those in good health. This finding is significant to recreation professionals in that it reveals that those more severely impaired may be precisely the ones who value activity the most, thus requiring more assistance to become involved.

Ragheb and Griffith (1982) found that the correlation between satisfaction with activities engaged in and life satisfaction was higher than that between frequency of participation and life satisfaction, and Mannell (1993) found commitment to an activity was important to life satisfaction.

These findings further support the link between the role of recreation participation and life satisfaction. More than number or frequency, it is important to deal with the meaning of activities to participants when attempting to improve life satisfaction. Findings such as those by Lomranz, Bergman, Eyal, and Shmotkin (1988) regarding the potential of activity involvement in impacting positive affect are significant to professionals in the field of recreation. Using the Affect Balance Scale, the researchers examined the relationship between activity and affect. For men, the level of activities was found to be a good predictor of affect, while for women, it was the satisfaction derived from an activity that best predicted affect.

An implication of such findings is that not only frequency of activities, but also their meaning to the participants should be taken into consideration during programming.

An Approach to Successful Aging

In an attempt to develop a prototypical strategy of successful aging, Baltes and Baltes (1990) and Baltes, Smith, and Staudinger (1991) have suggested a model called "selective optimization with compensation." According to the authors, this is an on-going, lifelong process that is intensified in old age. Schroots (1996) identified the central focus of the model as "the management of the dynamics between gains and losses i.e. a general process of adaption" (p. 745). The model is composed of three interacting elements: (a) selection, (b) optimization, and (c) compensation. The processes of selection, optimization, and compensation are defined below:

1. *Selection* refers to restricting one's world to fewer domains of functioning to focus on those domains that are high priority to the individual, domains that combine environmental demands and individual biological capacity, skills and motivations.

2. *Optimization* refers to engaging in behaviors to maximize their general reserves and to make it possible for individuals to pursue their chosen life courses. It rests on the assumption that maintaining high levels of performance is possible through practice and technology.
3. *Compensation* is relevant when the performance demands of an activity exceed an individual's current performance potential. At this point psychological and technological compensatory efforts are adopted.

The following example is provided by Baltes and Baltes (1990) to illustrate the elements above:

> Consider, for example, a person who has excelled as a marathon runner all his or her adult life and wants to continue this activity in old age. If this runner wants to stay at the same performance level, more time and energy will need to be invested in running. As a consequence, the person will have to reduce or give up other activities (selection). At the same time, the runner will have to increase his or her training and knowledge about optimizing conditions such as the influence of daily rhythms and dieting (optimization), and, finally, he or she will have to become an expert in techniques aimed at reducing the impact of loss in functioning (compensation). Which shoes to use and how to treat injuries are examples of such compensatory strategies. By combining these elements of selection, optimization and compensation, a high level of performance in marathon running might be retained into old age (p. 25).

Although at first glance, the selective optimization with compensation model may resemble some of the ideas within the disengagement and activity theories, a closer scrutiny will reveal that it more closely aligns with the continuity theory. The key issue in this differentiation is the notion of selectivity.

In this approach to successful aging, the individual actively decides what roles or activities are worth continued investment and moves to ensure their preservation and maximization. Dropping other roles or activities is thus a result of informed choice, based on what is deemed meaningful to the person. Contrary to the activity theory, this approach does not suggest mere substitution with new pursuits, although this is not ruled out. It postulates that, given personal and environmental restrictions, the older person will capitalize on remaining skills to meet lifelong interests. If new activities or roles are selected, the basis for selection lies in the perception that such activities or roles will fulfill the individual's need for continuity.

MENTAL HEALTH

According to Ebersole and Hess (1999), mental health may be defined as "a satisfactory adjustment to one's life stage and situation" (p. 743). The concept of adaptation appears to be intertwined with that of mental health. Those who adapt to subsequent stages in life retain positive mental health.

The majority of the elderly population is in good mental health (Cohen, 1990). Due to the gradual nature of the aging process, the older person has time to develop coping mechanisms to adjust to the physical and psychosocial losses characteristic of aging. However, the amount of physical and emotional energy consumed in adapting to the changes that result from such losses and recovering from the stress they cause may lead to behavioral responses such as loss of hope, decreased self-esteem, social isolation, feeling of burden, withdrawal, and inability to find alternatives.

Many factors will impact on the ability to cope with stress, such as availability of social support, adaptability of surrounding environment, previous levels of mental health, and the amount of stressors at a given period of time. An individual already vulnerable to stress may have his or her abilities to adapt severely depleted.

Although general statistics for mental illness in the elderly indicate about 22% of all individuals aged 65 or over meet the criteria for some form of it (Gatz, Kasl-Godley & Karel, 1996) the percentage for nursing homes may range from 70 to 90%. Hooyman and Kiyak (1993) provided additional information about mental illness in later life:

1. 20% of first admissions to psychiatric hospitals are individuals over 65 years of age;
2. older psychiatric patients are more likely to require longer periods of inpatient treatment and have chronic conditions;
3. older individuals are less likely to use community mental health services;
4. older African Americans are twice as likely as whites to enter mental hospitals, whereas older Mexican Americans and Native Americans are less likely to do so.

Some of the functional disorders most frequently found among the elderly are anxiety, chronic mental illness, and depression (Haight, 1991). Depression is one of the most common disorders encountered in the older population. One national study found that 27% of the elderly had some depressive symptoms (Gatz et al., 1996). An important distinction should be made between situational, or reactive, depression and clinical depression. Due to the amount of loss experienced by the elderly, reactive depression is not infrequent. With the passing of time, proper activation of coping mechanisms, and social support, the individual usually overcomes the feelings of sadness and resumes normal activities. Clinical depression, however, "is a more complex, profoundly immobilizing condition, stemming from unresolved conflicts, despair over one's life history" (Ebersole & Hess, 1990).

Whatever the classification, depression should not be taken lightly, especially considering the high rate of suicide among the elderly.

Although clinical depression is experienced differently by each individual, there are a variety of symptoms indicative of its presence. The most common symptoms of later life depression include: (a) a persistent sad feeling, (b) sleep difficulties, (c) weight changes, (d) feeling slowed down, (e) excessive worries about health problems and finances, (f) frequent tearfulness, (g) feeling worthless or helpless, (h) pacing and fidgeting (i) difficulty concentrating, (j) physical symptoms such as gastrointestinal problems or pain (National Mental Health Association, 1996). Of course any one of these symptoms may not be an indicator of depression. However, the existence of several may be cause for concern.

Suicide is a significantly more prevalent among the elderly than among the nation as a whole (Hooyman & Kiyak, 1993). Therefore, it is important to understand the factors that might precipitate such action. Men seem to be more at risk than women, perhaps because of the loss of control that may accompany retirement, or severe illness may be harder to accept for men than women, given socialization patterns both groups have been exposed to. Feelings of helplessness may lead to depression, and severe depression may culminate in a suicide attempt.

With the elderly, unlike among other groups, there are usually no threats; a suicide attempt is likely to be successful. Therefore, potential signs such as continued depression, sudden changes in sleeping and eating patterns, unusual behaviors such as giving possessions away, apparent disregard for previously cherished objects, persons, or activities, and comments such as, "I would be better off dead" or "Life has no meaning anymore" should be taken seriously.

There is also a need to be aware of risk factors such as illness accompanied by severe pain, loss of a loved one, declines in independence, and financial reversals (Hooyman & Kiyak, 1993), which may be precursors of suicide. Harbert and Ginsberg (1990) recommend that services such as telephone reassurance and being available to talk be instituted as needed.

COGNITIVE DISORDERS

The above paragraphs dealt with "functional" disorders, that is, disorders in which psychosocial factors such as personality and life stresses may lead to impaired functioning. Such disorders do not seem to have consistent biological causes. They differ from the "organic" disorders, which may be traced to physical etiology. The following section will explore the range of organic disorders among the elderly.

Primary and secondary brain dysfunction may result in psychological and behavioral disturbances. In the gerontological literature, reference is made to "acute" and "chronic" organic brain syndrome. In the past, a common differentiation between such terms was their reversibility potential. While "acute" was used to label "potentially reversible" disorders, "chronic" often referred to "irreversible cerebral impairment" (Ebersole & Hess, 1990).

The tendency to classify "chronic brain syndrome" as totally irreversible has changed over the years; today it is known that a small percentage of such disorders may be reversed if quick attention is given to their precipitating factors. Perhaps a better definition of each concept is offered by MacNeil and Teague (1987). According to them, "acute" brain syndrome "occurs at any age, often reversible, caused by agents such as trauma, infection, diabetes, congestive heart failure, drugs, alcohol," while "chronic" brain syndrome "occurs mostly in old age, usually irreversible, marked by psychological degeneration in the brain" (p. 111).

Rather than concentrating on the reversible or irreversible nature of organic mental disorders, the remainder of this chapter will utilize the terms "delirium" and "dementia" to describe the two major syndrome complexes experienced by the elderly.

DELIRIUM

Also known as acute confusional state or transient cognitive disorder, this syndrome is characterized by:

1. Disturbance of consciousness (such as reduced clarity of awareness of the environment) with reduced ability to focus, shift, or sustain attention
2. A change in cognition (such as memory deficit) or development of perceptual disturbances not better accounted for by a pre-existing, established, or evolving dementia
3. Development over a short period of time, usually hours
4. Symptoms that fluctuate during the day
5. Evidence that the disturbance is caused by direct physiological consequences of a general medical constitution (American Psychiatric Association, 1994)

Manifestations include memory impairment, language disturbances, learning difficulties, involuntary movements, abnormal mood shifts, and poor reasoning ability and judgment. Among the precipitating causes for delirium are (a) medication, (b) trauma, (c) infection, (d) malnutrition, (e) metabolic imbalance, (f) cerebrovascular disorders, (g) alcohol intoxication, (h) social stressors, (i) depression, (j) prolonged immobilization, and (k) sensory deprivation.

Delirium may effect over 20% of the elderly undergoing acute hospitalization (Ferri & Fretwell, 1992). Since episodes of delirium may be due to disorientation to the environment and lack of sensory input, it is recommended that a night light or a radio be left on during the night when environmental cues are dulled, aggravating confusion on the part of the elderly (Davison & Neale, 1986).

Usually, when the medical problem causing delirium is found, treatment is possible and the individual is able to return to previous levels of functioning without any sequel.

DEMENTIA

Dementia is an umbrella term including several disorders and limited almost entirely to the elderly (Gatz et al., 1996). The *Diagnostic and Statistical Manual of*

Mental Disorders (American Psychiatric Association, 1994) defines dementia as including the following:

1. Development of multiple cognitive deficits including memory impairment and at least one of the following: aphasia (loss or decrease in ability to speak, understand, read or write [burlingame & Skalko, 1997]), apraxia (inability to conduct purposeful, voluntary movements without the presence of impaired sensations, muscle weakness or paralysis [burlingame & Skalko, 1997]), agnosia (decreased ability to know familiar persons or objects [burlingame & Skalko, 1997]), or a disturbance in executive functioning (i.e. problem solving or abstract reasoning)
2. The decline must be serious enough to cause impairment in occupational or social functioning.
3. The decline must represent a decline from previously high levels of functioning.

Individuals with dementia exhibit a wide range of symptoms. Some of these include an inability to learn new information; loss of memory for information previously learned; difficulties with reasoning and abstract thinking; difficulties in ability to speak, carry out motor activities, and identify objects; personality changes; inability to carry out work or social activities; anxiety, depression, or suspiciousness; spatial disorientation; poor judgment and poor insight; and disinhibited behavior such as crude jokes or neglecting personal hygiene (American Psychiatric Association, 1994; New York Hospital Cornell Medical Center, 1996).

Dementia is not an inevitable consequence of the normal aging process. On average, dementia affects approximately 10 to 15% of the older American population. However, as age increases, so does the probability of developing dementia. Gatz et al. (1996) report the results of several analyses of the prevalence of dementia across the older population. Rates increase from under 1% among those aged 60–64 to approximately 30% of individuals over the age of 90.

The above facts are based on all elderly. Rates in institutional settings creep up to 50 to 70%. It is the primary cause for admission to institutional care and the fourth leading cause of death in the U.S., accounting for 150,000 deaths a year. Currently, it costs the country close to $90 billion a year, considering direct and indirect sources (AARP, 1986; Bowlby, 1993). The personal costs are also tremendous. As Rowe and Kahn (1998) state: "It robs people of their personalities, their ability to interact with others, and to function effectively" (p. 93).

DISTRIBUTION

It is estimated that Alzheimer's disease accounts for 50% of all cases of dementia. Another 15 to 20% of dementia cases are attributed to multi-infarct dementia. In approximately 20% of the cases, a combination of Alzheimer's disease and multi-infarct dementia is present. The remaining 10 to 15% of the cases result from potentially reversible conditions similar to the ones listed for delirium, or irreversible disease processes such as Parkinson's disease, Pick's disease, Creutzfeldt-Jacob disease, Huntington disease, Korsakoff's syndrome, multiple sclerosis, and AIDS (Aronson, 1988).

Some of these conditions may develop earlier in life, others are extremely rare, and not all will inevitably result in dementia. Two major causes of dementia among the elderly, multi-infarct dementia and Alzheimer's disease, will be examined next.

Vascular dementia. These types of dementia, formerly known as multi-infarct dementia, usually occur after age 65. They result from a series of infarcts in the brain, leading to tissue death. The infarcts are a consequence of interrupted blood supply to the brain due to vascular changes produced by arteriosclerotic disease.

The main characteristic of this type of dementia is its "stepwise" progression. In other words, symptoms usually begin suddenly and fluctuate with time. After the first evidence of decline, the individual may seem to improve or remain stable, until another infarct occurs, bringing about increased damage to the brain. Some of the telltale signs of vascular dementia include speech or vision problems and/or weakness on one side of the body. Vascular dementias (VaD) are differentiated from Alzheimer's disease (discussed in detail below) in several ways, including: (a) impaired motor skills are an early symptom of VaD, (b) brain scan shows evidence of stroke or stroke-related changes in VaD, (c) an underlying vascular disorder such as hypertension or heart disease is always present in VaD, (d) abrupt onset, often progressing in steps, with decline slowed by controlling the vascular disorder is characteristic of VaD, (e) some intellectual functions are affected to a greater degree than others in VaD (Alzheimer's Association, 1995).

Alzheimer's disease. The first case of Alzheimer's disease was identified in 1906 by Alois Alzheimer in Germany, but only in more recent decades has it been identified as a major disease. One explanation for this delay seems to be the previous distinction between "pre-senile" dementia and "senile" dementia. While the former was attributed to rare cases with onset before age 65 identified with Alzheimer's disease, the latter was thought to be related to normal aging or arteriosclerotic disease, thus the term "senile," meaning old (Bowlby, 1993).

In the past, it was not uncommon to hear the word "senile" used as a label for what was actually demented behavior. Such misuse of the term led to general stereotypes, equating "old" with "cognitive decline." Today, it is well known that Alzheimer's may occur either before or after age 65 and that vascular disease is not the sole cause of dementia in old age.

Alzheimer's disease is characterized by a progressive neurological decline, accompanied by the following pathological changes in the brain: (a) neurofibrilla, tangles (thick entangled nerve filaments), (b) neuritic plaques (abnormal deposits of neuronal breakdown products), and (c) brain atrophy (shrinking of the brain).

Such characteristics are only visible upon autopsy.

The *Diagnostic and Statistical Manual of Mental Disorders* (American Psychiatric Association, 1994) identifies Alzheimer's disease as:

A. Development of multiple cognitive impairments manifested by:
   — memory impairment marked by inability to learn new information or recall old;
   — at least one of the following:
   aphasia,
   apraxia,
   agnosia,
   disturbance in executive functioning.
B. The losses cause impairment in occupational or social functioning and are a significant decline from previous functioning.
C. There is gradual onset and continuing cognitive decline.
D. The cognitive deficits are not due to other central nervous system conditions that cause progressive deficits in cognition and memory, systemic conditions causing dementia, episodes of delirium, or by any mental illness such as depression or schizophrenia.

This disease affects approximately four million Americans. Approximately 10% of the 65 and over population have Alzheimer's disease (Alzheimer's Association, 1998). Its prevalence shows a dramatic increase with age; approximately 3% of individuals between the ages of 65 and 74 are affected, 19% of those between 75 and 84, and 47% of all individuals aged 85 and over (Alzheimer's.com, 1998). Since the over 85 age group is the fastest-growing segment of the older American population, a concomitant increase in the number of Alzheimer's cases is expected in the future. In fact, it is estimated that 14 million Americans will have Alzheimer's disease by the middle of the next century.

The financial costs of Alzheimer's disease are staggering. The cost per patient lifetime is approximately $174,000, and the total cost to the nation is $100 billion per year. Alzheimer's is the third most expensive disease, after heart disease and cancer. Typical family care costs are $12,500 per year, while care in nursing home is $42,000 (Alzheimer's Association, 1998a).

The search for the cause of Alzheimer's disease continues, and several causes are under examination. Some areas being considered include: chemical theories focusing on deficiencies and toxic excess, genetic theories, the autoimmune theory, slow virus theory, and the blood vessel theory which focuses on blood supply and the blood-brain barrier (National Institute of Mental Health, 1994).

The diagnosis of AD is done primarily by exclusion of other diseases. No current test is available to unequivocally detect the presence of this disease. Assessment includes: (a) complete history intake, (b) neurological examination, (c) physical examination, (d) psychiatric screening, (e) social-behavioral evaluation, (f) functional performance evaluation, (g) cognitive functioning evaluation, and (h) laboratory tests (Bowlby, 1993).

The life expectancy of an individual with AD is quite variable, ranging from 3 to as long as 20 years, with an average course of 7 to 9 years (Birchenall and Streight, 1993; Bowlby, 1993). The progression is gradual and is often classified into three stages according to the type of cognitive and behavioral deficits experienced by the individual as the disease advances as follows (Birchenall & Streight, 1993; Bowlby, 1993, Alzheimer's Association, 1998b):

EARLY

- some memory deficits for recent events, but good memory for past events
- deficits with episodic memory (recalling circumstances surrounding a specific event; e.g., what did you have for breakfast this morning?)
- deficits in semantic memory (recalling general knowledge about particular events or subjects, e.g., what are four food groups?)
- difficulty remembering names of people and objects
- slight judgment difficulties
- lack of awareness of personal difficulties
- lack of spontaneity
- time disorientation
- some deficits, but still functional in daily living skills
- confusion executing familiar tasks
- communication
- memory loss as greatest source of problems. Attempt to cover by: standard conversational and social skills, confabulation, flattery, and humor
- use of long pauses to "digest" information
- tendency to wander out of the topic
- trouble naming things, places, people
- confusion with words that sound alike (mouse/house), or are in same category (son/daughter)

MIDDLE

- intensification in previous stage's deficits
- new deficits such as disorientation, confusion, concentration, and limitations in performing tasks such as writing and calculating
- sensory impressions dulled
- restlessness at night
- decline in activities of daily living more noticeable, interfering with autonomy
- problem-solving deficits
- inability to maintain logical thinking for extended periods of time
- irritability and suspicion, mood swings

- isolation and flat affect
- wandering and pacing
- movement and gait disturbances
- communication difficulties: naming losses more pronounced. More complex, less frequently used words disappear first
- nouns and proper names replaced by pronouns or generic terms
- requests to repeat information are frequent
- great difficulty in following verbal directions
- language becomes increasingly "hollow"
- increased reliance on standard social phrases
- difficulty understanding figures of speech
- difficulty interpreting written directions
- difficulty concentrating
- difficulty initiating conversation
- forgetfulness regarding social conversational rules

ADVANCED

- progressive deterioration
- memory of past events impaired
- disoriented towards time, space, and people
- severely dependent in self-care needs psychological problems such as crying spells, aggressiveness, depression, anxiety, and psychotic reactions (hallucinations and delusions)
- communication: extreme difficulty in verbal communication
- if speaking, using short phrases, single words
- may "babble," use incoherent speech
- difficulty understanding even simple words

The above stages are not a rule for every individual affected by the disease. There is much variance regarding speed and level of decline seen among persons with Alzheimer's. Another important factor to remember is that these individuals maintain certain assets in spite of the losses. Based on a review of literature, Bowlby (1993) identified the following areas of persisting assets:

1. Emotional awareness—capacity to experience a full range of emotions in spite of difficulty in expressing them; need to give and receive affection, memory of feelings associated with past events.
2. Sensory appreciation—capacity to derive pleasure and stimulation from sensorial experiences.
3. Primary motor functioning—strength, dexterity, and motor control stable until later stages.
4. Sociability and social skills—persistence of overlearned, ingrained social

skills, such as shaking hands, exchanging social greetings.

5. Procedural memory and habitual skills—ability to remember "how to" perform certain activities by cuing into triggering aspects of the environment; e.g., being given a bowl with cereal and a spoon and using spoon to eat from the bowl.

6. Remote memory—ability to recall significant events from the distant past, or circumstances surrounding them.

7. Sense of humor—use of humor to cover embarrassing moments and to relate socially.

Remembering that the individual retains such abilities into advanced stages of the disease helps practitioners and caregivers focus on areas of intervention, to delay further deterioration, and to assure a better quality of life for the individual. Some suggestions for dealing with persons with Alzheimer's will be offered in the following section.

ULYSSEAN APPROACHES

Psychological vitality is important to Ulyssean living. The mind and body must function at the highest level possible to achieve a sense of accomplishment and happiness. The following material provides some examples of interventions used to create conditions conducive to Ulyssean living.

As a general principle, considering the potential causes of functional mental disorders such as depression, practitioners should examine the amount of social and psychological support provided by the environment. Individuals experience a great number of losses, some related to loved ones. Appropriate counseling should be made available to help cope with grieving. Support groups may be created for the elderly to share experiences and find solace among others undergoing similar pain.

Since loss of occupational status is so disturbing to some older adults, leisure education programs should begin prior to retirement and prepare individuals to find productive uses for their leisure time. Also, offering meaningful volunteering opportunities, such as involvement in civic associations or intergenerational programs, may help alleviate feelings of worthlessness and help maintain self-esteem.

Loss of health is often gradual and can be dealt with through approaches discussed previously in the chapter concerning biological aging. If sudden illness or disability set in, the individual will need psychological support through individual or group counseling. As noted above, involvement in recreational activities also has the potential to reduce negative feelings associated with declining health.

There are numerous interventions that may assist with mental well-being. Pet therapy, horticulture, music, and graphic arts are all examples of successful interventions in creating opportunities for socialization and enjoyment.

INTERVENTION TECHNIQUES

Aside from structured interventions such as reality orientation and sensory stimulation (discussed in detail in a later chapter), practitioners and caregivers dealing with the elderly need to be knowledgeable about the most successful approaches to working with such individuals, especially when they present challenging conditions such as dementia. As Hellen (1993) indicates, a thorough assessment is crucial for success when working with individuals with Alzheimer's disease. Activities must flow from the results of the assessment. The following are suggestions on how to work with persons with Alzheimer's disease compiled from a variety of authors (Bartol, 1979; Greenblatt, 1988; Weaverdyck, 1991; Bowlby, 1993; Hellen, 1993). They also are generally useful in working with older adults with a variety of cognitive impairments.

Communication:
1) Speak to the person as an adult, do not talk down.
2) Address person by proper title (Mr./Mrs.); use first name only after requesting permission.
3) Reassure by confirming the emotional message, even if verbal message makes no sense (e.g., "You seem to be upset about this, Mrs Smith").
4) Never argue or disagree if incorrect; instead find positive ways to validate feelings and orient to reality (e.g., if the person says she has not eaten all day, start by discussing types of food liked, then show the menu for the day, and refer to incidents during meal time rather than say, "You are wrong, you had steak for lunch just an hour ago").
5) Emphasize recognition, not recall.
6) For conversation topics, focus on "opinions" rather than facts (e.g., ask "How do you like to spend Christmas?" rather than "Where did you spend Christmas last year?")
7) Be aware of every aspect of presentation—tone, posture, facial expression—since the person may read non-verbal communication better than the verbal content of messages.
8) Alert the person by touching or saying his or her name before asking questions or giving directions. Make eye contact as you speak.
9) In social situations, always introduce other persons by providing name and orienting information so that the individual will not feel embarrassed for not recognizing others.
10) Eliminate background noise or confusion.
11) Speak slowly and clearly. Use short, simple sentences. Keep voice calm, low, moderated.
12) Do not use abstract language, confusing figures of speech, sarcasm.
13) When referring to names of places or objects, use full titles and descriptors (for example, we are going to the physical therapy room, the place you go for exercise every morning).

14) Use terms that are most familiar to the person in referring to objects (icebox vs. refrigerator). Use familiar phrases and mannerisms that were common in the person's life.

15) Allow ample time for response.

16) Be ready to repeat information; when doing so, use the same words.

17) Supply the words a person is trying to recall.

18) Avoid using "don't" or commands or ordering person. Instead, use clear directions such as "Mr Jones, I would like for you to throw the ball to me now."

19) Express warmth and caring. Listen even if the speaker is not making sense.

20) If the individual begins to ramble, refocus and rephrase what has been said so far.

21) Never speak about the individual to others in his/her presence as if not there.

Selecting and conducting activities:

1) Use overlearned, familiar activities.

2) Choose simple and repetitive, not overly challenging, but age-appropriate activities (folding napkins).

3) Emphasize sensory experiences.

4) Emphasize overlearned, persistent social skills.

5) Use activities to foster social interaction such as small parties.

6) Maintain exercise program. Encourage ambulation.

7) Stimulate cognitively. Do not assume potential participants are not able to perform activities. Use cuing, simplifying if necessary.

8) Allow for expression of emotions.

9) Take advantage of intact remote memory. Encourage reminiscing.

10) Explain the purpose of activities. Choose activities that are meaningful and have an obvious, practical purpose.

11) Use activities that relate to seasonal life themes and experiences from the work environment. Look for activities that reflect acceptable work themes for that generation.

12) Cue or prompt procedural memory by concrete, non-verbal instruction.

13) Break down complex tasks and give instructions in steps. Begin with a step participants can successfully accomplish.

14) If choices are required, offer only two manageable choices at a time.

15) Give immediate but not excessive feedback for responses or attempts.

16) Use consistent routines in the environment and presentation of activities.

17) When working in groups, do not expect to have everyone work on the same step independently. Use a "parallel" format, in which each individual completes each step of the activity in turn.

18) Plan the week or month around a familiar theme and schedule all activities related to major themes to increase consistency for the individual.

19) Use ample, familiar, concrete physical cues and memorabilia. Use multisensorial cues.
20) If participants get restless, reassure, call by name, and distract by asking for help with activity.
21) Use demonstration. Include high-functioning members to model. Keep supplies at hand for those capable of proceeding on their own.
22) When working with groups, sit around a table, maintain seat assignments for following group meetings.
23) Provide a bridge from the general milieu. When beginning groups, introduce participants, orient to time, place, explain reason for being there. Provide large name tags for participants.
24) Repeat successful activities often and maintain consistency in the schedule.
25) Schedule activities that demand verbalization and cognitive functioning in the morning and those requiring energy spending for afternoon.
26) Use small groups of three to five persons. Plan to meet no longer than 30 minutes.
27) Determine the best time of the day for a resident to do activities.
28) Read short stories and poems to simulate cognitive functioning.
29) Activities such as marching, clapping, walking, and dancing may be effective substitute for agitated and wandering behavior.

Environment:

1) Keep it safe by removing obstacles.
2) Remove sources of potential illusions, such as glare, unfamiliar noises or objects.
3) Allow space for walking.
4) Avoid wandering into dangerous areas; place warning signs.
5) Use environmental cues to help to help individuals find their way (e.g., photo on room's door).
6) Maintain environment structured consistently. Keep it unambiguous and understandable.
7) Avoid distractions. Keep things simple.
8) Make the environment as homelike as possible.
9) Compensate for physical deficits.

CONCLUSION

Psychological changes in the later years are varied within and across individuals. Most individuals adapt well to changes and are able to continue with patterns of behavior developed throughout life. The balance between continuity and change is typically maintained without major negative consequences. Unfortunately, another reality for some individuals is that pathological changes in personality and cognition will occur. The specter of Alzheimer's disease looms large in many families. However, even in these cases Ulyssean living remains a possibility through careful, well-planned interventions such as those discussed in this chapter.

Belief in the value of Ulyssean living requires it be a focus for all individuals receiving our services. People with cognitive impairments such as those described in this chapter may require greater effort to achieve the goals of Ulyssean living. However, they will also be among those who will benefit the most from this approach to life.

Chapter 6

◆

The Importance
of Leisure

What appears below is a letter received from a couple who attended an Elderhostel program given by one of the authors. It is reproduced exactly as written.

Dear Fran: A short report on leisure at Laurel Vineyards. The "work" part of our life is growing grapes, a vegetable garden and fruits as well as winemaking and selling grapes to home winemakers. Also the regular chores of keeping a home and personal finances in order. Actually leisure seems to be part of the above; a blend of leisure and work. A great deal of effort is made to keep 300 vines growing and producing, then made into wine—and gardening is not all fun, but many parts of our projects are leisure. There are frequent pleasant breaks from routine. A few of our leisure doings:

- Reading to learn or entertain
- A 20-minute walk before breakfast and a look at our beautiful world
- A leisurely second cup of coffee after breakfast with reading or conversation
- After lunch, reading and a nap
- Evening reading or TV (if any) Knitting or weaving with good friends one day a week—Mary Jane, A P.C. users meeting for Alan
- Lunch out or shopping
- Choosing books at the library
- Planting new plants and varieties of vegetables Watching the woods as seasons change
- Wine tastings with friends
- Tasting our wines two years after grapes were harvested
- Alan likes the challenge of developing techniques for solving problems using the P.C. Also learning to use new software.

THE ROLE OF LEISURE IN LATER LIFE

Is leisure a central focus in later life as Kelly (1987a) indicated, or is it a con foisted upon older individuals providing small compensation for losses in other roles? The answer is an elusive and often confusing one. This chapter will examine the role of leisure in later life.

Since the question is a multi-faceted one with several levels of answers, this chapter will be equally multi-faceted. There are several ways to examine the role of leisure in Ulyssean living; this chapter will examine its linkage to physical, psychological, affective, and social well-being.

WHAT IS LEISURE?

Dychtwald and Flower (1989) created a media furor with their publication of *Age Wave: The Challenges and Opportunities of an Aging America*. It was viewed as a major contribution in viewing life in the later years as something positive and to be valued. Leisure and recreation merited its own chapter in this highly entertaining book. Dychtwald and Flower view leisure as the "dominant national pastime for men and women over 60" (p. 119) and see it as "becoming progressively more active and adventurous, and physical as well as intellectual—in short, more intensely gratifying" (p. 115).

Clearly, we are concerned with something very important and even crucial in the lives of many individuals. However, understanding this phenomenon is difficult. Defining leisure is an impossible task. According to Barrett (1989), "Of all concepts that of leisure is one of the most intractable. Like the concept of time, in the words of St. Augustine, we know what it is when no one asks us, but when they ask what it is, we are hard put to find an answer" (p. 9).

There have been a variety of definitions presented for leisure. Generally, the definitions fall into three broad categories: time, activity, and state of mind (Kelly, 1996). It is tempting to adopt a time definition when examining leisure in the later years. The link between aging and leisure would be relatively easy to make, since in many cases old age is accompanied by retirement and its concomitant unobligated time. In fact, when asked to define leisure, responses from a group of older individuals included: that which occupies time not used to gain necessities; time when you can do what you want without thoughts of duties or obligation, time available when there is no required activity, time to relax and play, time to do things I want to do as contrasted to things I have to do, time to do things you wish to do without any pressure, unconstrained time, time to do things other than those essential, time left over, free time after I take care of responsibilities, time to do what you want, time when I have to answer to no one, unscheduled time.

If free time were synonymous with leisure, then the experience of that time would be superfluous to the leisure experience. That is clearly not the case. For example, 15 minutes immersed in a Clive Cussler novel or watching your favorite football team is not the same experience as 15 minutes spent in a dentist's waiting room. The first may be leisure, the dentist's office probably is not. Yet both are composed of unobligated time.

To limit the leisure perspective to time is to deny its potential centrality in life. It is not solely an event used to fill time. It can be more than that. While it is true leisure resides partly in the world of time, it also resides in a world of activity. In fact, typical definitions of leisure include: doing something you like to do in your spare time; an enjoyable activity that serves a purpose; relaxed reading; relaxation, doing what you desire, meditation; doing what you want at the time, reading; anything I choose to do for a change from work I have to do; things I like to do that aren't work; doing something special; completely different from everyday and/ or ordinary activities; sex; an enjoyable activity. This activity perspective is appealing and congruent with a common sense view. However, activity alone is not sufficient as a leisure definition. If it were, the same activity would always be considered leisure. For example, the experience of jogging would be the same whether it was to train for a race, an effort to lose weight, or a chance to interact with your friends. Again, this seems overly simplistic.

A third dimension that appears when older individuals define leisure is the perception of choosing to do something and enjoying it. Some examples provided by older individuals included: being last on the line at the grocery store and not caring; freedom of choice; doing what I want, when I want; a period of life that allows me to pursue a course of pleasure without many of the normal pressures of accomplishment; when you do what you want to do instead of what you must or what you think you must. These descriptions incorporate all three elements of time, activity, and perception.

There is general agreement that two central constructs of leisure are perceived freedom and intrinsic motivation. Perceived freedom is closely aligned with freedom of choice. The participant must feel the activity is chosen, not required. The other element, intrinsic motivation, indicates the activity is chosen primarily for rewards coming from the activity itself. Extrinsic motivation lies in rewards, such as trophies or other forms of recognition, which are external to the activity (Mannell & Kleiber, 1997). The importance of intrinsic motivation in Ulyssean living is discussed in greater detail in Chapter 7. We agree with Iso-Ahola (1989) who believes, "While freedom of choice or self-determination is a necessary condition for the occurrence of leisure, it is not sufficient . . . to have leisure one must experience enjoyment" (p. 256). Therefore, we view leisure as a freely chosen activity done primarily for its own sake, with an element of enjoyment, pursued during unobligated time.

As the letter that opened this chapter indicated, leisure is usually relatively simple. In fact, its allure is often in its uncomplicated nature. The Johnsons take obvious pleasure from the simple things in life. Their leisure revolves around everyday things, often integrated into their "work." But do not be fooled by the simplicity of leisure. It is also one of the most important arenas for personal growth and development for Ulyssean living.

Caudron (1997) addresses the changing nature of retirement and retirees. The baby boomers are entering the threshold of retirement and the impacts will be dramatic. Many boomers will return to work, in some form. Others will "reinvent" themselves through volunteer work, education, or other leisure involvements. The image of the retiree spending the years after work passing time in a variety of "leisurely" pursuits will be even less accurate than it is today. A retiree may decide to return to school, seek part-time employment, or join the Peace Corps. While these activities may not fit the traditional perspective of leisure, they clearly fall under our definition of leisure. In fact, the Ulyssean perspective demands a broader view of leisure than merely the passing of time in some frivolous activity. This huge group of individuals will enter their retirement years expecting a great deal out of retirement, including the opportunity to pursue a Ulyssean lifestyle. An understanding of the role of leisure in later life is crucial.

THE ROLE OF LEISURE

There is evidence that leisure provides a multitude of benefits to older participants (Mobily, Lemke & Gisin, 1991; Haberkost, Dellman-Jenkins & Bennett, 1996; Patterson, 1996). The underlying perspective of much of the research on leisure and aging has been the link between activity involvement and successful aging. Issues such as life satisfaction, interpersonal processes, social interaction, and health (Spacapan & Oskamp, 1989) have been included in the search for optimum aging. This chapter will examine the place of leisure in these processes. Several years ago Janet McLean presented an equation summarizing the factors that go into successful aging. With some modification, her formula was: Successful Aging = Health times Meaningful Activity times Being Needed times Financial Security. One way to examine the importance of leisure in later life is to examine its role in each of the components of successful aging.

HEALTH

Many view later life as a time of poor health. In fact this is not the case. (See Chapter 3 for more on this issue.) Health is defined as not only the absence of disease but also physical, mental, and social well-being, and therefore health is best viewed as an indicator of function and disability (Burdman, 1986). Although aging is accompanied by physiological decline, decreasing well-being is not a necessary concomitant of this process. Rather, the ability and willingness to take control of one's own health is crucial. According to Burdman, "To age is not to look forward to decrement and infirmity, but rather to continue to use and nourish all remaining capacities to the fullest" (1986, p. 106).

Actions, built around leisure, can be taken to increase health in later life. There is evidence that many elderly make efforts to achieve and maintain good health. The 1985 Health Survey indicates individuals over 65 years of age are less likely to smoke, report that stress has adversely affected their health, or be overweight than their younger counterparts. The bad news is that older individuals are also less likely to exercise regularly (U.S. Senate Special Committee on Aging at al., 1991). In fact, heart disease is the leading cause of death and major health problem in later life. Leisure can play a role in reversing the lack of regular exercise by older individuals and as a result increase physical health. Lifestyle is a major component of health. Exercise, as part of that lifestyle, is crucial.

Fortunately, many individuals realize the role of movement in their lives. Exercise programs are staples of the offerings at many senior centers. Many states have formalized the role of activity by holding annual Olympic games for older residents of their state. The culmination of this institutionalization of exercise is the development of the U.S. Senior Sports Classic. A recent report of the fourth annual version of this national contest, which had a total of 250,000 contestants over the age of 55, in *USA Today* (Dorsey, 1993) allows us a glimpse of the role of exercise in the later years. According to one of the competitors, 67-year-old sprinter Jim Law, "These games showcase a different slant of the aging process . . . It allows everyone to see that it is possible to age and be in control, contributing, creative, and competitive all at the same time."

Lois Scofield, a tennis player in the same event, echoed Law's message, saying, "We are proving that we are not a burden to society in the health sense. This whole industry is the best prescription for Clinton's (health care) administration. My advice to seniors would be to get off the bridge table and get onto the tennis court" (Dorsey, 1993, p. 12C).

Teague (1987) supported the need to get out and exercise. He cited evidence that "carefully planned physical activity programs can help prevent or diminish the severity of many chronic conditions affecting the elderly" (p. 60) and suggested activities to provide the five components of a balanced fitness program. They can serve as a guide in developing an effective activity program.

1. Aerobic training built around steady activity over several minutes. Teague includes activities such as cross-country skiing, jumping rope, cycling, rowing, tennis, and racquetball in this category.
2. Muscular strength and endurance activities including strength training activities incorporating free weights and weight machines.
3. Flexibility activities designed to prevent injury while reducing muscle tension. Teague identifies several stretching activities designed to increase flexibility.
4. Activities intended to improve balance should be included in the exercise program.

5. Teague's final fitness component is exercise for weight control. Exercise
    programs are one of the keys to happiness, and wellness, in later life.

Unfortunately, concerns about factors such as heart attack and injury may
prevent some individuals from initiating programs in this area. There are of course
cautions that must be followed prior to beginning an exercise program. (See Teague,
1987; Froelicher and Froelicher, 1991, for example.) In addition to being aware of
these cautions, it is recommended that recreation professionals instituting an exercise program seek the help of trained exercise experts, including the local physical
education teacher, university faculty, or exercise professional from local fitness centers, as the program develops. Although Paffenberg, Hyde, and Dow (1991) were
not specifically examining the benefits of physical activity to older individuals, many
of their conclusions are relevant to all age groups. They stated: "Epidemiological
evidence supports the concept that sedentary living habits are directly and causally
related to the incidence of hypertensive-atherosclerotic diseases, especially coronary
heart disease, sudden cardiac arrest, and stroke" (p. 50). They described the multitude of benefits accruing to regular exercisers, including:

- reduced resting heart rate
- lower blood pressure levels
- reduced blood glucose levels and possible decrease or delay in the development of noninsulin-dependent diabetes mellitus
- decreased fat body mass and increased lean body mass, lowering risk of
  obesity
- helps prevent osteoporosis and is rehabilitative for individuals determined to
  be osteoporotic
- increased muscular strength and improved structure and function of connective tissues thereby preventing chronic back pain
- potential prevention of various types of arthritis and benefit for individuals
  with osteoarthritis
- reduced depression and anxiety neuroses through improved social skills and
  self-image
- increased life expectancy

Goldberg and Hagberg (1990) provided an extensive review of the literature related to exercise in the later years. Their review supports its value. They conclude, "Recent studies demonstrate that some older subjects can derive major physiological benefits from regular physical exercise, including an augmented aerobic
capacity, reduced blood pressure, lower plasma triglyceride, reduced total and LDL
cholesterol, higher total HDL cholesterol, and improved glucose tolerance and insulin sensitivity. All these changes have the potential to reduce risk for coronary
heart disease, the major cause of morbidity and mortality in Western societies" (p.

423). Fried, Freedman, Endres, and Wasik (1997) found similar benefits accruing from exercise. They state, "Regular physical activity, both moderate and high intensity, are associated in older adults with lower frequencies of heart disease and diabetes mellitus, maintenance of weight, more beneficial levels of other cardiovascular disease risk factors, better physical functioning, and lower likelihood of disability and dependency" (p. 217). Clearly, exercise is a wonderful tool for Ulyssean living. It will result in increased health and well-being that is vital for a developmental approach to later life.

Health refers not only to physical health but mental heath as well. Just as there is strong evidence supporting the link between physical fitness and successful aging, there is also evidence linking mental well-being to success in later life. Engagement in leisure activities provides the cognitive stimulation and challenge needed for mental health. In fact, the Center for the Advancement of Health (Facts of Life, 1998) indicates that lifestyle choices are crucial to successful aging. Exercising, making friends, and engaging in activities are "three of the most powerful determinants of health and functioning in seniors."

MEANINGFUL ACTIVITY

Meaningful activity can take many forms. Meaningful may include instrumental use of leisure to reach goals and the expressive use of leisure to find meaning. It may be a way to find a new identity or a way to reestablish an old one. It may be an instrument for continuity or for change. In a sense, it is having something important to do.

According to Kelly and Godbey (1992), "Perhaps the most common stereotype is that retired older persons have nothing worthwhile to do" (p. 368). Ulyssean adults have much that is worthwhile to do. According to Miller (1965), retirement can be viewed as a crisis. It is a time when individuals are forced to leave a role that has been central to them, and they may be left without a replacement. This is probably congruent with the image many of us have of the later years. If an individual's image is based on what she or he does for a career, what happens when that career is no longer available? If there is any doubt that a job is crucial to many individuals' self-image, you only need to ask people what they do. In many cases, the response will be vocation oriented: I am a doctor, I am a carpenter, I am a truck driver. It is much less likely people will answer by describing avocational activity: I am a square dancer, I am a rock climber, I am a jogger. What then happens when individuals lose their vocational identity? Can leisure step up and fill this void? Is it fair to expect leisure to be that central to individuals?

Haggard and Williams (1991) believed people use leisure as a tool for identity creation and affirmation. They stated, "We began by demonstrating that leisure activities symbolize identity images. These images may be seen as an outcome or product of participation in a leisure activity" (p. 116).

Burdman (1986) related the story of a woman named Helen Ansley. She identified her own formula for mental health: the "A's" and the "FFIG's." They provide an excellent framework for understanding the role of leisure in later years. The "A's" were: Acceptance—there is a need to belong and experience the acceptance of others. Appreciation—everyone needs to be needed by others and make a contribution as an individual. Appreciation acknowledges the importance of diversity in contributing to the welfare of a group. Affection—there is a need to be affiliated with others and share in their success and achievements. Achievement—the setting and accomplishment of goals is an affirming experience. It does not lose its importance with increasing age. Amusement—according to Ansley, "laughter, fun, and games are an important part of the emotional diet."

Ansley's "FFIG's" are emotions that are potentially damaging to individuals. These include: fear, frustration, inferiority, and guilt. Ansley views the A's as being a counterbalance to the FFIG's. When an overabundance of FFIG's occurs, there is a need to act on them. Three techniques for combating an overload of FFIG's were identified by Ansley. Her prescription provides an excellent rationale for providing activities to older individuals.

The first is to seek out people and situations that provide the opportunity to experience the A's. Certainly leisure can provide an arena for that contact. Ansley's second suggestion is to take action, particularly exercise, to defeat the FFIG's. Finally, she recommends talking about the negative emotions with someone else. Burdman (1986) summarized Ansley's approach to healthful aging as "keeping interested in the world around us; keeping abreast of the times; caring and reaching out; developing a sense of independence; developing new interests and hobbies; and treating ourselves with dignity" (p. 102). These are sound examples of the potential leisure has an instrumental activity.

Csikszentmihalyi and Kleiber (1991) discuss the potential role of leisure as a tool individuals use "to explore the limits of their potentialities and to expand the range of their mental, physical, and social skills, what today we might call self-actualization" (p. 92). The importance of such a role in older adulthood for Ulyssean living is apparent. The Ulyssean adult is seeking to explore the limits, seeking to expand life, and seeking to self-actualize.

Csikszentmihalyi and Kleiber identify the activity requirements for self-actualization to occur: "Involvement must be deep, sustained, and disciplined to contribute to an emerging sense of self." They go on to describe the flow experience (see Csikszentmihalyi, 1975 and 1990, for a detailed description), which they identify as the context for self-actualization. The characteristics of this experience would appear amenable to programmatic intervention to assist in their occurrence.

The elements of flow include:

- The merging of action and awareness as the participant becomes part of the activity. The individual becomes lost in the activity and is not separated from it.
- The sense of complete involvement in the activity requires a balance between the demands of the activity and the skill of the participant. If an activity's

challenges are too great for the skills of the participant, a state of anxiety will result. When, however, the skills of the participant exceed the demands of the activity, boredom is the inevitable outcome. Locating the fulcrum between activity demands and participant's skills is crucial.

- The activity should provide a clear goal for the participant. The goal, whether it is to complete the marathon or finish painting the deck, provides an opportunity for feedback and sustains interest in the activity.
- Attention must be focused on the activity to the elimination of all else including worry and unwanted thoughts. If you have ever been so intensely involved in an activity that time seems to stand still and you find it hard to believe you have been doing it as long as the clock indicates, then you have experienced this level of intense involvement.

The combination of the above characteristics results in an activity becoming rewarding in itself, what Csikszentimimihalyi and Kleiber call autotelic. The flow experience emerges when there is an opportunity to explore alternatives and identify what is challenging and using that challenge as an opportunity for growth. Anxiety and boredom can be combated by the development of new skills and a concomitant opportunity for new challenges. Although program guidelines for facilitating self-actualization are not firmly established, the work of Csikszentmihalyi and Kleiber, as well as interpretation of their work, does provide some suggestions. These include:

1. Provide participants with opportunities for making choices and exerting control over their own leisure.
2. Provide a range of activities. Offering activities only at novice levels will result in boredom. Activities viewed as overly challenging will result in anxiety. Opportunities for activity progression must be made available so increasing skill levels can be accommodated.
3. Do not underestimate the abilities of older individuals. Myths and stereotypes should not guide program decisions.
4. Provide opportunities to discuss leisure and its importance. Help individuals identify how leisure can be used to challenge, not merely to pacify.
5. Csikszentmihalyi and Kleiber suggest that schools, and we would add programs for older adults, can assist in self-actualization by offering "opportunities for reflection, intellectual play, and exploration" (p. 98).

Further evidence of the importance of meaningful activity in later life is provided in the MacArthur Foundation Study of Aging in America (Rowe & Kahn, 1998). The study identified the three components of successful aging: (1) avoiding disease, (2) maintaining high cognitive and physical functioning, (3) engagement with life. The first two of these were discussed in earlier chapters. Engagement with life is at the heart of meaningful activity. As Rowe and Kahn wrote: "The task of successful aging is to discover and rediscover relationships and activities that provide closeness and meaningfulness" (p. 46). One of the roles of individuals working with the elderly is to assist in finding meaningful activities. Rowe and Kahn identify continued involvement in productive activities as a primary category of meaningful activity. In many cases these productive activities occur as a result of the third component of the successful aging equation: being needed.

BEING NEEDED

We are social individuals. Not many of us would be satisfied living alone in a cave, and few would be willing to enter the solitary life of a monk. We need other people and hope they need us. The process of being needed is reciprocal. It is an exchange between at least two individuals. Our focus in this section will be on two dimensions of being needed: volunteerism and friendship.

Volunteering by older individuals is a major use of free time and one that has been increasing. In 1989 41% of all Americans aged 65 and over had volunteered in the previous year. This included 47% of those aged 65 to 74 and 32% of those 75 or older (Chambre, 1993; Rowe & Kahn, 1998). The most common volunteer site for individuals 65 years of age or over was a church or other religious organization, followed by health care locations including hospitals, social/welfare organizations, civil/political organizations, and sport/recreation organizations. The average older volunteer donated approximately 4.7 hours per week over a 35-week period (U.S. Senate Special Committee on Aging et al., 1991).

The roles of volunteering in later life are varied. At the most obvious level, it is a mechanism to fill time and provide a regular schedule. It is also an opportunity to serve, to achieve recognition, to be active, to use skills, and to exhibit mastery and competence. Volunteering also provides an opportunity to achieve a sense of "giving back" to the community, an opportunity viewed as crucial to successful aging (Fried et al., 1997).

Being needed is also part of friendship. One of the consistent findings in the aging literature is the importance of friendship in later life (Crohan & Antonucci, 1989; Mullins & Mushel, 1992; Sabin, 1993). Social contact is an important aspect of well-being. Friendships provide support for coping with adverse events in life (Schultz & Ewen, 1993) feelings of attachment based on reciprocity and equality, can validate feelings of self-worth and social integration, and provide a role and meaning in life. However, factors such as changes in living arrangements, retirement, and other changes may make friendships vulnerable and threatened. Therefore, there is a need to introduce opportunities for friendship that may counteract the trend toward the diminishing quantity and quality of friendship. Leisure may provide such an arena.

Through planned social activities, programs to identify partners for activities ranging from tennis to travel, support groups and enduring friendships can be built. According to Antonucci (1990) friendships built on reciprocity and a fair exchange are more satisfying and positive than those built on asymmetrical exchanges. The leisure arena is one where reciprocity can be experienced. Participants are on equal footing and may negotiate the giving and receiving of support. There are no expectations that one individual will be the giver of support and the other will be the receiver. An activity, such as a card game, frees all participants to "give as good as they get" over the course of the game.

One of the authors can remember playing Scrabble with his 90-year-old grandmother. There was no need to be hesitant to try to win, no need to coddle or cater to "old age." There was only a need to try hard to win, usually with dismal results. This competitive arena was free of age bias, free of stereotypes, free of caregiving. It was an even exchange of effort, support, and benefits. As a result, it was a special time where age was irrelevant and friendship could develop.

Providers of recreation services can build opportunities for reciprocity into their programs by matching people of equal ability in activities. In addition, providing individuals with responsibility for their own programs can help provide an equitable exchange environment where everyone can bring his or her contribution to the rest of the group. It appears such an approach will assist in friendship formation.

FINANCIAL SECURITY

Some older individuals may use the free time available through retirement to develop a hobby that provides a source of income. This component of financial security may include making and selling crafts, starting a second career, consulting with business or individuals, or using skills such as woodworking to earn an income. Typically, the money earned will supplement Social Security income or a pension. Leisure service providers may be involved in this process through providing classes to teach skills, helping identify opportunities to use abilities, and matching individuals with needs with those able to provide the required services.

SOCIAL-PSYCHOLOGICAL BENEFITS OF LEISURE

George (1990) identified five major themes useful in examining the social psychology of later life. Each has implications for leisure services. The first, frequently identified in the leisure and aging literature, is the definition and achievement of "successful" aging. Issues such as morale, life satisfaction, and well-being are viewed as aspects of successful aging. George identifies the origin of the interest in successful aging as the debate over activity theory versus disengagement theory.

Although the focus has moved beyond these theoretical frameworks, the issue of social structure and quality of life endures. George (1990) defined subjective well-being as the individual's perception of the quality of overall life. Concepts such as happiness, morale, and life satisfaction fall under the umbrella of subjective well-being. George identified three social factors as exhibiting strong and consistent relationships with subjective well-being: socioeconomic position, attachments to social structure, and age density of the residential environment.

The second of these is particularly germane to the benefits of leisure in later life. George differentiated between formal attachments and informal participation in primary groups. Formal attachments include labor force participation and membership in formal organizations. Informal group involvement includes interacting with family and friends. The influence of loss of formal attachments appears to have a relatively unimportant linkage to life satisfaction. However, informal attachment involvement is a "strong and robust predictor of subjective well being" (p. 192).

The informal attachments that appear crucial to subjective well being can be developed through organized recreation programs. They are also part of the core of leisure identified by Kelly and Godbey (1992). Core activities are those inexpensive and informal things people typically do. They include socializing with friends, walking, reading, and going shopping.

Some of the greatest contributions to understanding the psychological benefits of leisure results from the work of Tinsley and his colleagues at Southern Illinois University. Although some of this work has been directly related to older adults (Tinsley, Teaff, Colbs, & Kaufman, 1985), much of it is more generic. However, that does not decrease its value to us.

According to Driver, Tinsley, and Manfredo (1991), "individuals should be able to structure their leisure so as to maximize life satisfaction, raise self-esteem, and facilitate increased self-actualization. To do so however, requires knowledge of the need gratifying characteristics of the various activities" (p. 264). This knowledge will also help professionals involved in the delivery of leisure services in structuring their program offerings.

The work of Tinsley and his colleagues resulted in the development of an instrument called Paragraphs About Leisure (PAL) designed to measure the extent to which involvement in an activity meets a range of psychological needs. The potential benefits of leisure described by Tinsley and measured by PAL include:

1. Self-expression—resulting from the use of individual talents and recognition of those talents;
2. Companionship—resulting from supportive interaction with others
3. Power—resulting from being in control and at the center of social situations
4. Compensation—resulting from experiencing something new and unusual
5. Security—resulting from the ability to experience a long-term involvement free from change and resulting in some form of recognition
6. Service—resulting from providing help to others
7. Intellectual aestheticism—resulting from intellectual and aesthetic experiences
8. Solitude—resulting from the opportunity to be by one's self

The work of Tinsley and Teaff (1983) shows the potential in using the PAL in program planning. Designing a program to ensure balance in activities will maximize the likelihood that needs will be met. For example, offering only activities high on companionship (bingo, bowling, ceramics, dancing, volunteer opportunities, and social group meetings) limits the likelihood of meeting a variety of needs.

Although activity provision will never be as simple as consulting a guide such as that detailed by Tinsley and Teaff, it provides an excellent starting point when designing programs. Actually using PAL with participants would further the process of finding balance in programs.

George's (1990) second theme in the social psychology of later life is social roles. A common perspective of later life is as a time of lost roles. Work roles, family roles, and community roles may be less prevalent with increasing age. Much of recreation for older individuals is viewed as an opportunity to replace these lost roles with a new role, a leisure role. The research findings related to the validity of this position is mixed.

George's third theme is the relationship of life events, such as retirement and widowhood, and well-being. The extent to which such events are likely to result in negative outcomes depends on how stressful the individual perceives such events to be. George states that "social resources, including socioeconomic resources, attachments to the social structure, and, especially involvement in supportive social networks, can lessen the impact of stressful life events" (p. 189). For example, Patterson (1996) and Patterson and Carpenter (1994) found some association between leisure involvement and stress reduction for recently widowed individuals.

Leisure can provide an arena for the development of social networks that may mediate the impact of life events. A great amount of leisure is social. Group travel, Elderhostel, potluck suppers, and volunteer work provide outlets for developing and utilizing social networks. They give individuals an opportunity to meet others who have experienced similar life events and identify skills and techniques to deal with them. As a result, the events lost some of their potency and become less deleterious.

Age-stratification theory is George's fourth theme. This theory was discussed in Chapter 2. Individuals are viewed as part of an age strata. These strata are viewed in a hierarchical manner. George cites evidence of avoidance by chronologically older adults to view themselves as part of that strata. It may be that leisure can provide a vehicle for decreasing the stigma of older age strata. For instance, the example that opens this chapter provides evidence of individuals whose age is unrelated to leisure achievement. This achievement can function to decrease the perceived stigma of being part of this age group. Achievement can take precedence over stratification.

George's final theme is aging and modernization. Although modernization theory is explored in Chapter 2, a brief restatement may clarify its relationship to leisure. Modernization "as indexed by urbanization and industrialization, leads to decreased social status for older adults" (p. 190).

It may be that this decreased social status results in decreases in the quality of life of some individuals. The extent to which an individual perceives decreased status may be related to decreases in happiness or satisfaction. If that is the case, vehicles for increasing social status must be identified. Within some groups of individuals, leisure may provide an opportunity for increased status.

The work of Leitner and Leitner (1985) supports the role of leisure in psychosocial well-being. Their review of the literature indicated leisure activity can provide a variety of benefits, including: "improved health; increased opportunity for social interaction; improved morale and life satisfaction; higher self-concept and improved body image; greater feelings of usefulness and self-worth; improved skills and better ability to function independently; and most of all, fun and enjoyment" (p. 21).

SOCIAL BENEFITS OF LEISURE

Although most of the focus on leisure in later years is on psychological benefits such as life satisfaction, morale, and self-esteem, leisure also has a social payoff. The relationship between leisure and the social system is often viewed from a perspective that leisure is dependent and the system is independent. That is, leisure is shaped by culture. However, in this section, leisure is viewed as the independent variable playing a role in shaping the system. An earlier section of this chapter discussed friendship, clearly a social benefit. However, here social benefits as they relate to the community, rather than the individual, will be the focus.

Unfortunately, this is an area where relatively little is known. According to Burch and Hamilton-Smith (1991) "the available systematic knowledge of the potential and actual social benefits of leisure is very thin and empirical evidence is especially lacking" (p. 369).

Burch and Hamilton-Smith (1991) identify three possible social outcomes of what they term "nonwork opportunities." These include bonding, solidarity, and integration. Bonding, or the establishment of "ties between intimates," results in loyalty to a group or association, as well as encouraging the performance of roles necessary for the continuation of the group. Social solidarity, described as "emotional commitment to a larger social role," results in enhancing individuals' role performance. Finally, social integration, or the linking of elements of society together, results in the efficient operation of the group. Leisure can play a role in all three aspects of the continuity.

Kelly (1991) views leisure as critical to "developing and maintaining bonds of commitment and sharing" (p. 422). A more recent study by McCormick (1993) in two southern communities clearly supports this conclusion. He examined the role of leisure in a residential, lakeside community populated mostly by retired northerners who selected the south as an area for retirement and a nearby rural community composed mostly of individuals who aged in place. A series of interviews with residents of these two communities indicated the crucial role of leisure in the formation of an identifiable entity in the lake community. Leisure played a major role in the bonding process.

Similar results were found by Hochschild (1973) in her study of Merrill Court. She identified the development of an "unexpected community" in this garden apartment development inhabited by older residents. She describes the beginning of the community in this small apartment building for retirees: The story of how a collection of near-strangers became a community has several versions. As Freda, the first "indigenous" leader tells it, "There wasn't nothin' before we got the coffee machine. I mean we didn't share nothin' before Mrs. Bitford's daughter brought over the machine and we sort of had our first occasion, you might say."

There were about six people at the first gathering around the coffee machine in the recreation room. As people came downstairs from their apartments to fetch the mail in the midmorning, they looked into the recreation room, found a cluster of people sitting down drinking coffee, and some joined in. A few weeks later, the recreation director "joined in" for the morning coffee, and as she tells it, the community had its start at this point. The evolution of a group of people from being a collection of individuals to being a cohesive community, marked by bonding, integration, and solidarity, began during a social event easily identifiable as leisure. The need many older individuals have for the establishment of social ties and to feel part of a community points toward the value of using recreation and leisure as a vehicle for social integration.

WORK, LEISURE, AND RETIREMENT

The examination of the importance of leisure in later life cannot be complete without an understanding of the role of retirement in peoples' lives. Some view retirement as one of the most significant changes experienced by older adults. Some fear it, others embrace it. The assumption that the work role is a major contributor to our self-worth may lead some to believe that retirement is likely to cause severe psychological distress or impact physical health. Miller (1965) claimed that retirement had the potential to trigger an identity crisis among the elderly. His position was based on the belief that occupational identity mediated most other roles of the individual, providing meaning to life and status to the person; leisure was not thought to replace work as a source of self-respect, productivity, and social acceptance. The stigmatization resulting from the loss of the ability to "perform" in society's eyes was seen as a cause for embarrassment, identity breakdown, and eventual withdrawal.

However, there is little evidence that retirement is a crisis. Rather, it is a process with much individual variation (Quinn & Burkhauser, 1990; Hooyman & Kiyak, 1993) marked by periods of satisfaction and dissatisfaction. Factors such as health, financial security, work experience, and the opportunity for meaningful activity involvement are related to satisfaction with retirement.

Ebersole and Hess (1990) identified six retirement issues of relevance to older individuals. They provide an indication of areas where assistance in adapting to retirement may be needed.

1. What provisions have been made for income in retirement? Assistance in financial management may be necessary.
2. What activities are important and available to the retiree? The required skills, abilities, interests, and resources need to be in place in order to participate in the activities.
3. What living arrangements are most appropriate? Factors such as size, physical access, cost, and geographic preference must be considered.
4. What accommodations for role changes are anticipated? Spouses may be spending more time together. Widowhood, grandparenting, and caregiving may become a reality.
5. What health changes can be expected? Health issues must be clarified and examined. Factors such as insurance, change in diet and exercise, and sexuality may be fertile areas of discussion.
6. Have legal matters, such as wills and inheritance taxes, been addressed? Programs to assist in the legal area may be needed.

A study by Bickson and Goodchilds (1989) gathered information from 79 older men regarding retirement. The group of men, half retired and half still employed, formed a task force to study issues related to retirement.

The retired members of the workforce in Bickson and Goodchilds' study (1989) were asked to identify the best things and worst things about retirement. Some of the responses regarding benefits were: (a) being creative, (b) no daily routine, (c) being your own boss, (d) no pressure, (e) relief of responsibility, (f) no obligations, and (g) Palm Springs! The most common advantage noted by the subjects was not having to live according to a set schedule. Although almost half the subjects said there was nothing bad about retirement, some of the disadvantages reported were (a) miss the work, (b) miss friends at work, (c) wife is worried about money, (d) wife's criticism of my activities, (e) getting wife to do things, and (f) making up mind about what to do. These responses point to both financial, social and personal concerns in retirement.

Interviews with the retirees and employees revealed that the former were significantly more satisfied with their overall use of time, particularly time spent with a spouse. This higher satisfaction of retirees with time usage seemed to be explained by their ability to vary how their time was spent. No differences were found between the two groups regarding time spent with friends. One interesting finding was that retirees were significantly more heterogeneous in their distribution of time for activities than employees.

In terms of family and social adjustment, regardless of employment status, those men who reported greater amount of time spent with their spouses tended to perceive themselves as happier with their marital arrangements. Of course, this correlation does not indicate the direction of causation. Is satisfaction a result or cause of spending more time together? The wives interviewed, however, instead of making reference to time, seemed to view adjustment to retirement as related to their need to preserve some personal space. In the social domain, the study showed that retirees made more friends during the project year than the employees. When asked how they would describe themselves, the retirees listed different roles retirees assume including: (a) collector, (b) churchgoer, (c) grandparent, (d) investor, (e) recycled teenager. Rather than representing a loss of meaningful roles, retirement to these men appeared to add new roles to their lives.

LEISURE COMPETENCY

The previous sections detail the role and benefits of leisure in later life. However, these benefits will not accrue unless individuals are able to participate in leisure. In addition, it is possible the role of leisure can be expanded if individuals learn how to become better "leisurites."

A paradox of leisure is that it may take work to achieve leisure. We are not necessarily born with the abilities needed to experience leisure. While a great deal of education is geared to vocational preparation, few efforts are designed to facilitate leisure involvement. The authors of this book are frequently presenters at pre-retirement seminars. One of the points they make is that leisure will not just happen. Free time will occur as a concomitant of retirement and other role losses, but some skill is needed to use this time for leisure. The Scuba divers' motto is "plan your dive, and dive your plan." Similarly, a motto for leisure in the later years may be "plan your leisure, and leisurely go about your plan." The following are ways that may be done. It is not the intent of this book to be a treatise on leisure education. However, leisure professionals working with older individuals will benefit from knowledge in this area. There are several useful books and materials that should be consulted for further information.

If leisure is used to develop feelings of competence, meaning, and mastery, then individuals need to learn how to do that. The presence of leisure opportunities is not sufficient to ensure leisure participation. Individuals also need to develop competence in the area of leisure. Competence assumes that the knowledge, attitudes, and skills required to participate in available activities have been acquired.

For example, Atchley stated that many older people are reluctant to engage in activities such as art, music, and writing, at least due in part to the individual's feelings of incompetence in activities.

The work of Bandura (1982) indicates a need for feelings of self-efficacy prior to entry into freely chosen activities. Self-efficacy is a belief that you have the ability to successfully participate in an activity. If an individual does not expect success in an activity, then participation is less likely to occur. Therefore, it is necessary to impart a sense of efficacy to individuals if participation is to occur. According to Bandura, efficacy can be increased through direct or vicarious experience with the activity.

There are four stages in Tedrick's (1982) leisure competency model. The first involves clarification of attitudes toward leisure and exploration of the role of leisure in life. Many instruments exist to assist in this exploratory phase. They include books and instruments such as the Leisure Diagnostics Battery. Such materials can be useful in exploring attitudes, values, and activity preferences. This exploratory phase will be concluded by decisions related to leisure, its role in life, and leisure goals.

The second stage of the leisure competency program involves the learning of new leisure skills and activities. Instructional classes and seminars may be effective techniques for this leisure education component. These can either be conducted in segregated settings, such as multi-purpose centers, or in age-integrated programs. It is possible that individuals may be more comfortable in an age-segregated setting; however, this is a decision best left to the participant.

The third phase of the program involves gathering information about leisure opportunities in the community. Some communities have directories of leisure opportunities. For example, Greenville, South Carolina, has a central clearinghouse where individuals can call to learn about outlets and opportunities. Such an information and referral service can be useful in identifying available activities. A search of the multitude of activity sources to be found in most communities can be used to develop a resource list. Sources of activity information are listed in Table 6.1.

The goal of the leisure competence program is to assist individuals in being able to take advantage of the leisure opportunities which exist. If successful, the opportunities to make choices and exert control over a major area of life will be increased. The program is a dynamic one marked by evaluation and feedback, and therefore, as individuals change and their circumstances change, the program will assist them in making alterations in their leisure lifestyle. It can be an effective approach to Ulyssean living.

The leisure education content model (Peterson & Gunn, 1984) provides an excellent overview of the components needed to "facilitate the development and expression of a satisfying leisure lifestyle" (Stumbo & Thompson, 1988, p. 18). The model includes four components: leisure awareness, social interaction skills, leisure resources, and leisure activity skills. The incorporation of these components into a leisure competence program will assist in preparing individuals for Ulyssean living.

McDowell (1978) developed an approach to achieving leisure well being. Although his work was done several years ago, the message is still a useful one. McDowell defines leisure well-being as "a measure of how well prepared you are to assume and maintain responsibility for an enjoyable, healthful, satisfying, and dynamic Leisurestyle" (p. 4). As a result of lack of leisure experience or failure to develop leisure skills over the life course, some older individuals may have a difficult time developing leisure well-being. McDowell's model can help facilitate its development.

Leisure well-being has four components. Each is crucial in developing effective leisure habits.

TABLE 6.1
SOME SOURCES OF ACTIVITY INFORMATION

Friends	AARP
Radio Station	Television
Newspapers	Board of Education
Libraries	Community Rec. Department
Churches	National Park Service State Travel or
Community Colleges	Visitors Bureau
County Extension Service	Adult Education Programs
YMCAs and YWCAs	Volunteer Action Center
Travel Clubs	Craft Groups
Elderhostel	Yellow Pages
Museums	Chambers of Commerce
Health Clubs	Travel Agencies
Bookstore	State Depts. of Parks and Recreation

Coping is the ability to manage boredom and guilt. In addition, it is the ability to move beyond what McDowell identifies as "I can't" compulsiveness. Some indicators of ineffective coping include: oversleeping, compulsive busyness, alcohol or drug abuse, watching television because it is easy, and not trying new activities.

McDowell's second component is leisure awareness and understanding. This includes an examination and understanding of the influence of work and duty on leisure. Viewing leisure as a reward for work or an event to re-create one to return to work is not an accurate perspective on this realm of behavior. It is particularly inappropriate for older individuals, many of whom are retired and therefore not able to "justify" leisure based on work. Individuals should be assisted in viewing leisure as valuable for its own sake. To do so requires realization of the value of leisure. Some areas to assist in examining leisure awareness include: reflecting on the role of leisure in life, examining the value of leisure in life, and looking at the excuses used for not doing activities.

Knowledge about leisure, including interests, resourcefulness, and fitness, is also part of leisure well-being. Issues such as the breadth and balance of leisure, knowledge of talents and interests, and the role of physical fitness are part of knowledge. Sample questions useful in identifying extent of knowledge include: What is one's leisure breadth and balance ? What common interests are shared with others? Is there time to be alone in leisure? Are the activities selected reflective of a variety of interests?

The route to leisure well-being is a personal one. Unfortunately, other people may make it a more difficult journey than it needs to be. McDowell's final component in his model is assertion. Assertion is built around McDowell's "bill of rights" including:

1. The right to do nothing
2. The right to procrastinate
3. The right to be uncertain
4. The right to be alone
5. The right to be playful
6. The right for self-expression
7. The right to be childlike

These seven items provide a strong statement of a "bill of leisure rights" for the later years.

A more recent program designed to enhance control and competence was described by Searle, Mahon, Iso-Ahola, Sdrolia, and van Dyck (1995). They designed an intervention that successfully enhanced feelings of leisure control and competence. The program included 12 units:

1. an examination of what participants did for their recreation;
2. an examination of participant's motives for activity involvement;
3. an analysis of the components, physical, mental, and social, required for each activity;
4. a self-assessment of abilities and their impact on activity involvement;
5. an explanation of how to adapt activities and equipment;
6. an examination of barriers to participation and how to avoid them;
7. a goal-setting session to make long- and short-term leisure plans;
8. an examination of alternate activities and the skills needed to participate in them;
9. an identification of support people and how to use them;
10. an assessment of personal resources such as finances and transportation;
11. an examination of community resources and how to take advantage of them;
12. a reassessment of leisure goals.

If individuals are to realize the meanings available in leisure, they must develop the competence needed to use leisure. The materials presented above can be used to develop programs to assist in doing that.

CONCLUSION

There are a variety of definitions of leisure, ranging from time to activity to state of mind. It is interesting that there is more agreement on the benefits of leisure than on its definition. Clearly, leisure can play a major role in the lives of older people. It has the potential for providing physical, social, psychological, and health-related benefits. Activities can provide vehicles to reach a variety of personal goals and are potentially a primary means of Ulyssean living. Leisure service providers can, therefore, assist in the search for Ulyssean lifestyle by facilitating the development of leisure competency.

Some individuals will choose leisure as a central life interest and use it to meet their social and psychological needs. Other individuals may not share the same degree of commitment to leisure, but it will still have a major impact on their lives and on their communities. Successful aging incorporates meaningful activity, and it is a misperception to view older adults as sitting around with nothing to do. Most older adults are active and find personal affirmation through their involvement. Ulyssean living requires nothing more and nothing less if it is to be a reality.

Chapter 7

◆

The Leisure Experience:
Motivational Factors

This chapter will explore leisure motivation and satisfaction. We will continue our search to understand leisure in the later years and how this leisure can be used to achieve a Ulyssean lifestyle. We will continue to explore the primary role of leisure in people's lives. The next chapter will directly relate leisure to the Ulyssean lifestyle, but here we are interested in focusing on further elucidating the richness of leisure and understanding its roots in earlier life. The model of motivation described by Mannell and Kleiber (1997) provides the definitional starting point for this chapter. The model postulates that behavior is preceded by a need or a motive. Engagement in the behavior may result in fulfillment of the need which originally motivated involvement in the activity. Feedback on the success, or failure, of the activity in meeting needs results in the continuation or cessation of the activity. Motives are a crucial part of the leisure experience. In fact, Losier, Bourque, and Vallerand (1993) identify motives as the most important factor affecting the leisure experience. This chapter will examine the motives which drive leisure choices. Let us start by looking at the leisure of Victor Logan.

> The light entered the workshop from one dusty window and fell on Victor Logan, playing in and about the grooves and wrinkles of his face as he bent patiently over a piece of wood on the workbench. The only sound was the scraping of Logan's chisel on the curley maple. The smell was of wood and dusty oldness. High on the dark shelves there were mysterious and wonderful boxes tied meticulously with string and labeled for nails, bolts, and screws. Well-used and worn tools of the trade lay in disarray.
>
> On a clothesline in one corner two violins hung, awaiting the final touch of the master craftsman. Logan was a master craftsman, a violin maker for more than forty years.

"I've never sold one," he said, tightening the strings of one of his violins. "Not that I haven't had offers. I do it for fun, and besides, I like having them just hanging around here."

His handsome red-headed wife stood outside the shop and gazed affectionately at her husband. "He's got the gift," she said. "He just loves to work with his hands."

He has never had any formal music training, but he taught himself and now "plays anything he can get his hands on." He is even the church organist at Bostic Presbyterian.

"I built my first violin in 1932. I had nothing to copy cause we farm boys had no money like that. So I borrowed one and built mine just by guess, and when it was done, well, it came out pretty close to the real thing," he said, dusting off the front piece of the violin he was working on.

Logan used only old wood and hand tools just as Stradivari did. Time in plentiful amounts and patience were the other shared ingredients. "I'd say it takes me about a year to build a violin," he explained, picking up his favorite.

He was slow to admit he could even play the violin, but finally picked up his favorite, tuned it carefully, and tucked it under his chin. His bow sawed across the strings, and the strains of "Christ the Lord is Risen Today" filled the workshop. He finished that piece and then went right into "In the Sweet By and By."

And so Victor Logan, violinist and violin maker, became Victor Logan, old-time fiddler. He let his right foot tap the tempo to the sprightly "Soldier's Joy," a haunting melody reminiscent of a highland bagpipe fling. His fingers flew like the feet of dancers he might have been imagining while he played the fiddle he had patiently built with his own hands years before—not for money, not for fame or glory, but, as he said, "just because I love the music" (Greenville News Piedmont).

Victor Logan is an individual who has been able to continue leisure patterns developed throughout life into his later years. This pattern of continuity is typical of many older individuals. Logan's involvement in creating musical instruments is a lifelong one. It is not a new leisure activity developed after retirement to help fill time. Rather, it is an activity he has found satisfying and fulfilling; it provides meaning in his life and is part of him. This chapter will examine the motivations and meanings of leisure and focus on understanding why people, such as Mr. Logan, do what they do.

LEISURE MOTIVATIONS

When we ask people why they engage in leisure activities, the typical answer is because they are enjoyable. That is seen as sufficient motivation—we do what we enjoy. However, there is a great deal of evidence that leisure is more than a pleasure provider. It is a rich area of behavior from which we should expect a great deal more than enjoyment. The Ulyssean approach requires a great deal more!

Examination of the meaning of leisure is a difficult task. Leisure revolves around personal, individualized activity and therefore is difficult to classify or categorize. Each individual brings his or her own history, physical and mental state, emotional needs, and intellectual perspective to an activity, and these influence the meaning of the activity. For example, participation in tennis may have five different meanings to five different participants. One person may do it for the status, another for the exercise, another to be with her spouse, one to emulate a role model, and one to socialize with friends.

The difficulty of attaching meaning to activities is further complicated by the differential nature of activities to the same person. An individual may jog because it is a fitness activity on one day and for socialization the next day. As Kelly summarized after examining the "career" of one activity, dancing, "In the end it is the meaning to the participant that is crucial. It is that meaning, that definition of the activity for a time and place, which determines whether doing the activity is primarily expressive leisure, social leisure, or activity that is required by social or professional roles" (1996, p. 25).

In spite of the difficulty in specifying leisure meanings, examination of this area will provide insight into leisure in the later years. Understanding why people do what they do has practical importance. Iso-Ahola (1989) indicated that knowledge of motivations can provide a powerful tool in program planning, since motives are linked to desired outcomes of participation. In fact, he views motives as internal factors driving behavior. As he stated, "If social interaction, for instance, is the main motivator among nursing home residents, then it would be foolhardy to plan recreation programs around activities that do not facilitate social contacts" (p. 247).

REASONS FOR PARTICIPATION

Some of the earliest work into the meanings of leisure was done by Havighurst (1961) as part of the Kansas City Study of Adult Life. He asked individuals to identify their favorite leisure activity and then classified these activities into 11 categories:

1. participation in formal groups including social clubs, fraternal organizations, and church groups
2. participation in informal groups

3. travel
4. sports participation
5. watching sports
6. television and radio
7. fishing and hunting
8. gardening
9. manual-manipulative activities such as sewing and woodworking
10. reading and imaginative activities
11. visiting friends and relatives

Havighurst then used these activity classifications to determine why people participated in activities. Eight leisure meanings were identified:

1. just for the pleasure of it
2. welcome change from work
3. new experiences
4. chance to be creative
5. chance to achieve something
6. contact with friends
7. make time pass
8. service to others

The meanings found were more determined by the personality of the individual than by age, gender, or social class.

EXPRESSIVE LEISURE

A major examination of the meaning of activities in later life was conducted by Gordon and Gaitz (1976). They defined leisure as "discretionary personal activity in which the expressive meanings have primacy over instrumental themes, in the sense that gratification of present needs, wants, desires or objectives is given precedence over practical preparation for later gratification" (p. 311). This definition clearly identifies leisure as being defined by meaning attached to an activity rather than the activity itself. The need therefore to understand why an activity is done becomes a necessity to understanding leisure.

Based on an extensive review of the literature, Gordon and Gaitz identified five major "objectives of leisure," including: relaxation, diversion, self-development, creativity, and sensual transcendence. They conceptualized these objectives as being ordered along a continuum of intensity of expressivity, with relaxation being very low and sensual transcendence being very high, and then categorized activities along the five dimensions.

Relaxation was defined as activities providing variety and recreation for the body. Activities such as sleeping, resting, and daydreaming were classified as relaxation. Activities providing a change of pace and relief from tension and boredom were classified as *diversion*. Light reading, hobbies, and socialization were identified as diversion . *Developmental activities,* such as learning to sing or dance, participation in clubs and organizations, and involvement in cultural activities, are often intrinsically enjoyable. In addition they result in increases in knowledge, physical capacity, and more abstract ways of interpreting daily experience. Activities such as playing an instrument or serious discussion about a topic were identified as *creative activities* and involve actively performing in a manner to create new cultural productions. The final classification, *sensual transcendence,* involves the pursuit of pleasure, including both sexual pleasure and activation of the senses.

Gordon and Gaitz do not imply any one type of activity has a higher value than any other since only the participant can decide value. However, before individuals are able to attach a value or meaning to an activity, they must be given the opportunity to participate. This indicates a need to provide individuals with a variety of activity opportunities, encompassing all five realms of meaning.

Limiting opportunities to some areas while eliminating others will limit the potential of leisure to contribute to life and Ulyssean living. For example, not providing opportunities for sensual transcendence, whether as a result of accepting a myth that old age is marked by a loss of sexuality or from a puritan ethic, deprives individuals of a needed leisure experience. The choice should lie with the participant, not the leisure provider.

Gordon and Gaitz examined the association between age and level of expressive involvement. They found that relaxation and solitude showed an upward trend, while developmental activity and creativity showed moderate declines across the life span, whereas diversion and sensual transcendence were marked by strong declines with increasing age.

According to Gordon and Gaitz, "These most 'pleasure oriented' and 'hedonistic' leisure categories in our sample are found to be almost the exclusive province of the relatively young" (p. 330). They interpreted this finding as indicating that older individuals had decided to trade the opportunity for high levels of happiness and joy obtainable from such activities for a more sedate existence. However, it may also be older individuals do not have equal opportunity with their younger colleagues for such activities, and these age differences are related to opportunity rather than desire. A further explanation may be that older individuals have never done such activities and therefore have not "traded" one activity for another, but have experienced continuity in their leisure.

In any event, it is worth noting that not all individuals in the Gordon and Gaitz study avoided sensual transcendence or diversion. Therefore, outlets to meet the search for those meanings in leisure should be provided.

Kelly and Godbey (1992) identified an alternative perspective on the search for leisure meaning by suggesting simplifying the definition of leisure to incorporate the global concept of "leisure activity," which transcends the environment and form of the activity. For example, they identify six components of meaning based on "leisure activity." These include:

1. psychological—a sense of freedom, enjoyment, involvement and challenge
2. educational—intellectual challenge and knowledge
3. social—relationships with other people;
4. relaxation—relief from stress and strain;
5. physiological—fitness, health, weight control, and well-being
6. aesthetic—response to pleasing design and environment
   (Kelly & Godbey, 1992, p. 234).

Lawton (1993) provided an updated explication of the meaning of leisure to older adults. His list of meanings supports the value of leisure in later life and included the following benefits:

1. solitude
2. intrinsic satisfaction
3. diversion
4. relaxation
5. intellectual challenge
6. health
7. personal competence
8. expression and personal development
9. creativity
10. social interaction
11. opportunity for service
12. social status (p. 29)

Other attempts to understand leisure motivations have focused on a smaller number of primary motivations rather than the more general approach illustrated above (Iso-Ahola, 1989). A series of motives, including competence, socialization, flow, arousal and seeking and escaping have been examined.

COMPETENCE

According to Kelly (undated) two main motivation dimensions have been identified in life course studies of aging. These provide an excellent starting point in the search for why people do what they do. The first is the "opportunity to develop, build, and demonstrate competence. Again, the more serious leisure that offers a challenge also offers the opportunity to be and become a person of demonstrable worth and ability."

Others have viewed competence as a primary leisure motivation. This primacy of a drive toward self-perceived competence is supported by Kamptner (1989). She wrote, "Theories of motivation emphasize that individuals have a need to feel effective and interact competently with their environment" (p. 170). However, declines in "autonomy and personal control which may come about by changes or losses in one's work or family status, income, social network, and physical capacities, or through social devaluation" may make it more difficult to achieve this sense of competence. Leisure can play a major role in the search for competence, particularly if individuals pursue the Ulyssean course.

Since leisure is freely chosen and largely self-determined, it provides an opportunity to select and succeed at activities that will result in perceptions of competence. Climbing a rock, creating a quilt, mentoring an at-risk youth, or completing the Sunday *New York Times* crossword puzzle allow participants to succeed or fail based on their ability and effort. Leisure maximizes the chance to succeed since the activity is selected by the participant and is not imposed by external agents. The result will be an affirmation of self-efficacy (Bandura, 1982) and mastery of the environment.

While people seek relaxation and escape in leisure, it is also an arena for action. Therefore, programs must offer opportunities for challenge and progression from introductory to advanced levels. In many cases, this progression will be most easily provided through age-integrated programs that provide all participants the opportunity to seek their own optimum level of action. However, it may also be necessary to start individuals at a very basic level and in an age-segregated setting until they have enough belief in their own ability that they will enter into age-integrated programs.

For example, a woman would only participate in a water aerobics program that was held in the swimming pool in her retirement community. The pool was for residents only and met her desire to be only with other older individuals. When asked why she did not participate in the program at the local YMCA, her response was that she was not comfortable being seen in her bathing suit in a public pool. It is possible she may have eventually progressed to the point of participating in the more advanced Y program, but the choice had to be hers.

Similarly, programs such as Elderhostel are designed to serve older individuals. Factors such as pacing, competition, and intensity are less than they might be in an age-integrated program. Certainly, many individuals in Elderhostel could do very well in regular academic classes, and many probably do, but the level of "action" provided in Elderhostel is that sought by many. If meaning comes from finding action contexts giving the opportunity to demonstrate competence and mastery, then the job of the leisure service professional is to identify, and if necessary provide, as wide an array of opportunities as possible.

SOCIAL INTEGRATION AS A MOTIVE

Kelly (undated) continues his examination of motivation in later life: "The second theme of motivation that draws consistent engagement is social, the developing and expression of community" (p. 10). Mannell and Kleiber (1997) also identified the need for relatedness as a key motivator of leisure. They view relatedness as revolving around being needed by others and having a sense of being part of something larger than oneself. The previous chapter addressed the role of leisure in community building. Since social integration is a primary motivation for leisure, strong programs will be those focusing on developing relationships. In fact, it has been said that one measure of program success when working with older adults is whether marriages occur between participants.

The author at one time worked in a camp limited to individuals at least 60 years of age. During the summer, a man and woman met during camp and became partners during the morning hikes. Hiking together blossomed into romance and the couple eventually wed. Clearly, this was a program success.

In another case, during the course of interviewing candidates for the position of center director, one of the authors was confronted with typical answers to the question: "If you were hired, what programs would you initiate?" Answers included travel clubs, potluck dinners, exercise class, and bingo. One candidate said she would start a dating service. She was hired. Kelly suggests programs providing opportunity for continuity (see Chapter 2 on theories of aging for more on the concept of continuity) in the personal and social realm are those that permit the "expression of ability and community." Clearly, competence and relatedness are important goals to include in programs.

FLOW

One of the most cited efforts to explain leisure behavior has been Csikszentmihalyi's (1975) notion of "flow." Flow is viewed as the state when individuals' skills are harmonious with the demands of the activity in which they are engaged. When an activity is overly demanding for an individual's abilities, anxiety will result. Contrarily, when skills exceed demand, boredom results. Individuals seek to optimize flow experiences and avoid boredom and anxiety-producing experiences.

This motivation can be effectively used in program design. For example, individuals with low levels of skill should be motivated to seek beginner-level programs. However, if the program does not become more demanding as they develop higher skill levels, boredom will result and dropping out of the program may occur. More odious than dropping out is the possibility the individual may continue to participate in the boring activity, thereby reducing the likelihood it will be a leisure experience.

If activities are viewed as too demanding, it is probable individuals will avoid them since the result of participation will not be personal or social development, but rather anxiety. Therefore, it is necessary that a progression is provided.

There is probably greater danger of underestimating the abilities of older individuals than overestimating their abilities as a result of myths, stereotypes, and ageism. The skills of many individuals are mistakenly viewed as diminishing and deficient. Programs based on those misconceptions will result in boredom. In fact, the low level of involvement in community-based "senior citizen" programs may be at least partly the result of programs viewed as boring by older individuals. If the focus was on meeting the motivation for flow, perhaps public programs would attract more participants. (See Chapter 6 for more on flow.)

SEEKING AND ESCAPE

Iso-Ahola's (1989) work supports a more focused perspective on motivation. In fact, he stated, "There are only two fundamental dimensions to leisure motivations: seeking personal/interpersonal intrinsic rewards, and escaping personal/interpersonal environments through leisure experiences. Leisure motivation is not a matter of either seeking or escaping, but of both" (p. 269).

These are two components of the intrinsic motivation that are necessary for leisure. In order to achieve the benefits of leisure discussed in the earlier chapter, individuals must be free to exercise choice and self-determination in their leisure, and this choice revolves around seeking and escaping.

The interpersonal realm refers to the social contacts, while the personal realm focuses on personal rewards, including competence, resulting from participation. Seeking and escaping are presented as motivational forces and not single motives. According to Iso-Ahola, both are present at all times in leisure behavior, but the strength of each varies. Figure 7.1 presents Iso-Ahola's model of seeking and escaping.

FIGURE 7.1
MODEL OF SEEKING AND ESCAPING BEHAVIORS

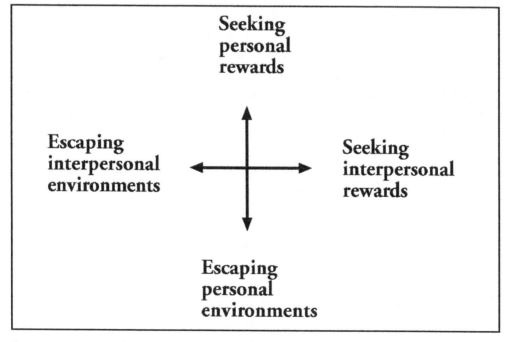

(ISO-AHOLA, 1989)

An example may help clarify this model. An individual may look forward to retirement and welcome the free time it will bring. However, she also views this time with trepidation, since boredom is not a desirable outcome. An opportunity to become a volunteer in an intergenerational program with at-risk youth is available in the local community. The individual would like to join since it would provide an opportunity to meet new friends (interpersonal seeking) while breaking away from work mates (interpersonal escaping) and an opportunity to use her skills in new ways while learning new things (seeking personal rewards) while disengaging from the work role (escaping a personal environment). However, she does not want the same demands on her time as work required, since the escape component is important. If the volunteer role became too rigid and structured, too work-like, she might cease volunteering if the opportunity for escape is no longer present. The wise project director will be aware of the seeking/escaping dimensions and work to keep them in balance.

OPTIMUM AROUSAL

Ellis (1973) identified optimum arousal as a primary leisure motivator. Individuals seek to be in a state of uncertainty and stimulation. This is often achieved through novelty in activities. The freely chosen nature of leisure makes this a behavioral arena where optimum arousal is likely to occur since participants have the freedom to alter their activities to introduce novelty, and the accompanying incongruity, into their activities. For example, an aquatics exercise program can be made stimulating by the introduction of new exercises, equipment, or members into the class. Similarly, challenging activities, such as rock climbing, backpacking, and kayaking, can be incorporated into an individual's leisure repertoire to allow opportunities for optimum arousal. Mannell and Kleiber (1997) indicated that arousal beneath, or above, an individual's optimum level is "unpleasant" and movement toward optimum arousal is pleasant. Therefore, people seek optimum arousal through novelty, incongruity, challenge, and uncertainty when they are sub-optimally aroused. When overaroused, supraoptimal arousal, individuals will seek things that are familiar and predictable.

Many programs for the elderly do not provide enough opportunities for optimum arousal. They are often made up of introductory level activities which underestimate, and underchallenge, the skill of the participants. The result is participants who are sub-optimally aroused. In these cases there is a need for stimulating, novel, challenging activities. However, the losses that accompany aging may result in a supraoptimal level of arousal in some individuals. If that is the case, familiar, predictable activities are most appropriate.

FINDING PERSONAL MEANING IN LEISURE

Reker and Wong (1988) provide an excellent examination of the search for personal meaning in the later years. They view the seeking of meaning in human existence as fundamental to life and are strong proponents of an interpretive science perspective on aging. This perspective has two major premises (p. 216):

1. Humans are viewed as "conscious, active, purposive, self-reflecting organisms capable of symbolization and symbol manipulation." The individual constructs reality rather than merely responding to reality. As a result "aging may be viewed as a process of change in personal construction over time." Aging is therefore an individual process "giving the person the power to accommodate and transcend both personal and societal limitations."
2. The physical attributes of the natural world are secondary to the meanings people attach to objects and events in searching for reality.

What is the role of leisure in finding personal meaning in later life? This meaning can only be identified by the actor. In fact, people are motivated by the search for personal meaning in life. Programs designed to assist in this search will help individuals find purpose in living. Although Reker and Wong are more theoretical than practical in their presentation, there are some clear paths to using the interpretive perspective for programmatic direction. Sources for personal meaning, resulting from values and beliefs, include:

1. personal growth
2. success or achievement
3. altruism
4. hedonism
5. creativity
6. religion
7. legacy

The development of meaning in life accrues from several values and as a result greater variety contributes to greater meaning. The result is what Reker and Wong call the breadth postulate:

"An individual's degree of personal meaning will increase in direct proportion to his or her diversification of sources of meaning" (p. 225).

Further postulates provide additional programmatic fodder. The *depth* postulate states:

"An individual's degree of personal meaning will increase in direct proportion to his or her commitment to higher levels of meaning" (p. 226).

The highest level of meaning rests in values that relate to the ultimate purpose of life and cosmic meanings. That is heady stuff that may be difficult to incorporate in a recreation program.

Victor Logan may have reached this level of meaning, but it is probably not accessible to all. However, the lower levels of meaning may not be as problematic. The lowest level of meaning is seeking pleasure and comfort. Many recreation programs are designed at this level. However, the depth postulate suggests a need to move beyond pleasure.

The second level of meaning is the devotion of time and energy to the realization of our potential. This would include areas such as creativity and personal growth. The Ulyssean perspective espoused in this book comes close to this level of meaning.

The third level of meaning revolves around altruism, and service to others with dedication to a larger social or political cause is part of this level. Opportunities such as mentoring, political action and community will contribute to this level of meaning. The depth postulate indicates the need to provide opportunities to find meaning at all these levels.

Individuals reflecting both breadth and depth in their personal meaning systems are viewed as healthy. They are able to cope and adapt in a shifting world while accepting personal limitations. In fact, the meaning system postulate addresses the value of a comprehensive meaning system.

The personal *meaning system of an individual who has available a variety of sources of meaning and who strives for higher levels of personal meaning will be highly differentiated and integrated. (p. 226)*

Although Wong and Reker develop other postulates, these are the most germane to the leisure topic. The finding of meaning in later life is personal. However, that does not mean individuals working with the elderly have no role in the search for meaning. In fact, the following postulates derived from Reker and Wong may explain our potential role:

Breadth Hypothesis: The opportunity to find personal meaning will increase in direct proportion to the number of potential leisure opportunities available.

Depth Hypothesis: The opportunity to find personal meaning will increase as activities providing opportunity to find higher meaning are provided.

Based on these hypotheses, it is recommended older individuals be offered a variety of experiences that will facilitate the finding of meaning in later life. Opportunities must exhibit depth and breadth if they are to be effective.

CONCLUSION

This chapter has examined the motivations underlying leisure involvement. Long lists of potential reasons for participating in leisure have been developed by a variety of authors. As this chapter has shown, these lists accurately reflect the multitude of reasons for being involved in leisure without telling us a great deal about why any particular person is involved at any point in time. The answer to why people do what they do is a deeply personal one. This is probably more true in leisure, one of the most personal of all behaviors, than in many realms of behavior. Therefore, the lists provided in this chapter should be viewed as points of departure rather than arrival. Obviously, they give us a perspective on the richness of the leisure experience. However, this richness demands activities be based on the needs and desires of participants rather than the judgments of leisure providers. Although people are pushed into activities by motivators such as competence, relatedness, arousal, and seeking and escaping, the nature of the activity selected to respond to the call for action will vary across individuals. It is crucial that leisure service professionals provide environments and opportunities where motivations can be translated into meaningful activities.

Chapter 8

◆

Time and Activities in Retirement:
On Being or Becoming Ulyssean

McLeish's Ulyssean concepts provide an interesting background to explore the activities and time uses of older adults during their retirement years. Similar to the Ulyssean notion of a journey noting a beginning and an ending point, we may wish to consider the analysis of time and activities for the 65 and over population not only as a fixed point in the early part of the 1990s, but also as a bridge to the future and to speculate about what might follow as adults age into the early part of the 21st century.

Demographic changes (higher levels of formal education for future older cohorts, for example) may portend change relative to the activity patterns of future retirees; perhaps some of these changes may move leisure in later life more toward the creative ideals espoused by McLeish.

Four styles of negotiating the aging process are outlined by McLeish (1976). The first group includes those who react to life and allow life to happen to them. They are happy to pay the mortgage, raise the kids, and perceive retirement as a period of free time, probably best used to relax. Others make an attempt at self-identification throughout life but are not successful in achieving the goal. These individuals may have started their own business only to put in many hours with only marginal success. Likewise their leisure throughout life may be characterized by grand plans and opportunities that never resulted in desired levels of satisfaction.

In the third group are those who attain success in a dominant arena of life (often the workplace) but upon retirement are in need of a challenge and new direction. Some members in this group continue to work and shun retirement, yet McLeish (1976) feels that something is lost when new ventures are never undertaken.

Finally, McLeish (1976) hails Ulyssean adults. Their journey through life is marked by adventure, mystery, beauty, and creativity. At mid-life they may abruptly change career direction and achieve success in a completely different field. During retirement they display courage—travels are undertaken, personal challenges add meaning to life, activities are pursued for the first time. Expanded leisure during one's '60s and beyond unlocks the doors of self-actualization in McLeish's view.

Yet what of the masses who struggle along in varying stages of "quiet desperation" and who are likely to tally even more hours in front of the television upon retirement? Has the Ulyssean concept no meaning for them? Indeed, one of the greatest challenges we face in the next decades is to upgrade the quality and meaning of leisure for adults in later life (as it is for all other age groups, as well). As time expenditure and activity patterns are explored in the succeeding paragraphs, an attempt will be made to point out changes or potential trends that might signal a movement toward a more Ulyssean approach to leisure.

A number of studies are highlighted and serve as the basis for discussion. An exhaustive review of the leisure and aging literature was not the intent here, rather included surveys were purposefully selected based upon their national scope or link to McLeish's concepts. Activity and time patterns during retirement are the primary thrusts; brief comments on the social psychology of leisure will be made.

Two caveats are offered. Discussion of findings or results of the studies included paint a broad stroke of what the "typical" or "average" older adult does during retirement. Such broad strokes can easily obscure a far different picture of lifestyle and leisure repertoire for those who possess characteristics that separate them from the norm. Excessive poverty or wealth, a constraining physical ailment, or one's race often bring significant alterations to normal patterns of leisure. The studies cited herein are also cross-sectional in nature. One must caution against the tendency to infer age-related changes when different age groups are compared. Differences observed in such cross-sectional studies may be cohort-related rather than age-induced.

AGING STYLES AND LEISURE

McLeish's (1976) typology of four aging styles reactivates the classic disengagement, activity, and continuity theory debates as to the ideal manner of navigating the retirement years. Clearly, McLeish's preference would be activity theory; e.g., the more novel activities undertaken during retirement, the better. Stress would be placed on the "newness" of pursuits if Ulyssean status is to be achieved.

Yet for the majority of retirees, continuity of activities with a slight decline in the high-output physical pursuits represents the leisure lifestyle. Kelly (1987) refers to a core of activities in adulthood that remain relatively stable over the years. Interactions with family, shopping, walking, television use, and reading are generally very accessible and don't require a high degree of organization.

This core in Kelly's (1987) scheme is balanced by "high-investment" activities that require greater degrees of effort, organization, and equipment and yield special meaning to the older participant.

Continuity of activities may also be suggested through the United Media Enterprises survey (1983). Here eight groups ranging from teens to singles to retirees are used to analyze leisure. When the numbers of different leisure activities are compared, the younger age groups are found to have a greater variety, with the number decreasing in adult groups to a low of 20 activities for those 65 and over (again, an inference based on cross-sectional research). This may suggest that during adulthood, favorite leisure activities are determined and certain pursuits are maintained.

The three highest-ranked activities are the same for all later adult groups (reading the paper, television, and talking on the phone). Comparisons later in this chapter generally support the notion of stability of leisure activities using different adult age groups. Counter to the notion of continuity is the finding that about one-half of participants in senior Olympics were unacquainted with their event until their 50s (Lindeman, 1991).

McLeish (1976) noted that some adults are content to be passive recipients, accepting whatever life brings. This style was also confirmed by Kelly (1987) in his survey of adults in Peoria. About 12% of the sample were labeled as "accepting adaptors." For them, locus of control was removed from self. Their contentment and strength lay in adaptability.

As for truly Ulyssean adults who meet the criteria of embarking on new paths during retirement, of seeking challenge, and of aspiring to the creative life, their numbers have not been accurately recorded. Anecdotal and case study evidence, however, points to a growing number of older adults who have accomplished significant deeds.

McLeish (1976) refers to Dr. Spock's transition from pediatric medicine to spokesperson for the peace movement in the late 1960s and early 1970s. One can frequently find athletic, volunteer, or arts accomplishments of the old-old portrayed in the print or televised media. Yet from this perspective (see Tedrick, 1989), there is a danger in focusing on the almost super-human achievements of the old (especially the old-old) as it may tend to separate them from the masses. They become oddities, and the message lost is that the potential for such deeds rests with many, not just a few, aging adults.

Two additional gerontosociologists who have supported McLeish's notion of creativity and heroism in later adulthood are Belle Boone Beard (1991) and Max Kaplan (1975, 1979). Beard's (1991) studies of centenarians reveal creativity and challenges undertaken in significant proportions. Likewise, Kaplan devotes a chapter to creativity in *Leisure: Lifestyles and Lifespan* and his cultivated order within the holistic framework of leisure speaks directly to self-actualization.

Kaplan himself might well represent the Ulyssean spirit. His broad sociological perspective, his ability to infuse examples from the world of music, and his references to great thinkers from many continents and historical periods lead to the assessment that creativity and exploring varied cultures have been integral parts of his life.

TIME USE

Robinson's (1991) time budget analyses yield much information about the structure of time in retirement. His 1991 findings based on diaries from older (65+) adults and 1998 indicate that more time is spent on housework during retirement, that older, and to a lesser extent younger, men are helping out more with house chores, and that television viewing dominates leisure time for older adults, as it does for all age groups. Older women, however, still do the bulk of house chores, about 60 % (Robinson & Godbey, 1997).

Abandoning the full-time work role yields an obvious leisure time benefit; those 65+ spend only 25% of the time that 18–64-year-olds do in paid employment (Robinson, 1991). Such an advantage in free time for older adults may well continue into the next decade as currently more are opting (or are being nudged by employers) for earlier retirement (Tedrick & MacNeil, 1991). In fact, the ages of 60 or 62 are probably more realistic as a norm for retirement than is the traditional 65 (Tedrick & MacNeil, 1991; U.S. Senate Special Committee on Aging, 1987). A notable trend reported by Robinson and Godbey (1997) is that through reduced working hours and early retirements, the group of 55- to 64-year-olds saw a decrease in work time of 18 hours a week from 1965 to 1985. Thus, retiring or partially retiring is becoming more commonplace in one's '50s

The United Media Enterprises study (1983) reported 43 hours of leisure time per week for the 65+ group or 11 hours more per week than the mean of 32. Older adults were similar to teenagers (41 hours per week) and in direct contrast with dual-career parents who had the least free time (23 hours per week).

Two other findings of interest from the study were that older adults were least likely to express the notion that they wasted free time, and two-thirds of the 65+ group said that time never weighed heavily upon their hands. The misperception of the aging sitting around with nothing to do should be put to rest with this finding.

According to Robinson (1991), in addition to spending more time in house-related chores, older adults are more likely than other age groups to enjoy leisurely meals, are more likely to sneak a catnap, and are less likely than those younger to go out to movies, sporting events, or other entertainment. Television viewing accounts for 20% of all leisure time for those 65+, with men averaging 25 and women 22 hours per week. Also, as gains in leisure time are seen, a very high percentage of the additional time is devoted to viewing (Robinson & Godbey, 1997).

Retirees socialize about as much as other adults with a slight decline when 65 and over persons are compared to 55- to 64-year-olds (Robinson & Godbey, 1997). Few differences were found between the time patterns of older adults from the period of 1975 to 1991 (Robinson, 1991). There are also few differences between the 65- to 74-year-olds and 75+ groups (Robinson, 1991; Robinson & Godbey, 1997), with the younger group a bit more likely to work some hours and the older group to eat out less and spend more time with the television and reading.

Robinson and Godbey (1997) conclude that differences in time use between the 75+ and 65 to 74 groups are not as great as are the differences between the total 65+ population and those aged 18 to 64.

LEISURE ACTIVITIES

One's retirement activities may be used as a benchmark in considering Ulyssean adulthood. Everyday patterns, changes over recent years, and trends that might continue into the future may be linked to concepts of creativity and adventure in later life. Such analysis does imply value issues. Increased travel pursuits, greater involvement with the creative arts, and higher levels of volunteering are probably more aligned with Ulyssean notions than is listening to the radio or television. Yet, what about sitting quietly and thinking or reflecting? Some might classify this as a null or void activity along the lines of stereotypes of the aged rocking on a porch with nothing to do.

Some leisure analysts, however, deGrazia (1962) and McLeish (1976) among them, would be quick to count thinking and solitude as among the most cherished uses of time. McLeish (1976), in fact, offers many examples of mental gymnastics to be performed to keep mental powers agile. Thus, evaluations of retirement engagements are likely to include a degree of bias depending on the observer/reviewer.

Included in Table 8.1 are findings from seven different surveys (The Pennsylvania Survey includes two older age groups) relative to leisure activities of the 65+ population. The first three used large, representative samples. The TIAA-CREF study of former professors and college administrators was chosen because of the higher education levels and adequate financial resources of the group. Improvements in educational levels (see Tedrick & MacNeil, 1991) of future older cohorts are predicted and this study's findings might serve as a harbinger of the future.

The last three (Pennsylvania State, CIGNA, and Sports Illustrated) focus on physical activities. While summary comments will be made, the reader should be aware of methodological inconsistencies. The nature of the exact question asked and the method of collecting data can bring about varying results. A diary of time use and a question seeking to know what one's favorite activity is (not how much time is spent doing various activities) may yield differences. Also, certain physical or fitness activities probably would not be expected to take up a large portion of leisure time; three sessions of 40-minute intensified exercise may be all that is needed to provide fitness benefits. Aldana and Stone (1991) do discuss differences in perception as to how much regular or high-intensity exercise respondents report. Remember, further, that these aggregations will not reflect differences based upon key characteristics such as poverty, lack of transportation, etc.

In summary, the data support Kelly's (1987) description of a core of activities that are accessible and do not involve extensive resources or high levels of organization.

TABLE 8.1
LEISURE ACTIVITIES OF THE 65 + POPULATION

Percent participating	Age group	Activity days	Percent participating	Age group	Activity days	Percent participating	Age group	Activity days	Percent participating	Age group	Activity days
	45-54			55-64			65-74			75+	
%			%			%			%		
64.7	Jogging/walking for fitness	96.7	64.7	Sightseeing	18.2	65.9	Sightseeing	26.0	48.5	Jogging/Walking for fitness	74.8
64.4	Sightseeing	17.0	60.3	Jogging/walking for fitness	82.6	62.3	Jogging/walking for fitness	97.6	45.9	Sightseeing	25.8
62.8	Picknicking	7.3	54.0	Picknicking	4.5	59.8	Picknicking	4.6	38.5	Picknicking	2.0
53.4	Swimming	12.0	34.9	Swimming	8.6	31.7	Hiking	22.7	21.5	Birdwatching	44.3
41.9	Hiking	14.1	34.9	Hiking	15.4	26.6	Swimming	12.5	17.8	Hiking	10.5
34.5	Bicycling	14.0	22.3	Birdwatching	39.3	26.0	Birdwatching	45.6	9.6	Swimming	4.1
27.2	Fishing	6.1	20.5	Bicycling	11.6	18.9	Bicycling	10.7	6.7	Bicycling	3.6
26.6	Boating	–	19.2	Fishing	4.3	18.3	Fishing	4.9	5.9	Boating	–
21.7	Birdwatching	35.5	16.3	Boating	–	13.8	Boating	–	5.2	Fishing	.4
15.0	Hunting	2.9	13.6	Hunting	2.2	10.5	Hunting	3.0	4.5	Camping	.4
14.8	Camping	2.7	13.0	Golf	3.2	8.1	Camping	2.2	3.7	Golf	2.8
13.6	Golf	4.0	12.3	Camping	1.6	3.9	Baseball/softball	.4	1.5	Baseball/softball	.1
11.3	Baseball/softball	1.8	4.4	Tennis	1.2	2.7	ORRV's	.5	1.5	Basketball	.1
7.4	Basketball	1.3	4.2	Baseball/softball	.6	2.4	Snow skiing	.4	0.7	Tennis	.7
7.4	Tennis	1.9	3.9	Basketball	.7	2.1	Tennis	.7	0.7	Hunting	.1
6.5	Snow skiing	.6	2.8	Snow skiing	.3	2.1	Ice skating	.1	0.0	Football/soccer	0
6.3	ORRV's	1.7	2.5	Ice skating	.1	2.1	Basketball	1.3	0.0	Horsebackriding	0
4.7	Horseback riding	1.4	2.2	ORRV's	.1	1.5	Horseback riding	.1	0.0	Football/soccer	0
4.4	Ice skating	.1	1.1	Horseback riding	.1	.3	Football/soccer	.1	0.0	Snow skiing	0
.3	Football/soccer	.1	1.1	Football-soccer	.1				0.0	Snow skiing	0
24.4 (Mean)		225.2 (Total)	19.4 (Mean)		197.6 (Total)	18.6 (Mean)		242.6 (Total)	10.6 (Mean)		170.0 (Total)

The impact of television and other media requiring listening or reading can be seen. Television viewing ranks number one in nearly all of the age categories in the United Media Enterprise study (1983), and the over 65 group was more likely to view on a daily basis than any other group, although reading the newspaper ranked even higher for older adults. Television and radio use was not ascertained in the TIAA-CREF survey. Robinson and Godbey (1997) report, as well, that gains in free time experienced by the 65+ population are gobbled up through increased television viewing. Its importance as a foundation of leisure time cannot be disregarded for older adults in retirement.

The rankings also reveal that the majority of elderly have contacts with others, over the phone or through visiting. Hobby, game, and creative arts activities appear often in the mid-rankings.

As for exercise, the studies are fairly optimistic. In the CIGNA survey, the over 65 group gave the highest response rate (68%) of all adult groups when queried about regular exercise. Most retirees appear to be walking, although with differences in intensity. Jogging, however, is much less popular (CIGNA, Sports Illustrated). A new trend may be the use of exercise machines (Sports Illustrated). Sightseeing, picnicking, bird watching, and hiking are also highly ranked physical forms of recreation (PA Survey). It is interesting to note the low level of participation (28%) in education-related pursuits from former college professors and administrators; perhaps they see retirement more as an opportunity to break away from previous engagements (a compensatory notion) rather than maintenance of the familiar.

Analysts of retirement are also fond of comparing two or more older age groups with the notion of detailing expected changes over later adulthood. As previously noted, differences may be age-related or due to cohort variations if cross-sectional data are observed.

Robinson (1991) found greater differences in activity patterns between those over 65 and those 18–64 than he did between the two older adult groups (65–74 and over 75). The oldest group (75 and over) spent less time in paid employment, ate at restaurants less often, and participated in sports and travel less than did those 65–74 (Robinson, 1991). Television viewing (eight hours per week more for retirees) and reading (over three hours more per week) are the activities that occupy substantially more time for retirees than for adults 18–64 (Robinson, 1991). This latter finding is also supported in data from the 1986 Gallup Poll.

In comparing respondents over 65 with three other adult groups (empty nesters, traditional parents, and dual-career parents) from the United Media Enterprise survey (1983), the popularity of television and newspaper use is once again apparent. Those over 65 are more likely to spend time with hobbies or reading a book than the other adults. Older adults are just as likely to exercise as are other adults, while less time is spent during the retirement years on listening to records and tapes and on fixing the house (Enterprises, 1983).

Recent data concerning physical activities and exercise during retirement appears to be encouraging (see last four columns in Table 8.1). Older adults (over 65) were more likely to engage in regular exercise and to walk slowly than were adults in other age groups in the Aldana & Stone (1991). Participation in jogging for those over 65 is much less according to the Aldana & Stone (1991). Differences between walking and jogging cannot be ascertained from the Becker and Yost (1991) as the two are combined. Those 65 and over swim and do calisthenics more often than other adults, except those under 25 (Aldana & Stone, 1991). In 11 out of 14 categories in the CIGNA Survey, the 65 and over group participates more actively than does the 45-64 group.

Data from the Sports Illustrated poll are not as encouraging. When the over 65 group is compared to the next youngest group, 50- to 64-year-olds, significant drops in participation can be seen in nearly all activities. Golf is an exception with nearly identical participation for both groups.

Other findings can be seen in Table 8.2 that compare outdoor physical activities for four adult age groups in Pennsylvania. In many activities participation is greater for the 65–74 group than it is for the 55–64 or 45–54 age groups. Total activity days are greatest for the 65–74 group. This is probably due to the much lower level of involvement in full-time employment for the 65- to 74-year-olds as contrasted with the two younger groups.

Sightseeing, jogging/walking, picnicking, hiking, and swimming are highly ranked for all adult groups. It is interesting to note the low level of participation for tennis, generally considered a lifetime sport. Numbers are small both in percentages participating and in activity days (Becker & Yost, 1991).

It is evident from the preceding discussion that many positives can be gleaned when the activities of retirement are explored. The freedom retirement brings in the sense of available time to pursue desired activities is borne out in comparisons of those over 65 with adults of middle age. Time spent and numbers participating in selected activities are frequently higher for the 65 and over group.

It is probably unwise to categorize all retirees under the label of "65 and over." With extended periods of retirement for most, a division in the early to mid-70s and also one in the early to mid-'80s would be most useful when late life leisure is explored in the future. Shifts can be seen in outdoor activities using such age demarcations (see Table 8.2). Yet Robinson and Godbey (1997) maintain that differences in leisure activities between the 65 to 74 group and those 75+ are marginal; the younger group is more likely to be involved in some form of paid employment and even more time is spent with the media (television, reading) as one moves through the 70s and beyond.

Kelly's (1987) description of a leisure "core" is substantiated throughout these studies. Television, reading, phone use, and other social contacts are frequently done by most retirees. Is the overall pattern of leisure in retirement as presented here to be considered Ulyssean? That question deserves consideration as we also ponder the future.

TABLE 8.2
OUTDOOR PHYSICAL ACTIVITIES PENNSYLVANIA STATE SURVEY[1]

Robinson[1]	United Media[2]	Gallup[3]	TIAA-CREF[4]	PA State 65–74[5]	PA State 75+[6]	CIGNA[7]	Sports Illustrated[8]
TV 23.5 hrs.	Newspaper 87	TV 47	Reading 92	Sightseeing 65.9	Jog/walk 48.5	Regular 68.0	Exercise machines 20
Reading 5.95 hrs.	TV 81	Reading 19	With friends 75	Jog/walk 62.3	Sightseeing 45.9	Walk (total) 55.6	Fishing 18
Visiting 3.85 hrs.	Talk-phone 47	Resting 13	Gardening 71	Picknicking 38.5	Picknicking 39.5	Slow walk 40.5	Swimming 16
Non-determined activity 3.85 hrs.	Hobbies 39	With family 7	Travel 66	Hiking 31.7	Biking 21.5	Fast walk 24.8	Bicycling 12
Convers-ation 2.8 hrs.	Books 35	Games/cards 7	Hobbies 61	Swimming 26.2	Hiking 17.8	Swimming 17.6	Bowling 12
Hobbies 2.45 hrs.	Exercise 34	Visit friends 6	Creative Arts 43	Birding 26.0	Swimming 9.6	Calisthenics 15.0	Golf 11
Sports/Outdoors 2.3 hrs.	Garden 30	Dine out 3	Church 37	Biking 18.9	Biking 6.7	Biking 13.7	Boating 10
Religion 1.75 hrs.	Talk-friends 30	Movies 2	Volunteer 35	Fishing 18.3	Boating 5.9	Dance 11.8	Hunting 9
Resting 1.75 hrs.	Records 20	Dance 1	Sport/Fitness 33	Boating 13.8	Fishing 5.2	Aerobics 7.8	Calisthenics & aerobics 8
Games 1.63 hrs.	Magazines 20		Prof. Organ. 32	Golf 12.3	Camping 4.5	Jog 5.2	Jogging 8
Travel/Social 1.4 hrs.	Fix home 12		Civic/Frat. groups 31	Hunting 10.5	Golf 3.7	Run 5.2	Hiking 5
Radio/records .82 hrs.			Education 28	Camping 8.1	Softball 1.5	Weightlifting 3.3 Basketball	Billiards 5

[1]See Robinson, 19991, Hours per week spent on activities
[2]See United Media Study, 1983, Percent engaging in daily participation
[3]See Gallup, 1986, Favorite way of spending an evening in percent
[4]See Milletti, 1984, Percent engaging in the activity
[5,6]See Becker and Yost, 1991, Percent engaging in Physical Activities
[7]See Aldana and Stone, 1991, Percent engaging in Physical Activities
[8]See Lieberman, 1991, percent participating within the last 12 months

MOVING TOWARD ULYSSEAN LEISURE

As noted by McLeish (1976), certain conditions are more plentiful during retirement that should permit older adults to utilize their creative forces and thereby approach Ulyssean leisure. The first is the availability of time. Indicated earlier was the advantage that the over 65 population enjoys here in comparison with other adults. While for many seniors their days are quite full, they are more often than not able to enjoy a self-directed, leisurely pace. This issue of pace is as important to creativity as it is to leisure. Creative ventures often require reflection, time to reanalyze, and reworking a thought or action until a level of satisfaction is reached. Unhurriedness is compatible with retirement. Likewise, many would agree that the quest for satisfaction in leisure is as much wrapped in the style and manner of what is undertaken as it is in accomplishments gained or number of things done. Leisure should involve more than a race to check off a recreation "To Do" list, and retirement allows one to develop a self-paced rhythm.

Three additional characteristics (McLeish, 1976) held by the majority of aging adults are: the varied and rich experiences gained and stored over the years, the ability to be unorthodox without the fear of being a slave to others' perceptions (or misperceptions), and the talent to deeply sense or feel (even if the biological senses aren't as keen as they once were).

These conditions are well-matched with creative endeavors. McLeish (1976) gives numerous examples of exercises designed to get one out of familiar ways of thinking and going about daily life. For him, adults must be open to new ways of perceiving the world; he recommends that repetitive journeys be broken by finding a new path or route to prevent boredom. He even challenges the orthodoxy of moderation: eat dessert at breakfast and lunch, and instead of viewing one movie on a given day, binge and see three.

While the empirical support for this notion of celebrating the unorthodox may allude some, it is easy to recall many senior adults who were far too busy having a good time to worry about what others thought of them.

Do research findings support in any way McLeish's (1976) concepts of challenge, new journey, breaking with the commonplace, and creativity during the later years? Challenge could be exemplified through the focus on fitness that increasing numbers of older adults are adopting. The societal trend of attention to wellness, healthy lifestyles, and regular physical exercise has captured the mature market as it has younger and middle-aged adults.

As reported earlier, walking, swimming, sightseeing, hiking, picnicking, and calisthenics are forms of exercise undertaken by many older adults (Aldana & Stone, 1991; Becker & Yost, 1991). Few would project that this trend will diminish soon. Competitions such as senior Olympics, master's swimming meets, and golf and bowling tournaments for those over 65 are notable and should continue growing. Challenge can be illustrated through the physical forms of recreation being performed by substantial numbers of senior adults.

The issue of appearing to be unorthodox is addressed elsewhere (Tedrick, 1989). Images of healthy, active senior adults can be used in the battle to overcome the negative stereotypes of old age. Media stories of champion athletes in their '80s, of a female weightlifter in her late '70s, and of frail, wheelchair-bound nursing home residents participating in a modified Olympic contest attest to the fact that aged adults are accomplishing physical feats.

Such exposure is becoming more common, yet the danger in these images is that too many observers will see such elderly competitors as only exceptions to the rule; they will fall victim to what others (Ward, 1984; Hess, 1974) have termed "pluralistic ignorance."

Those selected by the media are perceived as super-human, and such participation is not thought to be within the realm of the average retiree. The next breakthrough will be the emancipation of the older competitor to such a degree that the potential for all to undertake such physical challenges will push the fascination with the "oldest" or the "fastest" into the background.

In terms of competitive participation, the numbers are compelling. At the most recent national gathering in Syracuse, the U.S. National Senior Sports Organization hosted 5,000 senior athletes; this number is overshadowed, however, by the 200,000 who participated at the local, regional, and state levels (Lindeman, 1991). Add to this masters' swimmers, older marathoners, golfers, bowlers etc. in retiree leagues, and the total level of participation creates an image that far surpasses the talents of a singular, aged athlete.

The next threshold to overcome—and movement is proceeding in the proper direction—is releasing the potential held by all older adults to enjoy healthy, physical competitions. Local recreation providers will be pressed to add "over 50" and "over 65" leagues just as they have for the "over 30" group who have begun to mature.

Travel as a Creative Venture

Travel as a leisure pursuit has received increased attention from older voyagers and those who market and package such services to retirees. Change of routine and gaining new experiences are among the benefits sought. Ostroff (1989) notes a segmentation of the older travel market. Older singles, grandparents accompanied by children and grandchildren, those with disabilities requiring special services, and older couples who want to tour Disney World by themselves are identified targets of tour companies. This desire to leave the familiar and explore new surroundings matches with higher levels of education and discretionary budget dollars held by more and more retirees.

As to the reasons for taking vacations or trips, they appear to be as varied as the backgrounds of the seniors themselves. Four studies are in agreement that the older travel market is a diversified one comprised of many different groups who are not all being reached effectively by tour companies (Backman, Backman, & Silverberg, 1999; Blazey, 1987; Hawes, 1988; Shoemaker, 1989).

Blazey (1987) focused on differences between older participants and non-participants in a senior travel program in Washington State. Participants were more likely to be female, in good health, and between the ages of 65 and 74. It was hypothesized that those 55–64 might have been reluctant to join because they didn't want to be associated with older "senior citizens" (Blazey, 1987).

While lack of money was mentioned as a barrier, poor health, lack of a companion, and not wanting to drive home in the dark were also given as constraints. Blazey (1987) suggested that the stigma issue, or younger retirees not wanting to be associated with "senior" programs and people, is one that all leisure providers should attend to.

Shoemaker (1989) identified three clusters of older travelers. The first, labeled "family travelers," enjoyed being with family members, were 64 or younger, and slightly more likely to be male. They took shorter trips; golf and shopping were favorite activities.

Another group was termed "active resters." They sought spiritual and intellectual enrichment, liked to meet people, and enjoyed quiet times, although visiting sites and special events were of interest.

The last group, the "older set," were more likely to be 65 or older and enjoyed staying in resorts with everything accessible. They often returned to favorite places, and historic sites were favored by this group. Shoemaker (1989) projected that learning weekends would become more popular with senior travelers. The focus would be the intellectual enrichment through the site visited.

Using data from a national survey, Hawes (1988) examined travel profiles of older women. Five age groups (50–54, the youngest, and over 70, the oldest) were created; factor and cluster analysis techniques were used to identify different groupings of female travelers and characteristics associated with them. General trends included younger groups being less likely to have traveled abroad but with a strong desire to do so. Those under 60 were generally less satisfied with their overall leisure. Overall, the group did not approve of the idea of taking a trip on credit; they wanted the trip paid for prior to leaving.

Factor analysis yielded three different groups (Hawes, 1988). "Travelers" hold a strong orientation to vacation trips. They had traveled more and wanted to visit more places compared to other older females in the sample. They were most often single or from a small household, had active lifestyles, enjoyed excitement and uncertainty, and were higher in income and education level than other women.

The second group, "laidback travelers," enjoyed travel but were more inclined toward domestic trips. An unhurried, relaxing pace was expected, and they would not go into debt to take a trip.

The last group, "dreamers," had a fantasy notion of travel. Television was a primary source of stimulation for them, and this fact distinguished them from the other two groups. Hawes (1988) analyzed media preferences and found each group to differ. He concluded that television was not a primary pastime for "travelers" and the "laidback"; marketing efforts for them would be more successful if aimed at printed media.

Similar to Hawes' (1988) approach of identifying profiles, Backman, Backman, and Silverberg (1999) analyzed senior (55+) nature-based travelers using factor analysis to identify five different psychographic types of participants. These were described as: education/nature, camping/tenting, social, relaxation, and information seeking. The profile predicted the style of nature-based travel and the benefits sought. It was also found that younger senior travelers were less interested in the educational/nature benefits and older seniors were less inclined to favor camping/tenting.

The studies and projections mentioned would appear to predict a very strong decade continuing into the year 2000 of travel involving senior adults. Older travelers are a heterogeneous group with differing motives and characteristics. As the baby boom cohort ages, it will be interesting to follow their travel interests. If increased education is associated with travel and if prior travel is associated with future travel (Hawes, 1988; Shoemaker, 1989), then a sustained period of adults visiting domestic and international points of interest should ensue as baby boomers move beyond middle age into retirement.

Creativity is related to travel, as well. The variety of ways that adults travel indicates originality and thoughtful planning. Some desire the group tour, stopping at traditional tourist venues; others want to control when and where they go.

The media has highlighted some retirees who sell their houses and are constantly on the road living out of recreational vehicles. Home is literally where they stop on a given day. The link of education and travel is intriguing; perhaps formal schooling that was less than stimulating will be replaced in later life by actually seeing and experiencing things firsthand.

Will the varieties of senior travel also incorporate those on limited budgets? Might state parks be used as a kind of hostel for the economy-minded? Will we see groups of seniors on the roadside taking two- or three-day bicycle trips? Will seniors start their own travel companies and combine avocational and vocational interests? These possibilities are exciting. Creativity and travel are highly compatible and will be most visible as numerous older adults literally seek their Ulyssean journey on the roadways here and abroad.

CREATIVITY IN LATER LIFE

Creativity was considered in Chapter 4 as part of our examination of cognitive changes in later life. That chapter focused on the components of creativity and age differences in these components. In this chapter, our focus is more directly on the place of creativity in leisure and later life.

As we consider the variety of ways that adults can be creative in their retirement years, perhaps we should even refocus on what "creative" means. Typical dictionary definitions emphasize associations with the original or the imaginative or doing something in a new way. There appears to be enough latitude in these descriptions to incorporate activities that many older adults could pursue. Too often "creative" is only linked to the arts with some specific output as the evaluative criterion. Daily life can be creative! Indeed many older adults have used much imagination and degrees of problem-solving skills in navigating the day-to-day travails of living. Simply surviving through adaptability should be seen as a creative process for some.

Likewise "creative" leisure encompasses more than an award-winning sculpture, poem, or short story. New directions and endeavors, new friends and places, all have a place within the realm of creativity. McLeish (1976) seems firm on this point: Creativity is not only for the select few; it is a concept to be applied to all.

Although much of the work cited in Chapter 4 applied the question of peaks in achievement or creativity, generally, to the vocational area, the issue does have relevance to the current discussion of creativity and leisure in the retirement years, particularly if one considers the work of Csikszentmihalyi (1990) regarding flow experiences in work and leisure settings.

The measure of creativity or achievement as quantity or quality is an ongoing concern. Studies have indicated that the two are linked; in fact, Simonton (1988) notes that many of the most accomplished have a career pattern of starting early (gaining accolades at a relatively young age), producing much, and sustaining that productivity over a long period of time.

There are exceptions as Abra (1989) details, often in the arts; Gauguin only began painting near his fourth decade. Abra (1989) also raises an interesting point on the definition of creativity. Perhaps it is not so much originality that should describe the creative process as refinement. Here it would seem that the combination of leisure and experience shown in older age could provide a powerful force to creative ventures. It may take years to work the vegetable or flower garden into the desired state. An artistic style for the amateur water colorist may be the result of many years of experimenting with different techniques.

Should we focus during retirement on how much is done or only the degree of originality in finished products? Certainly there must be room for inclusion of creativity in the process of doing. The senior athletes who engage in a new event exemplify this spirit; hopefully our definition of creativity can accommodate the process of doing.

The proposed psycho-biological and motivational factors responsible for peaks in creativity also appear to have implications for the realm of retirement leisure. These factors have been frequently framed in a human development perspective (Abra, 1989).

As categorized by Abra (1989), differences in creativity between younger and middle-aged adults and those beyond middle age might be accounted for by: flexibility of thinking (does originality suffer because older adults are more rigid in thinking—a decrease in fluid intelligence?); persistence (do motivations change throughout the life cycle such that achievement is viewed differently in late life?); mortality (as death becomes more of a reality, how do concepts such as Erickson's (1950) generativity affect creative endeavors?); even gender (do the sexes age differently with men becoming more "feminine" in late life and older women assuming more responsibility; is creativity enhanced for both groups, but in different ways?).

Simonton (1988) even suggests an extrinsic/intrinsic framework that might explain declining achievement over time in the work sphere; as we reach a certain point in salary or awards, do the extrinsic motivations become less important? And if we become more inner-oriented (Neugarten, 1968) or intrinsically motivated as we age, how is creativity affected?

Given the link between intrinsic motivation and leisure (Iso-Ahola, 1980; Neulinger, 1981), we might expect certain forms of creative leisure to be boosted by decreased extrinsic motivation. As the body of literature emerges both from the perspectives of the social-psychology of leisure and the motivational factors underscoring creativity, hopefully theory will be developed to better understand the nature of creativity in later life.

To conclude, let us return to McLeish (1976, pp. 282–284) and some practical suggestions for enhancing the creative spirit. We should, he urges, look at the world in fresh ways, through the eyes of a child. Oh, to gain that spirit of a carefree kid during recess! Surely we could benefit through the absolute devotion to the joy of the leisure moment. Further suggestions include: generating new ideas from familiar situations (could we make daily or weekly occurrences more interesting?), keeping a pad by the bed to write down "semiconscious" ideas, keeping a daily journal and reflecting upon it, and being creative in idle minutes when we have five minutes and we are awaiting someone. It's also a good idea to gain new points of view and observe situations through others' eyes.

CONCLUSION

This chapter has examined the line between activity involvement and Ulyssean living. The availability of unobligated time experienced by many older individuals allows self-direction. The opportunity for choice provided by this time can facilitate a Ulyssean lifestyle, since creative methods of looking at life, unencumbered by external obligations, can be explored. The need to break out of traditional ways of seeing the world and examining new paradigms underlies Ulyssean living. Loss of the work role and seeking the challenges of new roles can help accomplish this.

However, looking at the world in new ways may not be easy. Merely having the time and freedom is not enough. Creativity is also needed. Recreation professionals working with older adults can help in the development of creativity. Creativity groups, based on the activities described in this chapter, may be initiated. These should focus on efforts specifically designed to introduce new ways of thinking and seeing. Reading, personal exploration, and seeing the world through the eyes of others will also assist in this process.

The Ulyssean journey during life implies creativity. With retirement comes discretionary time, and with aging comes experience—two qualities suited to the creative process. By broadening our definition of creativity beyond originality and beyond achievement through quantity, more older adults should be able to adopt the Ulyssean way. Let us encourage this spirit and celebrate the daily process of living.

Chapter 9

◆

Ethnicity and Gender:
Impact on Leisure
for Older Adults

If the Ulyssean journey through older adulthood stands as a central theme of this book and its application to leisure and retirement is a corollary concern, then the effects of ethnicity and gender upon that journey, particularly with regard to activities and their meaning, deserve consideration.

With a broad, sweeping stroke we may describe "typical" retirement, but as will be shown, differences due to one's ethnicity have been reported in the types of leisure pursuits enjoyed and their functions or meanings on a personal level.

Similarly, gender in virtually every investigation completed has been used as an independent variable when activity participation is being analyzed. Hence, the purpose of this chapter is to (a) review current literature in the areas of ethnicity and gender as applied to activities in adulthood (particularly older adulthood), (b) address major theories that have evolved surrounding one's race or ethnic background and how leisure is impacted, i.e., ethnicity, marginality, acculturation, or assimilation, and the more recent differential access model (Taylor, 1992), (c) offer a critique of the strengths and weaknesses of the current research and theory at this point in time, and d) explore leisure through the context of aging, ethnicity, and gender as noted in recent work (Allen & Chin-Sang, 1990; Allison & Geiger, 1993; Boyd & Tedrick, 1994; Brown & Tedrick, 1993; Tedrick & Boyd, 1999).

Strengths/Weaknesses of
Existing Research Knowledge

Discussion of cutting-edge theory related to leisure, aging, ethnicity, and gender is hampered by two major flaws related to samples drawn for research studies: (a) few studies are specifically concerned with older adults and therefore "adult" is often operationally defined as anyone over 18 or 21, and (b) if "older adulthood" is a focus of the study and ethnic background is introduced as a variable, sample sizes typically end up being smaller than desired, even when oversampling of certain ethnic groups occurs.

There are exceptions to the above, yet studies with smaller numbers of minority members such as Brown and Tedrick (1993) are more common. Here a nationwide outdoor recreation survey was used for secondary analysis; while 1,600 older adults (60+) were among those sampled, older blacks totaled only 136. Existing qualitative studies (Allen & Chin-Sang, 1990; Allison & Geiger, 1993; Boyd & Tedrick, 1994) obviously contain small samples while stressing the interpretive paradigm.

The first factor, lumping all adults together or excluding older adults, must be weighed carefully as life-cycle theory and cohort effect are considered. Findings from research exploring activities, meaning, and ethnicity where adults 21 to 70+ are aggregated can provide only hints or speculation when leisure and aging in later life is of concern.

Assimilation or acculturation for a 25-year-old recently immigrated to the United States might be very different from that of a 70-year-old who arrived in this country 50 years ago. In short, we must be very cautious of applying the work on leisure, ethnicity, and gender to older adults when the samples comprising these studies have excluded this subpopulation.

The second issue, small sample sizes of older ethnic groups, frequently compromises generalizability. Floyd (1998) noted small samples in ethnic studies may lead to "false homogeneity" by reducing demographic variability and may eliminate the use of sophisticated multivariate statistical procedures which require large sample sizes. If ethnic groups are further sub-divided (educational level, social class, or gender), cells can become very small. Thus, it must be kept in mind that generalizability in studies involving older adult ethnic groups and their leisure may be less than ideal.

Furthermore, activity lists used in many of the larger-scale outdoor recreation surveys are designed for a younger adult population and are used for purposes of resource management, planning, and visitor use strategies. These lists do not capture the essence of daily (outdoor or otherwise) activity for many older adults, and frequently the lists appear inappropriate for aging or ethnic adults (Taylor, 1992).

For example, one study (Brown & Tedrick, 1993) using a nationwide survey included: horseback riding, outdoor team sports, kayaking, primitive camping, motorized vehicle use off improved roads, ski touring, and snowmobiling as possible activities for senior adults. While these pursuits certainly reflect outdoor management considerations, they are less than desirable in capturing typical retirement interests.

Another failing present in the empirical work on leisure and ethnicity is that conceptual clarity is often lacking when key terms such as: race, ethnicity, or ethnic background are used. Race and ethnicity may be interchanged incorrectly (as variables or in narrative discussion); often a checkmark in the demographic section of a questionnaire serves as the basis for identification (Floyd, 1998; Taylor, 1992).

Kelly and Godbey (1992, pp. 163, 164) note that race differs from ethnicity and includes social identification that cannot be altered; racial identification is permanent. Ethnicity or ethnic background on the other hand is a complex term and includes feelings or perceptions on the part of the subgroup member. The depth of feeling one has regarding ethnicity may vary for each person. Terms such as ethnic identity, acculturation, ethnic consciousness, generational status, structural assimilation, etc. have been used in measuring and discussing the concept of ethnicity (Carr & Williams, 1993; Floyd & Gramann, 1993; Taylor, 1992).

Recent studies involving leisure have carefully looked at individual perceptions of ethnicity (Allison & Geiger, 1993; Carr & Williams, 1993; Floyd & Gramann, 1993; Shaull & Gramann, 1998; Stodolska & Jackson, 1998; Taylor, 1992), yet in many others the above-mentioned confusion or oversimplification can be found.

Other weaknesses within the existing body of knowledge include the use of theoretical models that are simplistic; too often race and class are used when number of activities is the dependent variable and other intervening factors are never considered (Taylor, 1992). Another failing is the monolithic aggregating of all subgroups into one, e.g., the group "Hispanics" is not further divided to include the considerable variation based upon country of origin (Floyd, 1998; Floyd & Gramann, 1993; Taylor, 1992); Taylor (1992) notes that black leisure participation has been perceived as deviant, perhaps stemming from studies of outdoor-wildland participation that have shown "underutilization" by blacks. This ethnocentrism or "norming" of activities based upon a white, middle-class orientation has been mentioned by others (Allison & Geiger, 1993).

Considered together, these weaknesses should not overshadow what has been reported about ethnic variation in leisure pursuits. Specialists in outdoor recreation (Baas, Ewert, & Chavez, 1993; Carr & Williams, 1993; Dwyer & Gobster, 1992; Ewert, Chavez, & Magill, 1993; Floyd, 1998; Floyd & Grammann, 1993; Johnson, Bowker, English, & Worthen, 1998; Stodolska & Jackson, 1998) have contributed much toward an understanding of how ethnicity impacts upon selection, use, and meaning of outdoor-related activities.

The largest gap remaining, from our perspective, is the speculation and hypothesizing that must occur because of the dearth of studies including older adults, their leisure, and ethnic considerations. For example, how did assimilation play out 30 or 40 years ago when ethnic group members of today's elder cohort were making leisure choices in a different period of their lives? How did location, access, and historical time shape their leisure then and perhaps for years to come? Likewise, how were female roles different years ago, and did the feminist movement affect leisure positively for those 60 or 75 today?

An interesting approach to the above question is a recent study by Bialeschki and Walbert (1998) which combines historical and leisure studies perspectives in contrasting the leisure of white female textile workers with that of African American females employed in tobacco factories during the period of 1910 to 1940. Historical factors such as the attitudes of factory owners concerning the provision of company sponsored leisure and the role of the Church and early union efforts give meaning to leisure opportunities and choices for these women in the industrial new South.

There aren't many retrospective studies that can fill in the leisure timeline from early adulthood through the retirement years. We do have studies that report the current status of leisure for ethnic groups and for males and females; we must, however, be cautious in applying findings about leisure and ethnicity to the older adult population when they have been largely excluded from samples.

Theories Explaining Leisure Participation

This section reviews the dominant theories proposed and empirically tested concerning leisure (most often outdoor-related) and subgroup variation. Marginality, ethnicity, assimilation/acculturation, and the differential access model are presented with commentary and synopses of supporting studies. The reader is again cautioned that generalizations to older adult populations involve risk as few studies have sampled aging persons.

Marginality

Marginality theory is closely linked to socioeconomic status and the negative consequences stemming from limited access (Taylor, 1992; Washburne, 1978). Recreation resources available at the local level are likely to vary greatly; poverty and various forms of discrimination brought on by meager financial means have direct impact on the kinds of leisure opportunities available or not present. Styles and meaning of participation are therefore affected. Marginality theory embraces constraints and barriers as powerful shapers of personal leisure. Related to the wildland outdoor experience, it proposes that many urban poor adults grew up with very limited chances to enjoy overnight camping, visit state or regional parks, or learn to appreciate outdoor recreation. Cost, transportation, availability of adult supervision, and nonexisting instructional programs could all have been barriers. In summary fashion, Floyd, Shinew, McGuire, and Noe (1994, p. 156) describe marginality in the following manner, "Stated differently, by occupying a subordinate class position, minorities have had limited access to society's major institutions which negatively affects life-chances and lifestyles, which is reflected in reduced participation in certain forms of leisure."

Washburne (1978) tested the marginality thesis using a California survey of urban residents that oversampled blacks. Without controlling for residence or other socioeconomic factors, blacks were shown to be more involved in team sports and spectator sports, while the participation for whites was significantly higher for wild-land-outdoor recreation, travel outside of their community, camping and day camping, and walking, hiking, and climbing. When residence and socioeconomic status were controlled (matching whites and blacks on these indicators) differences in participation still held for most activities based upon race. Wasburne (1978) concluded that support could not be found for the marginality theory, and the latter analysis appeared to favor differences based upon race.

Two other research thrusts are linked to marginality. Leisure sociologists as early as the 1950s used social class as a predictor variable when comparing lower-, middle-, and upper-class groupings. Among them, Burdge, (1969); Cheek, Field, and Burdge (1976); Clarke (1956); and White (1975); all found differences in participation based on social class.

Gottlieb (1957), as an example, explored the use of taverns by the lower class. Gerontologists concerned with ethnic factors have also contributed to the dialogue on marginality. Rather than comparing ethnic groups while controlling for social class, their approach has more often been to look at constraints and barriers and demography in explaining service underutilization and other quality of life factors.

Double or triple "jeopardy" has been used (Jackson, 1972; Jackson, Kolody, & Wood, 1982) to describe the forces of ageism, racism, and poverty as daily life is considered for many minority aged persons. The notion pertaining to leisure would imply restricted access, limited opportunity, and difficulty in working within existing systems. Yet, as will be shown later in this chapter, older minority adults do develop meaningful leisure patterns and are able to overcome many obstacles.

Brooks-Lambing (1972), who implicitly considered marginality, found differences in the leisure of three groups of retired blacks; those with the fewest economic resources displayed the narrowest range of activities.

Floyd's (1998) recent review of marginality theory as represented by the work of leisure researchers noted the following weaknesses: often the concept has not been clearly defined and it has not been shown how socioeconomic differences (middle- versus lower-class, for example) affect the theory. Further, discrimination has not been analyzed as a factor in most marginality studies, and while participation rates have been used as the dependent variable, rarely have meanings and values been tied explicitly to marginality theory.

ETHNICITY

Ethnicity theory related to leisure patterns attempts to explain differences (between minority groups and the majority population or among varying ethnic subgroups) in participation based upon the values, orientations, norms, and socialization processes inherent within the subcultures being examined (Allison & Geiger, 1993; Floyd et al., 1994; Kelly & Godbey, 1992; Taylor, 1992).

Also referred to as the "subcultural" theory or hypothesis, it is a multi-faceted framework that has frequently been treated in a simplistic fashion without exploring the meaning of what ethnicity means to those participating in the study (Allison, 1988; Allison & Geiger, 1993; Kelly & Godbey, 1992; Taylor, 1992). Attitudes, behaviors, and lifestyles stemming from the cultural origins of subpopulations are of interest, as is the context in which leisure activity occurs. Floyd (1998) also noted that ethnicity is often treated in a static manner and that researchers have not been able to capture the changing, dynamic nature of ethnicity.

Critics have faulted some research for failing to analyze intragroup variation, e.g., results are presented under the label of "Hispanics" or "blacks" when ancestry (Mexican American or Cuban, African American, or Jamaican) may be a crucial concern (Kelly & Godbey, 1992: Taylor, 1992). Taylor (1992, p. 97), for example, reported differences in participation in ethnic festivals between Jamaicans and African Americans. The notion of a black subculture pertaining to leisure has also been challenged (Taylor, 1992) in that variation can be found when the black population is sub-divided.

Many studies have lent general support to the ethnicity theory (a word of caution is introduced again—some studies have not probed ethnicity sufficiently and have failed to uncover the degree of ethnic identification, ancestry, generational status, etc., instead relying only on a "race" designation as part of a questionnaire).

Frequently cited is the Stamps and Stamps' (1985) investigation of 750 urban adults, 2/3 black due to oversampling, which found relatively high correlations in activities for lower-class whites and blacks ($R = .79$) and middle-class blacks and whites ($R = .55$). A higher correlation, however, was found between lower-class and middle-class blacks ($R = .89$)

Blacks ranked socializing/partying, television/radio, sports participation, reading, and listening to music as their top five activities, while whites ranked listening to music, television and radio, outdoor recreation, sports, and sewing/needlework as their favorite activities. Comparison by race and class showed middle-class blacks favoring socialization/partying and resting/relaxation, while middle-class whites ranked outdoor recreation significantly higher. These were the only significant differences out of 22 activities. Lower-class blacks and whites differed in only two areas, whites favoring reading to a greater degree, and blacks ranking resting/relaxation higher.

Washburne (1978), noted earlier, while exploring marginality, found differences between blacks and whites when social class was controlled, which aligned with theory based upon ethnic differences. Other notable investigators include Dwyer and Hutchinson (1990) who used regression analyses for a sample of Chicago residents. Race, gender, and age were included in the regression equations, and while only small amounts of variance were explained by the combination of variables, race was significant in 3/4 of the analyses.

The Pennsylvania Outdoor Recreation Survey (Becker & Yost, 1991) showed participation rates higher for whites in many of the outdoor activities (birdwatching, boating, fishing, golfing, hunting, sightseeing, and swimming), while blacks participated significantly higher in basketball and football. Comparable levels of participation existed for baseball/softball, bicycling, horseback riding, jogging or walking, and picnicking.

Using a stratified, nationwide sample of 1,600, Floyd et al. (1994) explored both race and social class. Class was determined subjectively by study participants. A moderate level of association was found regarding the activities of whites and blacks (R = .53), with blacks ranking social activities and exercise activities higher, and whites favoring outdoor/individual pursuits. Associations between middle- and lower-class blacks (R = .73) and middle- and lower-class whites (R = .86) were higher. Low associations were found for lower-class whites and blacks (R = .42) and black and white females of lower class (R = .23), leading the authors to conclude that ethnicity theory may operate differently at the lower socioeconomic levels, and that gender should be analyzed, particularly when meager economic resources are present.

Recent, late 1990s studies have continued to use ethnicity as a framework in exploring leisure. Stodolski and Jackson (1998) focused on discrimination of ethnic whites (Polish) by using qualitative and quantitative techniques. In contrast to earlier studies, little discrimination was experienced in leisure settings; more often the workplace or governmental bureaucracies were the locations of jokes or references to language difficulties. The concept of "ethnic enclosure," participating in leisure or other social contacts only with those of similar ethnic ties, was discussed as a possible outcome of discrimination.

Marginality and ethnicity were examined in a study focusing on wildland recreation visits in the rural South (Johnson, Bowker, English, & Worthen, 1998). A series of logistic regression models incorporating a variety of sociodemographic variables were used to estimate visitation to outdoor sites. In contrast to the findings of previous research, poorer rather than higher-income African Americans were found to visit wildland sites more often, although, overall, whites visited more frequently. It was suggested that rural urban differences should be accounted for in marginality and ethnicity studies and that the two orientations probably work in combination to explain racial differences.

ACCULTURATION/ASSIMILATION

Closely linked to work on ethnic variation is the acculturation or assimilation perspective, which describes the degree to which ethnic groups "blend" with the dominant or majority population. Labeled the "melting pot" thesis by Allison and Geiger (1993), acculturation has received scrutiny from many different social scientists. Pfister (1993) notes that generational status, education and income, age, years of residence in the adopted country, ethnic density of the neighborhood of residence, occupation, religion and kinship networks may all be crucial factors influencing acculturation. A type of ethnocentrism may also exist on the part of the dominant ethnic group (Allison & Geiger, 1993) in thinking that assimilation is or should be a goal of all ethnic subgroups; some members may embrace the idea, while others will resist attempts except where absolutely necessary. Generational differences may exist, with first and third clinging to the native culture in contrast to second generation children and adults making a conscious effort to adopt the lifestyles, dress, and behaviors of the majority group (Kelly & Godbey, 1992).

Of particular interest here is the role played by recreation and leisure regarding assimilation. Leisure may enhance assimilation, or it may take forms associated with native customs and thus help to perpetuate a strong sense of ethnic identity (festivals, celebrations, dishes, reading material). For a group of elderly Chinese Americans, leisure was found to both support assimilation (reading English and watching popular television shows) and to assist with ties to ethnic culture through activities such as Tai Chi, mahjongg, or reading newspapers printed in Chinese (Allison & Geiger, 1993).

Assimilation and acculturation are complex concepts and may be viewed on a continuum ranging from resistance (retaining the native or "old" ways) to complete acceptance with overt attempts to adopt the diet, language, customs, habits, and religion of the majority. Floyd and Gramann (1993) note that structural assimilation refers to the process of ethnic group members entering into the mainstream through participation in the workforce, education, and civic affairs. This involvement occurs through warm, personal ties with members of the majority group (primary structural assimilation) and through less intensive contacts made in institutional or community settings (secondary structural assimilation) such as attending school functions or non-intensive relationships in the work setting. Recreation, due to its often social forms, obviously offers opportunities for primary and secondary structural assimilation.

Using the above conceptual framework as a base, recent studies (Carr & Williams, 1993; Floyd & Gramann, 1993; Gramann, Floyd, & Saenz, 1993) have probed outdoor utilization and meaning as related to the degree of assimilation present on the part of the various ethnic groups. This research thrust improves upon the earlier noted weakness of many studies that failed to explore ethnicity in any detail. In measuring assimilation for Mexican Americans in the metropolitan Phoenix area, two techniques were used (Floyd & Gramann, 1993; Gramann, Floyd, & Saenz, 1993): the degree to which English was used and understood as the primary language and the degree to which friends of the same or other ethnic groups were selected for recreational visits (primary structural assimilation).

Results suggested the notion that assimilation is a factor that should be considered in analyzing recreation patterns. Mexican Americans who scored highest on the acculturation scale were similar to Anglos in four out of five activity categories, while the least acculturated groups participated significantly less than Anglos in all but one category (Floyd & Gramann, 1993).

When benefits were explored (Gramann, Floyd, & Saenz, 1993), differences were noted between Mexican Americans (divided into three groups based upon acculturation scores: least, intermediate, and highest) and Anglos. Mexican Americans highest in acculturation valued family togetherness significantly more than did Anglos or the other two groups of less-acculturated Mexican Americans. Some benefits were perceived in the same fashion by all groups, but distinctions were evident in most categories based upon acculturation. The authors concluded that selective acculturation may occur where certain views mirror the majority population, yet others remain distinct from the dominant group.

Degree of acculturation was also a part of a three-pronged approach in describing ethnicity (ancestral group membership and generational status were the other elements) in a study of Hispanics of Mexican and Central American origin and Anglos in the national forests in Southern California (Carr & Williams, 1993). Mexican Americans were found to be more acculturated than Central Americans and variations were found both in activity usage and reasons for participation. Visits with extended family described Mexican Americans, while Anglos were more likely to be visiting with friends. Variation within Hispanic groups was a theme both in leisure style and perceived benefits. Meanings and activities (baptisms, for example) linked to religion were found in the forest.

In an attempt to explore the earlier noted weakness of leisure ethnicity research, its lack of focus on values and meanings (Floyd, 1998), Shaull and Gramann (1998) compared Hispanics and whites regarding values placed on family-related leisure experiences and meanings attached to nature-based activities. Assimilation-acculturation was assessed through a self-reporting of English or Spanish use and comprehension. Hispanic participants were divided into three groups ranging from least (Spanish most often used) to most (English used predominantly) acculturated. Hispanics classified as bicultural (between the two extremes) held higher family values regarding leisure than did whites, although the least and most acculturated Hispanics did not differ from whites in this orientation. Also, the least acculturated Hispanic group were most favorable toward nature-related values when compared to whites and more acculturated Hispanics. It was cautioned that a monolithic perspective, viewing any ethnic group in a homogeneous fashion, may fail to capture intragroup differences.

Since the work described above with the exception of the Allison and Geiger study (1993) does not focus on adults of retirement age, interesting considerations emerge when aging is added to the descriptions of acculturation and its relationship to leisure. Length of time in the adopted land and one's age at the period of immigration would be two factors worthy of study.

Perhaps retrospective studies where older adults could describe leisure at different ages would be helpful in clarifying assimilation connected to aging. Immigration at 15, 25, or 40 might be expected to reflect different patterns of leisure and the desire to assimilate. The age at which African Americans, for example, experienced the civil rights movement or overt discrimination in attempting to use recreation resources could be expected to shape attitudes and activities that might well carry on for years. Woodard's (1988) analysis showed factors such as age, discrimination, prejudice, and urban or rural upbringing were responsible in shaping the leisure patterns of black Americans.

Did structural assimilation hold a unique interpretation when separate but equal was the order of the day? These and other questions are ripe for exploration when the effects of aging are added to what has been written about acculturation/assimilation and leisure.

DIFFERENTIAL ACCESS MODEL

Another recent interpretation having a tie to earlier work on ethnicity is Taylor's (1992) differential access model, which sees life's chances being affected by the different or unequal manner in which individuals are or are not able to tap a variety of resources in the community. Taylor (1992) describes these discrepancies as follows:

Unequal life chances arise because of differential access to societal resources. Inequalities emanate from systematic, institutionalized historical and contemporary discriminatory practices based on factors such as racial characteristics, ethnic origins, social class background, and gender. These factors in addition to family and friendship networks, place of residence, life cycle stage, and community ties are important factors in leisure participation (pp. 15–16).

As far as leisure is concerned, the unequal circumstances may affect leisure in five ways: (1) knowledge of and (2) participation in recreation activities, (3) the breadth or repertoire of activities, and (4) the distribution and (5) quality of recreation resources available. Using a sample of 144 residents in New Haven, Connecticut, including two groups of blacks, African Americans and Jamaican Americans, and two groups of whites, Italian Americans and other whites, Taylor (1992) analyzed ethnic leisure participation (hangouts, cooking, media use, and festivals) and local park use according to the variables of race, class, neighborhood and time at the residence, life cycle, marital status, age, gender, family, friends, and most importantly, ethnic identity.

The latter was assessed by ancestry and whether respondents perceived themselves more as members of ethnic groups or as simply more generic "Americans." Ethnic identity accounted for 16% of the significant effects relative to leisure participation. Gender was a successful predictor in the areas of knowledge of ethnic hangouts (males), ability to list hangouts (males), and participation in festivals (females). Race and gender were important when park use was analyzed; twice as many females (43%) as males said they did not use neighborhood parks, and black women (52%) had the highest reported non-use of parks of any group. In terms of age, 46–99-year-olds had the lowest visitation rate of local parks. Both race and self-assessed ethnic identity were noted as important in predicting leisure as measured by ethnic pursuits and park usage.

Using Taylor's differential access model as a theoretical foundation, Juniu (1997) explored the work and leisure lives of 18 adults who had immigrated to the U.S. from South America. Obtaining adequate leisure was a problem for most as work assumed a primary importance in their lives. Access to leisure and types of activities were related to a variety of factors, with social class and the ability to use English being primary discriminators. Middle-class and professional immigrants were much more likely to associate with the mainstream culture in personal and work-related engagements, while working class individuals participated most often with extended family and others of South American descent during free time. Gender, age, and family situation also accounted for differences in leisure. Similar to Taylor (1992), Juniu's analysis supported a framework consisting of many variables to understand the behaviors and meanings attached to leisure for this group of South American immigrants.

GENDER AND LEISURE

Leisure participation as differentiated by gender has been an object of concern for social scientists and recreation planners alike for decades.

Feminist perspectives (Henderson, Bialeschki, Shaw, & Freysinger, 1989, as one example) have created an awareness of the special leisure concerns of women (access, cost, availability based on schedules, crime and attendant fear, lack of opportunities, etc.) and have challenged the status quo. When looking at older women, the effects of cohort—Was working "outside" the family encouraged? How was the feminist movement interpreted personally and at what age?—mixes with gender as changes in such areas as increased athletic opportunities at the interscholastic and intercollegiate levels have been enjoyed by today's younger women but were absent for many females years ago.

Before exploring gender differences connected with leisure, this brief capsule of typical retirement is introduced. Ordinary retirement, as described in two reports by Kelly (Kelly, 1987; Kelly & Westcott, 1991), was characterized by continuity of roles and interests, with a core of activities being enjoyed by both males and females. The samples were primarily whites in blue-collar occupations having lived in the Midwest. Adults were relatively satisfied with retirement living, poor health and disruptive family circumstances (death of a spouse, divorce) having expected negative impacts. Daily patterns had stabilized after a honeymoon period, and family contact was at the center of social involvements.

As for activities, a core of accessible, low-cost pursuits dominated leisure for most (Kelly, 1987; Kelly & Westcott, 1991). Television, contacts with others, informal entertaining, home and yard projects, and selected crafts (primarily women) were the most popular free-time engagements. Fitness or high-exertion activities, such as swimming or hunting, were not favored, and little involvement was seen in formal organizational offerings (senior centers, etc.) or volunteer work.

For this sample of seniors, male-female differences emerged in the following; men were more likely to have a fix-it type project in progress around the house and to drive more often. While family involvements were important, the role played by men differed from that of their spouses. Women occupied the nurturing or organizational roles in dealing with family, and they spent more time in conversations with friends and family. Kelly (1987) notes this role division of men as "providers" and women as "caretakers" being a significant factor over the life cycle in regard to leisure and family interactions.

Finally, high-investment activities requiring special equipment or locales, friends, or high levels of skill for participation provide the "balance" to the "core" of home-based activities that dominate leisure in retirement. Camping, hobby clubs, and sports such as golf require such an investment.

FEMINIST PERSPECTIVES ON LEISURE

A group of authors/researchers has focused recently on the special concerns of women in regard to leisure (Allen & Chin Sang, 1990; Bialeschki & Henderson, 1991; Henderson, 1990a, 1990b, 1992; Henderson & Rannells, 1988; Henderson, Bialeschki, Shaw, & Freysinger, 1989; Horna, 1991; Melamed, 1991; O'Neill, 1991; Teaff, 1991). The major themes have been the inequality of women regarding leisure, a basic difference in the way that men and women conceptualize and experience leisure, and changes both societal and within the delivery systems of leisure that should be made to better meet the circumstances of women.

Females beyond their teen years often face the task of keeping the family operating in addition to holding down a full-time job; the disparity in unobligated time for males and females has been frequently reported (Henderson, 1990a; Hochschild, 1989; Horna, 1991; O'Neill, 1991; Robinson, 1989a, 1989b).

Because of upbringing and the traditional role of nurturer, many women feel they have no right to enjoy leisure; the concerns of others must come first (Henderson, 1991). The very meaning and interpretation of leisure may differ for men and women; Deem (1986) suggested that women emphasize friendship and togetherness, less competition and decreased aggression as compared to men, and enjoyment of the simple experiences during free time.

Leisure constraints or barriers differ by gender, as well; time pressures due to family obligations, personal safety, and health issues are viewed as primary concerns for women (Henderson, 1991). Taken together, these issues, concerns, and female-male differences are significant when leisure participation is examined.

To what extent did the issues raised in this section affect the older women of today, particularly in regard to leisure? Certainly, prescribed roles in the family, rather rigid in years past, influenced leisure greatly for women. The time budget studies have shown a trend over the years of greater male participation, although females do a disproportionate amount of work around the home (Robinson, 1989b).

The notion that "a woman's work is never done" rang true for most of the current group of older women, even to the point of blurring the distinction between work and leisure when free time did exist. Canning, baking, quilting, or crafts with a utilitarian purpose were often done when regular chores were completed. During interviews, many older women have relayed to this writer that husbands were in complete control of finances and were not expected to lift a finger around the house. Shared decision making, whether present or not, would affect leisure as it would other homemaking tasks.

Attitudinal barriers kept many women from pursuing desired interests, particularly in regard to sports or competitive activities. It was simply not expected that a young woman might desire to excel in the competitive arena. Even if attitudes could be overcome, lack of opportunity or poor equipment or coaching faced many women who desired to be athletes. Lack of exposure might then carry over into adulthood.

Did the feminist movement have positive effects for cohorts of now-retired women? Was there liberation that resulted in broader or changed notions of leisure? As with most movements, the degree of influence here most likely varied due to personal and philosophical circumstances, yet the connection to leisure is intriguing and is worthy of exploration, perhaps through retrospective interviews.

Patterns of labor force participation for females 60 and beyond today as contrasted with the current higher percentages of working women with a career orientation is another factor to consider. Staggered working cycles arranged around child rearing or calls to work in wartime are descriptive of some 70- and 80-year-old women. How leisure blended with cyclical working schedules is a topic worthy of speculation.

Finally, race or ethnicity and socioeconomic variables must be factored into consideration of feminist perspectives on leisure. The contrast of working class women, black and white, in the South as explored by Bialeschki and Walbert (1998) is an example of how meanings for church activities or simple monotony-breaking techniques at work, like singing, can differ based upon race. As has been noted previously and will be emphasized in the following section, race, cultural norms, and educational and economic status exert significant influence upon leisure for females and males. Availability of recreation resources, discrimination confronted, and influences of the church differ for selected subgroups of women. Studies such as Taylor's (1992) employing multivariate techniques have been helpful in untangling the web of forces that determine leisure behavior.

THE INTERSECTION OF AGING, ETHNICITY, GENDER, AND LEISURE

One of the earlier studies to focus on the leisure of retired blacks used three categories: professionals, former semiskilled workers, and a group on public assistance

(Brooks-Lambing, 1972); all were living in Florida. Findings revealed strong social class differences, with the former professionals expressing the broadest repertoire (12.8 average activities) with greater involvement in civic and community roles and intellectual activities than the other two groups.

Travel was important to the former professionals (mainly teachers), and they also differed from the others in expressing a greater desire for new activities in retirement. The former semiskilled workers displayed a much narrower range of activities (6.3 average, half of what the professionals noted) consisting primarily of television, radio, reading the Bible, and house projects. They were active in the church but not typically in leadership or organizational roles, and many had ceased participating in activities since retiring.

Those on public assistance had a very narrow range of activities (mean of 4.1) with radio, television, reading, and Bible study being dominant activities. Among the desired new pursuits were learning to sew and improving reading and writing skills. Gender differences were noted; women tended to fish more often, with the authors noting that the social aspects were important as fishing tended to occur in groups.

Women also favored handicrafts such as quilting and sewing, while men typically worked on home-related projects and in the garden. Also of note was the restriction on card playing from a religious perspective. Both education and income were positively correlated with activity participation, yet health status showed no effects.

The 1982–84 Nationwide Recreation Survey was used for secondary analysis comparing older black and white groups on outdoor activities and constraints (Brown & Tedrick, 1993; McGuire, O'Leary, Alexander, & Dottavio, 1987). In terms of leisure constraints, older blacks were significantly more likely than whites to experience the following barriers: money, transportation difficulties, safety concerns, lack of information, and lack of an activity companion. Older blacks, compared to whites, favored picnicking, fishing/crabbing, spectator sports, traveling, volleyball, visiting zoos, jogging, and training animals. Overall, however, it was concluded (McGuire, O'Leary, Alexander, & Dottavio, 1987) that similarities, not differences, characterized the two groups.

Using a composite of number of activities and frequency of participation, Brown and Tedrick (1993) compared older whites and blacks on 22 activities (some from this nationwide survey were probably inappropriate for this population; possible activities included primitive camping and use of off-road vehicles). Comparable to other studies reporting lower levels of outdoor/wildland activity for blacks, this analysis showed significantly greater participation for whites, with fewer than 25% of the older blacks reporting any participation at all.

When income, age, education, and gender groups were compared, racial differences still were found. Older black females had the lowest participation score of any age group analyzed. The authors (Brown & Tedrick, 1993) concluded that the special concerns of older blacks should be considered relative to outdoor leisure planning and participation and that problems exist when pre-established activity lists are used to assess certain subpopulations.

OLDER AFRICAN AMERICAN WOMEN

Leisure in the lives of older African American women has been explored in two recent studies using qualitative techniques (Allen & Chin Sang, 1990; Boyd & Tedrick, 1994). The interrelationship between a lifetime of work and leisure was the foundation for Allen and Chin-Sang (1990) when interviews with 30 older (average age 75) women involved in urban nutrition and activity programs in Florida were analyzed.

Perhaps it was not unexpected that only 13 of the group said they had experienced any leisure prior to retirement and half of those described their leisure connected to work or service. Work had typically started in childhood on farms, and throughout life, farm labor, domestic jobs, and food and health care service were the most common types of employment. When retirement came for these women, leisure was appreciated and perceived as something earned. In late life, leisure was defined by 2/3 of the group as free time or time for personal enjoyment. Other definitions included relaxation or taking it easy, having no work, or time for the church or Bible study.

When looking at descriptions of current activities, leisure overlapped with work activities (things such as house duties and service-oriented pursuits). Favorite leisure engagements (in rank order) were attending a senior center, television, church or prayer meetings, crafts, and exercise. Church was viewed as a context for leisure and service, and in the senior center, work and leisure roles were combined. Many spoke of center activities they enjoyed and important roles such as helping others or doing tasks around the building.

According to Allen and Chin-Sang (1990), these women were survivors, having displayed decades of self-reliance. Leisure, in purpose and in function, was linked to a lifetime of work and represented in later life a continuing way to serve others.

Similar to the above study, Boyd and Tedrick (1994) conducted in-depth interviews with 11 older African American women attending an urban senior center. A life course framework was used to discuss leisure, work, and family histories. In addition, leisure meanings, attitudes, satisfactions, and barriers were discussed.

Life satisfaction was tapped using a formal instrument, the open-ended Life Satisfaction Index B (Neugarten, Havighurst, & Tobin, 1961). The older women (aged 65–94) were predominantly widowed, living on their own with meager financial resources, and had contact with children and grandchildren. With one notable exception, the women rated high in life satisfaction. Statements such as, "I feel fortunate to have lived this long" captured the essence of aging at this point in their lives. Friends, family, grandparenthood (or great-grandparenthood), and God or the church were themes interwoven with questions about life satisfaction.

Using Kelly's (1987) conceptualization, 7 of the 11 represented a straight-arrow life course (life events occurring at about the same time as others of their age); the other four had experienced a major life trauma such as a personal injury or family problem that had forced them to make a major readjustment. As with many of their birth cohorts living in the North, eight had moved from the South prior to their '20s. Descriptions of life growing up centered around school, the family, church, and a rural or farm lifestyle.

Childhood activities were noted as playing ball, short trips to a park or zoo, church-related social and religious gatherings, and games, both indoor and outside. The decade of their '20s was marked by marriage and childbearing; few mentioned paid employment. The late teens and early '20s were the most active leisure period with social (friends and courting) activities; parties, gatherings, picnics, movies, dancing, and church functions were mentioned.

Middle life, as described by the older women, tended to blend as did re-membered leisure pursuits. Descriptions of children growing, housework, and paid employment were given, and activities with their children mirrored their own early years going to parks, zoos, picnics, outside activities, and church events.

The fifth or sixth decade brought change such as health problems (cancer) personally or for a spouse, stoppage of work for the husband, and leisure, as de-scribed, was not much different from earlier periods.

Widowhood intruded in the '60s and '70s, which forced new social pat-terns—the senior center became a focus of interaction for most and continuing involvement in the church or Bible study, although actual church attendance began to drop and previous roles (singing) were given up, most often because of health issues.

Beyond church or center involvement, leisure in later life centered around a "core" (Kelly, 1987) of home-based, somewhat passive activities headed by televi-sion and radio (often religious-oriented programming), praying, and less frequently, visiting others and sewing. One older female carried on a type of street corner ministry, attempting to reach teens. The youngest of the group was decidedly more active with a much broader repertoire including travel, cooking, and riding a bike. Regular exercise as an activity was rarely mentioned.

Major themes or findings from the interviews included the following (Boyd & Tedrick, 1994). (1) Family and religion had served and continued to serve as major focal points throughout their lives; both were directly linked to leisure, and this was in agreement with other researchers (Allen & Chin-Sang, 1990; Taylor & Chatters, 1986). (2) A core of leisure activities existed that centered on home-based experiences as well as the center and church. (3) Leisure, as a concept, was not easily described (free time or time without obligation was the primary notion), yet it was seen as enjoyable, important, and connected with relaxation; leisure appeared to permeate or intermingle with other aspects of daily life. (4) Few desired to attempt or pursue new activities, and barriers were noted as health problems, lack of money, and neighborhood crime. (5) One older African American woman stood in marked contrast to the others; her life satisfaction was extremely low because she had been separated from family early in life, was unable to access appropriate services as an adult, and was not accepted at the center. The value of qualitative methods was emphasized as her descriptions of life provided much meaning relative to leisure in a way that would have been much different had quantitative methods been employed.

OLDER AFRICAN AMERICAN MEN

As a follow-up to the previously cited study on females, older African American men were interviewed to explore their leisure and how it might differ from women (Tedrick & Boyd, 1999). An urban senior center was again selected as the site and 15 men comprised the sample. Beyond male-female comparisons, the study focused on current and past time use patterns, leisure activities, and meanings. Preliminary findings resulted in the identification of three themes. The first of these was labeled "opportunity" and described differences in life circumstances which had made it easier or harder for the males to access leisure at different times throughout their lives. As an example, migration to the North resulted in different leisure patterns/opportunities during the life course. Those who had grown up in the South often described life on the farm and having little free time. Dropping out of school to work was common. Those who had moved North at a younger age typically remained in school longer, which meant opportunities in school sports. Military experience was common in the latter group, which meant exposure to travel which carried on to a degree during post-military adulthood. While having an effect on the breadth of leisure opportunity, those who grew up on the farm spoke positively of this life which was linked to a certain type of leisure style. Family and church were important and served as a focal point for leisure time. There was no indication that leisure opportunities were missed because of life on the farm.

A second theme revolved around the connection of active church involvement and what Kelly (1972) termed "relational" leisure. Men who were active in volunteer roles or assisting at their churches mentioned the notion of being with or helping others—the relational motive. "If you just go to the service and then leave, you're not contributing." For many there had been a high level of involvement in organized religion throughout their lives, and even as health declined or the aging process made it more difficult to attend services, the desire to help in any way remained strong. As told by one older male, "The Lord has been good to me and my family and I said if I were able to retire and lie long, I'm going to put something back into the system. People are my life." By comparison, while many African American women in later life were also active in supporting roles in their churches, they spoke more frequently of the personal impact of church/religion through worship at services, prayer, Bible reading, etc. Men most often recounted an active role or visiting someone when the topic of religion arose.

A third theme derived from the interviews was the role of the senior center in their lives and how participation was influenced by health status and the presence of physical ailments. Center attendance provided a structure to daily time use; most came four or five days a week, and the routine of getting up, awaiting transportation, eating a meal at the center, and returning in mid or later afternoon was a pattern they described frequently. Daily time use was centered around this important activity. Participation style at the center was greatly affected by health status. "When it comes to activities, I can't do so much because of my heart." The relational motive (Kelly, 1972) was again present in connection with the senior center, "I come here to help those who can't help themselves."

Further analysis will focus on male-female differences, but it was clear that connections exist between religion/church and leisure for both older African American men and women, although purposes or reasons for involvement may differ slightly. Males also spoke of the social club, a topic less frequently voiced by women. As expected, certain personal factors—health status as a prime example—shape leisure participation and meaning. The social or relational aspects of senior centers, religious organizations, and other forms of leisure are valued by both African American men and women in retirement.

CHINESE AMERICAN ELDERLY

Allison and Geiger's (1993) examination of elderly Chinese Americans is noteworthy for two reasons: the lack of empirical work with this population regarding free time pursuits and the analysis of leisure as a means to maintain cultural identity and a way to seek assimilation through sharing the popular activities of the majority population.

The authors cite a previous study by Cheng (1978) showing gardening, relaxing at home, reading, television, and crafts to occupy the bulk of leisure time activities for older Chinese Americans.

The pattern uncovered by Allison and Geiger (1993) was similar, yet broader. As a group (10 males, 15 females ranging in age from 64–85 at a senior center) television, walking, reading, and exercise were top rated. Men were more likely to read, walk, and watch television, and women were a bit broader in their free time, including interests such as sewing, helping others, Tai Chi, mahjongg, and church activities. Reading materials were used to maintain ties to China (71% read Chinese papers, etc.) and to "learn the American way" (40% read items printed in English). Television was also used to become a part of the mainstream culture. It was noted that further studies examining assimilation should explore the ways in which leisure is used as a link to the old and the new.

The Ulyssean Journey for Older Ethnic Adults: Concluding Thoughts

For many older minority adults, daily life exemplifies the Ulyssean journey: indeed, "triple jeopardy," being exposed to the negative influences (constraints including access to serves) due to age, ethnicity, or gender, may be a challenge faced by many of this group.

In the context of McLeish's (1976) notion of life defined by adventure and creativity, leisure offers the opportunity for self-actualization. That is not to say that the bulk of the leisure repertoire of older minority adults is filled with jaunts across the globe, rock-climbing expeditions, and creating various artworks in the garage studio. The core of daily leisure is a more mundane, home-based series of activities emphasizing accessible media, tasks (many blending work and leisure motives or functions) that are generally enjoyed and done without pressure, and maintaining social contacts through family and friends. The more adventurous or challenging engagements, taking on a new hobby or an extended trip, punctuate the pattern of daily life, providing balance (Kelly, 1987).

The finding by Allison and Geiger (1993) that older Chinese Americans use leisure to maintain Chinese identity (reading material about China and printed in Chinese, mahjongg, Tai Chi) and to learn about America (television, local newspapers printed in English) deserves further consideration and exploration. Investigators should undertake similar interviews using a life course perspective with other ethnic group members of older age. Many intriguing questions arise: How does age impact upon the desire to assimilate (or not), and what forms of leisure are used at different ages to maintain ethnic ties or to embrace the culture of the majority population? Do answers to the above questions differ when various ethnic groups are compared? How do minority adults who have immigrated to America use leisure as a link to the past and as a bridge to the new culture if assimilation is desired? Hopefully, further investigation will determine if what is generally accepted about ethnicity and leisure holds true for aging persons.

Taken as a group, the theoretical perspectives of marginality, ethnicity, acculturation/assimilation, and the differential access model all offer speculation into late life leisure for ethnic subgroups, although few studies have sampled the elderly specifically. Viewed together, rather than singularly or as competing explanations, they offer much insight. Marginality, focusing upon constraints, barriers, and limited opportunities, is particularly relevant when low socioeconomic status is present.

As examples, older blacks on public assistance (Brooks-Lambing, 1972) spent most of their free time on radio, television, reading, and the Bible; for urban, older, African American women (Boyd & Tedrick, 1993), activities beyond the home, church, and senior center were not frequently mentioned.

Ethnicity theory is particularly helpful in noting intergroup differences; Stamps and Stamps (1985) reported higher correlations in activities for lower- and middle-class blacks than for whites and blacks of the same social class. Intragroup differences have been explained by the level of acculturation or assimilation on the part of ethnic subgroups. The ways in which Hispanics of differing ancestries use the outdoors has been a theme (Floyd & Gramann, 1993; Gramann, Floyd, & Saenz, 1993).

Taylor's (1992) recent analysis leading to the differential access model was significant in a number of ways. Ethnic leisure was a focus (festivals, reading matter, cooking, etc.), and care was taken in assessing ethnicity from the perspective of the respondent.

A future goal tied to both research and policy formulation is to better understand leisure throughout later life as related to gender and ethnicity. Ulyssean leisure implies a journey interpreted most appropriately in individual terms. Thus, consideration must be given to qualitative methods emphasizing symbolic interactions (Samdahl, 1987) and the subjective. Measuring the Ulyssean journey through life stories blending age, ethnicity, and gender is a task worthy of our attention.

Chapter 10

◆

Living Environments

Providers of services to the elderly operate in a variety of settings, and the structure of the environments in which an individual functions is becoming an increasing concern to gerontologists. Rather than viewing the environment as a static setting into which people come to perform activities, it is being seen as a dynamic milieu that can be either penalizing or prosthetic. Therefore, it is important that people working in the environments of the elderly understand its impact and learn how to use it in such a way that it will be a positive factor in Ulyssean living.

This chapter will provide an introduction to the role of the environment in general as well as its specific role with older individuals. This chapter will be followed by two brief chapters focusing on three environments, the age-integrated community, the age-segregated environment, and the long-term care facility.

Before examining the role of the environment in the lives of older individuals, it is necessary to determine the link between leisure and the environment. In many cases, the environment as it relates to leisure is often limited to the outdoor environment. However, that perspective does not provide the level of understanding we seek.

According to Wall (1989), "a full understanding of recreation is unlikely to be achieved in the absence of an appreciation of the attributes of the places in which people recreate, and of the ways in which environmental factors contribute to and detract from the qualities of recreational experiences" (p. 451). He identifies three components of the recreation experience: the individual and his/her attributes; other people; the environment where the activity occurs. Although all three elements are interconnected, the focus in this chapter is on the third element.

In its most elemental form, the environment encompasses the settings where activities occur. Water is needed for swimming, outdoor areas for hiking, a lighted area for reading, and a field for baseball. However, environment is more than that. It includes "all aspects of the world around us" (Wall, 1989, p. 454). Unfortunately, the examination of environment and leisure has not developed beyond an understanding of the natural environment.

Environmental Concerns

Human behavior is a complex phenomenon influenced by a variety of factors. This complexity contributes to the difficulty in studying behavior. However, there are approaches to interpreting behavior that are helpful. The field of environmental psychology provides an established approach. According to McAndrew (1993), environmental psychology "is the discipline that is concerned with the interactions and relationships between people and their environments" (p. 2). The focus is on the content of the environment as well as the reactions of the individual. For example, we will examine how the built environment of a long-term care facility shapes the behavior of individuals in that environment. However, we will also examine how the individual influences the environment.

McAndrew identifies several types of environments. Each can influence behavior and should be considered when examining the experiences of older individuals. The ambient environment includes factors such as sound, temperature, illumination, and odor, which provide a constant sensory input that influences affect and physical well-being. Think of the conditions you experience every day: the temperature of your dorm room, the smell in the cafeteria, the color of the walls in your classrooms, or the lighting in the library. You may not be aware of these things until there is a problem. At that point, you may feel uncomfortable, unable to reach your goals, or may actually get sick. These factors may affect older individuals in the same way. Color is an excellent example of how the ambient environment can influence individuals. McAndrew's review of the literature on color reveals several interesting findings (pp. 65–66):

1. Colors are associated with moods in the following ways:
   blue—secure, comfort, serene, calm
   red—defiant, exciting, protective
   orange—upset, distressed
   purple—dignified
   yellow—cheerful
   black—despondent, powerful
2. Lighter-colored rooms are perceived as more spacious and bigger than dark-colored rooms.
3. Colors differ in their ability to arouse. Red is a highly arousing color. For example, research has found people walk faster in hallways of warm color (red or orange) than in cool-colored hallways, and pink rooms reduce anxiety more than red rooms.

Factors such as noise and crowding can have equally significant impacts on behavior. Excessive levels of either can result in psychological and possibly physical distress. Individuals working with older people need to be aware of the environment and its effect on behavior.

Parmelee and Lawton (1990) indicate that little empirical work has been done in the area of environments and aging in the past decade. Much of what we know developed in the 1960s and 1970s. However, the older work has contemporary value and provides an exciting overview of this field.

According to Parmelee and Lawton, the primary dialectic in the field is between autonomy and security. Autonomy is defined as "the state in which the person is, or feels, capable of pursuing life goals by the use of his or her own resources; there is thus minimal need to call upon other people's resources" (p. 465).

The heart of autonomy is perceived freedom and independent action. However, the counterbalance to autonomy is security. This is defined as "a state in which pursuit of life goals is linked to, and aided by dependable physical, social, and interpersonal resources. The term thus emphasizes not only physical safety or psychological peace of mind but also the communality rather than the separateness of the person" (p. 465). The authors view the autonomy-security dichotomy as being at the heart of person-environment relations since the independence and freedom of early and middle life should continue into later life. We all need to exercise choice and control over daily activities. Autonomy is crucial to happiness in the later years.

Parmelee and Lawton indicate that personal safety and security are major concerns among the elderly. In fact, fear of crime is a major factor in limiting involvement by older individuals. The earlier chapter on physical aspects of aging in this book indicated that factors such as poor vision, balance problems, hearing difficulties, and slower reaction time may put older individuals at greater risk of accidents than their younger counterparts.

Clearly, a balance between autonomy and security is needed. Steinfeld and Shea (undated) stated, "An environment that provides a high level of safety and security is likely to have a lower level of privacy, independence and choice" (p. 1). Absolute security might be guaranteed by a closed environment with a great deal of control by facility managers, but this would minimize autonomy. Contrarily, completely independent living in an age-integrated community may assure autonomy but ignore security needs.

The approach to balancing these two needs is often presented within a person-environment fit model, which seeks the point at which the demands and characteristics of the environment are congruent with the needs, preferences, and ability of the individual. The ultimate goal related to the environment is to achieve congruence between the demands of the environment and the abilities of older individuals (Lawton, 1989).

The environmental press model (see Figure 10.1) depicts this ideal situation. The "zone of maximum comfort" is the condition where the environmental demands are lower than the competence of the individual. Lawton describes this as the zone "characterized by the maintenance of appropriate behavior, together with a favorable level of psychological well being consisting of restfulness, relaxation, or pleasant lassitude" (p. 139). The area where the demands of the environment are

FIGURE 10.1

ECOLOGICAL MODEL OF ADAPTION AND AGING

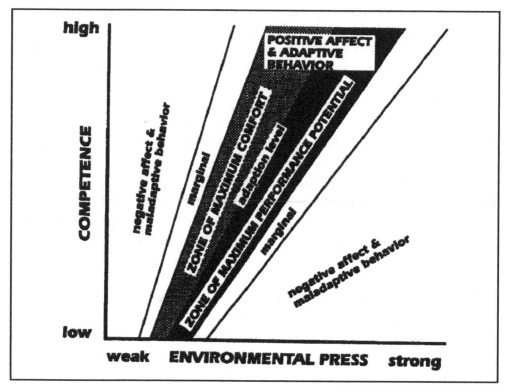

(LAWTON, 1989)

greater than the individual's competence is labeled the "zone of maximum performance potential." Lawton indicates: "Provided the mismatch between demand and competence is relatively small, this situation is one where new learning and novel experience occurs" (p. 139). Either of these zones will be desirable based on the needs of individuals.

When the congruence between the demands of the environment and the competence of the individual is out of balance, individuals enter a state of stress (beyond the zone of maximum performance) or boredom and atrophy of skills (beyond the zone of maximum comfort). Seeking renewed congruence is necessary. The following part of this chapter will discuss how this might be achieved.

FACTORS INFLUENCING THE ENVIRONMENT

An understanding of behavior relies on an examination of the forces that operate in the environment. Crandall (1980) differentiates between the "people effect" and the "thing effect" in the environment. The people effect includes five components:

1. The type of people in the environment: Are they alert or feeble? Are they old or young? Are they open- or closed-minded?
2. The number of people in the environment: Are there enough to interact with? Are there so many it is stressful?
3. The type of interaction that occurs: verbal or nonverbal, equal or one-sided, personal or impersonal?
4. The amount of interaction: too much or too little, constant or sporadic?
5. What are the norms of behavior in the environment?

According to Crandall, the "thing" effect of the environment consists of two parts: the physical aspects of the environment, such as the arrangement of furniture, temperature, and wall color (these are similar to aspect of the ambient environment discussed above) and the non-physical aspects of the environment, such as privacy and territoriality. All these aspects of the environment influence the behavior and well-being of the individual. Crandall cites research indicating the environment plays a role in an individual's physical and mental health.

Territoriality is a crucial aspect of privacy and safety. There is a need to have space we can identify as our own. As you will see in the chapter on long-term care environments, this need is often met by allowing individuals to retain some of their furniture and use it in their rooms.

Environments can also be differentiated as either "micro" or "macro" environments. The micro environment can be viewed as the identifiable places in which a person lives or interacts with others. Examples include an individual's house, a multi-purpose center, or a long-term care facility. The macro environment encompasses a broader living milieu such as the neighborhood, community, or city (Schwartz, 1975). Examination of the environment at both these levels is necessary to an understanding of behavior.

An increasing number of older people are "aging in place." In fact, approximately 70% of older Americans spend the rest of their lives in the place they celebrated their 65th birthday (Barbara Krueger & Associates, 1996). Successful aging in place requires environments that are safe, accessible, usable, predictable, and accommodating. Pynoos and Golant (1996) identified four strategies useful in helping people age in place: increased financial assistance, more helpful household arrangements, home modification, and responsive home and community services. Household arrangements will be discussed in Chapter 12. The sections of this chapter that follow focus on modifications of the micro and macro environments.

THE MICRO ENVIRONMENT

Several authors (Charness & Bosman, 1998; Ebersole & Hess, 1991) expounded on the value of environmental modification as a pragmatic intervention strategy. It

is clear that purposive intervention into the microenvironment can play a significant role in the development of Ulyssean lifestyles.

Understanding the role of living places in individuals' lives is also important in understanding the role of the environment in later years. According to Cox
(1993), the elderly are more restricted to their home environment than any group
other than small children and individuals in institutions, and as a result, the "house,
neighborhood, and community environment, is, therefore, more crucial to older
persons than it is to other age groups" (p. 214).

The place where older individuals live provides opportunity for mastery,
competence, interaction, privacy, and stimulation. Clearly the living environment
is more than a static setting providing an envelope for living. It is a dynamic creation that is a factor in the quality of life experienced by individuals. Therefore, it is
important to understand how the environment can be improved. Although much
of the work in this area has specifically applied to the living environment, it is likely
many of the suggested manipulations can apply in other environments.

Schwartz (1975) provided very specific interventions useful in using environments to improve the quality of life. Although offered several years ago, his
suggestions are still appropriate today. According to Schwartz such interventions
are important in development of positive self-regard. He wrote:

> The essential concept in the design of micro-environments for the aged
> must be aimed not only at ameliorating stress, minimizing the effects
> of losses, and compensating for deficits, but must do so in ways which
> enhance the individual's effectiveness, support their competence, and
> thus maintain self-esteem (p. 289).

According to Schwartz, three dimensions are relevant when considering
environmental intervention: environmental cues, environmental stimulation, and
environmental support. Environmental cues are necessary:

1. to identify spaces and distinguish personal or private spaces from public and
   shared spaces;
2. assist people in finding the way to individual areas;
3. anticipate unforeseen hazards such as stairwells, changes in slope, and slippery spaces;
4. locate needed persons;
5. locate service areas, utilities, and materials and supplies.

Suggested techniques to provide necessary cues include:

1. signs with recognizable symbols, easily read from walking or wheelchair eye
   level;
2. reinforcing signs at frequent intervals when crossing large spaces;

3. use of brightly colored doors and symbols to identify entry ways, utility areas, service areas, etc.;
4. use of lighting to enhance quiet areas;
5. use of textures to identify hazard areas;
6. auditory cues such as chimes to signal events such as meals, activity time, and other events;
7. automatic devices, such as sliding doors and elevators, as needed;
8. large print newsletters, calendars;
9. other program cues.

A second area of concern is environmental stimulation. According to Schwartz, it is important to:

1. promote the use of all the senses;
2. enhance new learning behavior;
3. introduce variety into the environment;
4. challenge individuals through activities;
5. provide success experiences;
6. maximize associative inputs.

Environmental stimulation can be increased by:

1. use of bright colors;
2. use of contrasting colors;
3. introduction of changeable materials such as plants and art work into the environment;
4. enhancement of bare walls through paintings, murals, wall hangings, and the like;
5. use of multimedia programs for entertainment, discussion, and information;
6. use of materials such as oversized books to compensate for sensory losses;
7. initiation of formal sensory stimulation programs;
8. introduction of exciting foods, beverages, and spices into meals;
9. introduction of pets for stroking, observing, and loving;
10. opportunity for intergenerational contact.

The final area of concern is environmental support. Such supports are necessary to assist individuals in establishing control and competence in their environment. It can be built into the environment through techniques such as:

1. providing programs that allow real choices and control;
2. individualizing programs, activities, and leadership approaches;
3. providing prosthetic devices to compensate for losses;
4. "non-infantizing" of individuals;

5. providing opportunities for self-management even if some risk is involved;
6. designing furniture to be assistive rather than penalizing, including seats with arms or lift devices;
7. using oversized knobs and handles on doors and windows;
8. using in-house phone system to reach staff and activity areas;
9. personalizing living and activity spaces;
10. meeting personal preferences in eating, activities, seating, etc.;
11. providing access to reading lights that are low glare, magnifying glasses, earphones for radio and television;
12) providing personal I.D. for staff and others with whom the elderly will have contact.

The above listings are not comprehensive. Rather, they should be viewed as illustrative. Any intervention that will assist individuals in the mastery of their environment is legitimate.

Weiner, Brok, and Snadowsky (1987) and Ebersole and Hess (1998) echoed Schwartz's earlier concern about providing prosthetic environments to older individuals. However, Weiner et al. recommended an approach focused on more general features of helpful environments. These included:

1. prostheses for life-maintenance activities focusing on safety concerns such as non-slip floor;
2. prostheses for perceptual behavior emphasizing use of visual stimulation in the environment;
3. prostheses such as color-coded doors and hallways to aid in cognitive behavior;
4. prostheses to aid in self-maintenance skills in areas such as cooking and toileting;
5. prostheses to enhance morale;
6. prostheses to aid in retaining a sense of time (clocks and calendars), sense of self (mirrors and retention of personal objects), and autonomy (space for privacy);
7. prostheses to encourage social interaction with staff and others, including the engineering of space.

The gradual decline of the senses, discussed in Chapter 3, requires a higher threshold of sensory input be provided for stimulation. Sounds, sights, smells, and tactile sensations may need to be heightened. Older individuals may experience sensory deprivation in a dull, monotonous, nonstimulating environment. This can result in impaired thought processes, childish emotional responses, and organic deterioration. As a result, there is a need to create stimulating environments.

The living environment must be designed to incorporate sensory stimulation through the use of lighting, shapes, changeable materials, lively conversations, and any other techniques needed to activate the senses.

Facilities may need to be designed to compensate for limited mobility of the resident. The use of one level in facilities, if at all possible, is recommended. If that is not possible, an elevator may be needed for residents to use programs and facilities on the second floor. Thresholds into rooms should be eliminated to facilitate movement by wheelchairs. Good lighting in corridors and over any existing steps are important in reducing accidental falls. Handrails in traveled areas and in bathtubs are useful prosthetic devices. Slippery surfaces and loose rugs should be avoided. Logic should prevail in the design of facilities, and any potential hazard or barrier should be eliminated. In addition, it is important to include individuals with mobility impairments in planning and designing facilities.

All individuals need privacy. Crandall (1980) suggests two ways of providing privacy: physical barriers and the establishment of social rules. Setting areas apart through walls and dividers would be examples of physical barriers. Rules identifying areas as quiet areas or certain times as quiet times are examples of the use of rules.

The final area discussed by Crandall is comfort. The individual needs to feel at ease and comfortable in the environment. Aspects such as safety, temperature, and color are all aspects of the environment that contribute to its comfort.

Concern with environmental intervention has become evident even in the popular culture. It is no longer the domain of gerontologists and architects. Dychtwald and Flower's best selling book (1989) included a chapter entitled "Redesigning America," detailing environmental modifications that help make life more livable. Their suggestions are extensive and too numerous to identify here. However, a partial listing will help establish their focus:

1. covering floors with carpeting or textured surfaces to reduce glare;
2. automobile dashboards with fewer reflective surfaces;
3. steering wheels with controls for lights, heating, etc. in the center;
4. elimination of high-glare fluorescent lights;
5. talking appliances, providing orally what currently is only available visually;
6. custom-programmed television and radio to compensate for hearing difficulties;
7. specially designed kitchen utensils;
8. non-skid surfaces in bathtubs and kitchens;
9. bathtubs made of resilient materials providing safety and comfort while keeping water hot;
10. street lights that change more slowly, giving pedestrians ample time to cross;
11. verbal command systems in the house and the automobile.

Charness and Bosman (1990) identify the credo for design of environments: "Know the user." Earlier chapters of this book detail changes experienced by individuals as they age. Physical, social, cognitive, and affective factors should be considered when examining environments. Charness and Bosman provide extensive resources for environmental modification, and although space does not permit complete reporting of their information, several of their suggestions are particularly useful and will be detailed here. Their guidelines for the visual environment include (p. 452):

1. avoid sudden and large shifts in illumination;
2. control glare by shielding light fixtures and using non-reflective materials on walls, ceilings, and floors; place furniture away from sources of glare; use overhangs on windows; do not locate windows at locations where falls are more likely to occur;
3. difficult color discriminations should be avoided including discriminations in the blue-green range and colors of the same hue;
4. the size of visual objects should be enlarged; use increased contrasts to identify hazards.

A series of modification in the auditory environment are also listed:

1. background noises such as air conditioning and piped-in music should be controlled;
2. high-frequency sounds (defined as above 4,000 Hz) should be avoided;
3. the volume of important sounds should be increased;
4. visual cues should be used in addition to auditory cues.

A group of housing researchers, planners, and designers met in 1990 to address the issue of environments that would adapt to the changing needs of individuals as the age. Among the suggestions generated at the conference were 12 principles helpful in designing for older users. These included:

1. privacy;
2. social interaction;
3. choice, control, and autonomy;
4. orientation and wayfinding;
5. safety and security;
6. accessibility;
7. stimulation and challenge;
8. familiarity;
9. aesthetics;
10. personalization;

11. adaptability;
12. sensory aspects.

These design principles can be incorporate into activity areas, day care programs and recreation facilities as well as living areas.

While the goal of providing a non-penalizing environment is an important one, it is just as important not to do too much. If all risk and challenge are removed from an environment, individuals will not be challenged. The result of such an environment will be boredom and stagnation.

Baltes, Wahl, and Reichart (1991) recommend applying the principle of "just manageable difficulty" when deciding how much help and compensation is needed. This principle suggests that the demands placed on older individuals be "just manageable" by them and that their success be determined by the ability to effectively negotiate the environment at that level. Demanding too much or expecting too little are both contrary to this approach.

According to Schwartz (1975), "Any environment which tends to infantize the older person will subvert his sense of self worth and self-esteem, and will ultimately defeat many of the positive effects which can be envisioned for an environmental design program for older people" (p. 291). The goal in environmental design is to provide a setting that allows an individual to be as independent as possible while also meeting needs for safety and security.

THE MACRO ENVIRONMENT

Ebersole and Hess (1998) include an extensive discussion of the role of the environment, specifically as it relates to safety and security. They divide space into personal and life space and suggest that the needs of each are different.

Personal space is viewed as the individualized component of multiple life spaces and is more private than the largely public life space. Much of the discussion above focused on personal space. However, it is also important to focus on the larger milieu.

Ebersole and Hess identified two crucial life space concerns that are particularly germane to Ulyssean living: transportation and fear of crime.

Transportation is a crucial concern when working with older individuals. Many older people may be deprived of transportation, a "critical link in the ability of the elderly to remain independent and functional" (p. 426). Lack of a car, failure of public transportation to meet needs, poor driving skills, and economic constraints may result in limits in mobility. It is noteworthy that Ebersole and Hess view transportation for pleasure and recreation as a crucial need that often goes unmet. Some suggested solutions to transportation problems include:

1. use of volunteer drivers;

2. reduced or subsidized fares on public transportation;
3. transit systems designed for older users and including appropriate routes and schedules;
4. charter bus trips;
5. sponsorship of safe driving programs.

Programs that fail to take transportation needs into account will exclude many participants. Planners need to always keep this crucial service in the forefront when planning programs.

A second crucial life space issue is crime. Many older individuals identify this as a major concern, greater than safety and health concerns. This fear can deprive an older person of opportunities for Ulyssean living and therefore should be addressed by service providers. Crime prevention programs may be excellent additions to the list of recreation opportunities available to older individuals. In addition, care should be taken in scheduling activities since evening programs may be problematic for many.

The life space concept is related to Regnier's (1975) concept of critical distance. Although the work he cited was done over 20 years ago, it does point toward a focus we should retain. Critical distance is the distance individuals are willing to travel for a service. For example, some services are viewed as "core" and the desire is to have these within walking distance. A bus stop, grocery store, drug/variety store, bank, post office, and church are included in this core. If transportation is not available, the core can be expanded to include hospital, senior center, park, library, dry cleaners, and luncheonette/snack bar. Other services and facilities, including movie theater and bar, may be located farther than walking distance and still be viewed as accessible.

The distance at which services and facilities become inaccessible will of course vary as a result of factors such as health and fitness of the individual identifying the critical distance, topography, and weather. What is important is that service providers be aware of the impact of the location of things in the macro environment and plan accordingly.

Weiner, Brok, and Snadowsky (1987) introduced the concept of "radius of activities" to address issues similar to those identified within the critical distances framework. Understanding an individual's spatial world allows service providers to identify ways to expand that world since environments may restrict the sphere in which people operate.

Weiner et al. suggest discussing the radius of activity with individuals in hopes of identifying restricting factors and broadening involvement. They recommend focusing on the variety of locations where activities occur and identifying the potential barriers to behavior within each. These locales include:

1. Home
2. On my block

3. Within a five-block area of home
4. Neighborhood
5. Other neighborhood in town or city
6. State
7. Outside state
8. Outside the United States

Reviewing the activities and barriers within each locale will provide an effective tool for expanding the possibilities for Ulyssean living. For example, one of the authors of this book recalls working with a senior center which was moved from the activity room in a high-rise apartment for older residents to a nearby building that had been converted from a school to a multipurpose center. The new location was a much better facility than the earlier one. It had more space, more services, and more activities. However, many people who had attended the programs at the original site did not come to the new location. After much speculation about why this had occurred, it was decided to question those who had stopped attending. It was found that a traffic light on a street that had to be crossed by many individuals who wanted to walk to the center did not stay green long enough for them to safely cross. Changing the timing on the light had a dramatic effect on participation.

Identification of locales may point toward self-imposed limits on movement that may restrict Ulyssean living and should be removed. Weiner et al. (1987) concluded: "Anyone who works with an older population must pay particular attention to the influence of environmental factors on observed behavior. *This is especially true if the aim is to help motivate an exploratory attitude*" (p. 25—emphasis added). It is this exploratory attitude that facilitates the Ulyssean lifestyle.

Howe (1992) discusses the need for "linkages" in the macro environment. If any part of the environment is inaccessible or penalizing, the entire environment is suspect. As Howe indicated, a state-of-the-art bathroom in a senior center that has a gravel-topped parking lot is of no use to an individual in a wheelchair. Similarly, an excellent program at a facility that does not provide transportation will not be successful. Involving older individuals in the planning and design process is one way to ensure all elements in a facility are linked and usable.

Cox (1993) identified several techniques for deciding what environmental modifications are desirable. The extent to which older individuals are involved in the process varies. These approaches can be revised into the following three perspectives.

1. The older individual plans and initiates changes in the environment. This self-directed approach is desirable for Ulyssean living. If older individuals are made aware of the role of the environment in their lives and educated in ways of manipulating the environment, the likelihood of this approach occurring will be increased.

2. The older individual can work collaboratively with other individuals in redesigning the environment to achieve a desired goal. Architects, planners, recreators, social workers and counselors could play a role in the design process.

3. Experts, such as architects, design the environment for older individuals. The outsiders design a prosthetic environment based on their knowledge of the needs of older individuals.

All three approaches could yield designs conducive to Ulyssean living.

Howe (1992) summed up the need for designing user-friendly macro environments: "Planning for an aging society means planning for people. It means recognizing the diversity within our population and facilitating the development of a built environment that accommodates rather than confronts this diversity. Keeping in mind the needs of older Americans will help create vital communities that are good places in which to live and grow old" (p. 7).

CONCLUSIONS

The environment in which individuals live and play has a significant impact on behavior. Ulyssean living can be enhanced by the creation of prosthetic environments designed to help compensate for the physical and cognitive losses that accompany the aging process. In most cases, the creation of optimal environments will not require a great deal of effort. In fact, minimal changes are often preferable to major renovations that may reduce autonomy. Individual needs should determine the extent of environmental modification. Issues of choice, control, independence, stimulation, security, and safety must all be considered.

Changes may be needed in environments that are essentially personal, such as living spaces, as well as the larger environment, such as a neighborhood. Optimum modification will consider both levels while retaining the individual as the central focus. This will ensure modifications follow the principle of "just manageable difficulty" and are therefore prosthetic without overcompensating for losses.

Chapter 11

The Long-Term Care Facility

There is a need for some alternative for individuals who are unable to live alone and have no community services to assist them in remaining in the community. The long-term care facility provides that alternative for approximately one million individuals aged 65 and over.

The decision to relocate into a long-term care facility is a difficult one for all involved. It may be accompanied by guilt on the part of family members and "relocation trauma" by the individual entering the facility. However, in many cases this is a necessary decision that will benefit the resident as well as the family.

CHARACTERISTICS OF LONG-TERM CARE FACILITY RESIDENTS

Approximately 5% of all individuals aged 65 or over are in nursing homes at any one point in time (Pynoos & Golant, 1996). However, over the course of a lifetime, many more than 5% will be in a long-term care facility. It is estimated that 43% of the people who were age 65 in 1990 will use a nursing home at some point in their lives (U.S. Senate Special Committee on Aging et al., 1991). Dunkle and Kart (1990) indicate that "the consensus among researchers seems to be that the total chance of institutionalization before death among normal aged persons living in the community would be about one in four" (p. 233). Clearly, the specter of institutionalization will become a reality for many individuals.

Three levels of care are provided in nursing homes. The level of service will depend on the needs of the individual. Tedrick and Green (1995) identify the levels of care as:

a. skilled nursing care—intensive, 24-hour-a-day care, supervised by a registered nurse and under the direction of a physician;
b. intermediate nursing care—involving some nursing assistance and supervision but less than 24-hour nursing care;

c.   custodial care—room and board, with assistance in personal care, but not necessarily health care services.

The average resident of a long-term care facility is a white widow, 80 years of age with a variety of chronic conditions. She has been in the facility for 18 months and was a patient in a hospital or other health care facility prior to admission. Women are twice was likely as men to be in a nursing home (U.S. Senate Committee on Aging et al., 1991).

The majority of residents need help bathing, dressing, using the toilet, and transferring. Many also need assistance in eating and are incontinent. In addition to physical impairments, many residents also experience cognitive difficulties. About 63% of the 1985 residents were memory impaired or disoriented, and 47% experienced senile dementia or chronic organic brain syndrome (U.S. Senate Committee on Aging, 1992). Many residents also exhibit hearing, visual and communication impairments (Resnick, Fries, & Verbrugge, 1997).

Cohen (1990) and Smyer, Zarit, and Qualls (1990) indicated that the prevalence of mental disorders in residents of nursing homes is rising and as many as 70 to 80% of residents experience psychiatric problems as their secondary or primary diagnosis. Furthermore, entering residents are sicker now than previous admissions. Typical residents of long-term care facilities have been described as poorly adjusted, depressed, disoriented, unhappy, disabled, docile, slow moving, alienated, dependent, submissive, isolated, and withdrawn (Crandall, 1980). Not only are residents of long-term care facilities likely to be among the sickest of the elderly, they are also likely to be among those with the least social support. According to Tedrick and Green (1995), fewer residents of nursing homes are married, fewer have daughters, and fewer have at least one adult child when compared to older adults not in long-term care facilities.

O'Brien (1989) provides a glimpse into daily life in the long-term care facility. Some factors that emerged from his study of life in "Bethany Manor" included:

- residents learned to get along by not rocking the boat;
- friendships, with other residents as well as with staff, were important to residents;
- contact with family was valued;
- privacy was important;
- reminiscence was a favored activity.

O'Brien was able to construct a topology of how individuals adapt to a nursing home. Some individuals, groups labeled "socialites," "guardians," "free-lancers," and "single-room occupants," all find value in activities occurring in the facility. The socialites are involved in the full range of activities and are deeply involved in their homes, whereas guardians focus on supporting others and focus on this assistive role. The single-room occupant is a participant, but primarily limits involvement to his or her room. Free-lancers combine the active participation mode with passivity and privacy. Activities should be designed to accommodate all these types.

REHABILITATION IN THE
LONG-TERM CARE FACILITY

Recent legislation, primarily the Omnibus Budget Reconciliation Act of 1987 (OBRA), has changed the nature of care in long-term care facilities. "Warehousing" individuals while focusing on custodial care is not acceptable. Tedrick and Green (1995) wrote, "Nursing homes now are expected at least to maintain the residents' present level of functioning, possibly restoring or improving it, taking into consideration new problems or progressive conditions" (p. 7). The question of what role a long-term care facility can take in improving quality of life, as opposed to merely making life comfortable, is of major importance when examining ways to make later life Ulyssean. Can residents of long-term care facilities grow and develop? Can they experience old age in a positive way?

One approach to facilitating growth in residents of long-term care facilities is altering the environment. Ebersole and Hess (1998, p. 501) list 11 approaches to modifying the long-term care facility—approaches in which activity personnel can participate:

1. individualize care;
2. learn who the patient was;
3. foster a sense of control;
4. recognize strengths;
5. provide environmental cues or orientation (see Chapter 10 for more in this area);
6. maintain home-like schedules as much as possible;
7. communicate;
8. adapt schedules of diagnostic procedures to patients' needs;
9. time the giving of information to the patients' needs;
10. maintain consistency in interaction;
11. maintain activities of daily living using patients' resources and social supports.

These recommendations were supplemented by factors identified as contributing to the satisfaction of nursing home patients. Awareness of these factors, and addressing them whenever possible, appears crucial to developing Ulyssean lifestyles in residents:

1. keeping personal possessions;
2. something is done about complaints;
3. privacy is available;
4. staff show a personal interest and care about residents;
5. the facility is cheerful;
6. physicians can be seen as needed;
7. help comes in a reasonable time;
8. rooms and surroundings are clear;
9. good food;
10. life is boring (negative factor);
11. personal belongings disappear (negative factor);
12. large amount of bothersome noise (negative factor).

A national movement, called The Eden Alternative, specifically focused on creating a new nursing home environment, has begun. Its founder, Dr. William Thomas, defines the movement as "the creation of a human habitat where people thrive, grow and flourish, rather than wither, decay and die." Simply put, The Eden Alternative creates long-term care facilities that are as "home-like" as possible. Animals, cats, dogs, birds, and rabbits co-exist with residents in Eden Alternative facilities. Plants are prominent in the plan to normalize the living environment and children are frequent visitors. The intent of creating this environment is to reduce the use of medication while increasing the residents' contact with the outside world. An Eden Alternative facility follows 10 basic principles (Eden Alternative, 1999):

1. Realizes loneliness, helplessness, and boredom account for the bulk of suffering among the frail elderly.
2. Commits itself to surrendering the institutional point of view and adopts the human habitat model which makes pets, plants, and children the axis around which daily life turns.
3. Provides easy access to companionship by promoting close and continuing contact between the elements of the human habitat and the people who live and work within.
4. Creates opportunities to give as well as receive care by promoting elders' participation in the daily round of activities that are necessary to maintain the human habitat;
5. Imbues daily life with variety and spontaneity by creating an environment in which unexpected and unpredictable interactions and happenings can take place.
6. De-emphasizes the programmed activities approach to life and devotes these resources to the maintenance and growth of the human habitat.
7. De-emphasizes the role of prescription drugs in elders' daily life and commits these resources to the maintenance and growth of the human habitat.

8. De-emphasizes the top-down bureaucratic authority in the facility and seeks instead to place the maximum possible decision-making authority in the hands of those closest to those for whom we care.

9. Understands that Edenizing is a never-ending process, not a program and that the human habitat, once created, should be helped to grow and develop like any other living thing.

10. Is blessed with leadership that places the need to improve resident quality of life over and above the inevitable objections to change. Leadership is the lifeblood of the Edenizing process and for it there is no substitute.

These 10 principles fit nicely with the Ulyssean perspective espoused in this book. The clear focus in Eden Alternative facilities is on the resident. His or her well-being is primary and it is achieved through active involvement in a facility as home-like as possible. The facility, and its staff, exists to help residents achieve maximum functioning and the highest quality of life possible.

The potential for rehabilitation exists in the long-term care facility. There are several general goals that, if met, will contribute to Ulyssean living. There should be an attempt to reduce dependence on staff and, as a result, increase independence. In addition, contact with reality, perceived control, continued involvement in life, and family contact are important components of Ulyssean living. The following discuss these areas in greater detail.

INCREASED INDEPENDENCE

Carruthers, Sneegas and Ashton-Shaeffer (1986) view the achievement of a leisure lifestyle as important to residents of long-term care facilities. It is an opportunity to achieve some autonomy and independence in a restricted environment.

They suggested a comprehensive program (see Figure 11.1) designed to provide a balanced leisure experience based on needs of individuals in nursing homes. It provides an excellent guide to a therapeutic approach to leisure and a direction for planning a comprehensive program.

An example of a more focused approach to enhancing independence is a program designed to reduce dependence is that designed by Sperbeck and Whitbourne (1981). They stated that "one of the most damaging effects of institutionalization of the elderly is dependence on staff, characterized by apathy, passivity, and the eventual reduction in self-maintenance behaviors" (p. 268).

Their study was based on a belief that staff are partly responsible for unnecessary dependencies in residents. They believed that "to the extent that staff possess inaccurate assessments of older person's abilities and further hold stereotypic beliefs about the aging process in general, prolonged exposure to such an environment in the form of institutionalization will inevitably lead to a maladaptive dependent inter-relationship between staff and elderly residents" (p. 268).

FIGURE 11.1
OVERVIEW OF COMPREHENSIVE PROGRAM

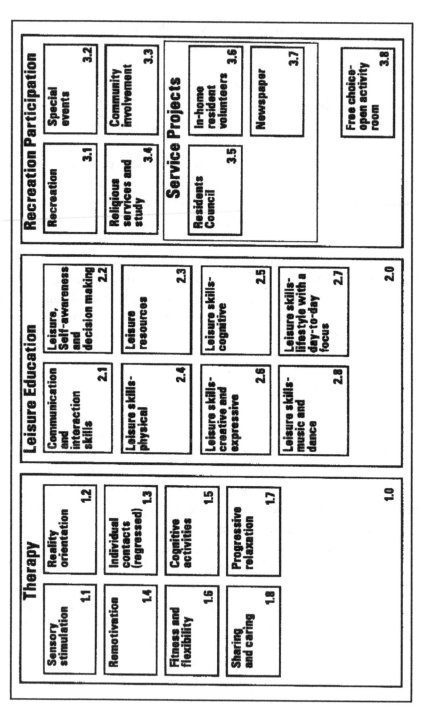

(CARRUTHERS ET AL., 1986)

Staff were put through a three-phase training program. Phase one consisted of a cognitive restructuring program that focused on increasing the staff's knowledge of older person's abilities. During this phase emphasis was placed on the importance of situational determinants of dependency behaviors. The second phase involved the teaching of principles of operant behavior. The final phase involved the application of behavior management principles with four residents identified as functionally dependent. A brief description of each of these individuals and the program used follows.

Subject A—He had refused to walk for over six months. His unwillingness to socialize was used in designing the behavior management program. The staff approached him once a day and agreed to leave him alone about walking if he walked the targeted number of steps for that day. In addition, the required number of steps was increased by two each day.

As a result of the subject's increased sociability, the program was adjusted to include verbal reinforcement and staff attention contingent on the exhibition of the targeted behavior.

Subject B—He exhibited non-shaving behavior. Staff was instructed to provide a physical prompt by placing a hand over the resident's and help him shave. Verbal reinforcement was also given when he exhibited independent shaving strokes. Finally, all the staff in the training program complemented subject B on those days he shaved himself completely.

Subject C—He also depended on staff to shave him. Although he refused to shave himself, the subject complained about the job done by the staff member who shaved him. This was used in the management program. The staff member gradually shaved less of the subject's face in order to provide him with a legitimate complaint. Upon complaining that the staff member was not doing a good job, the subject was asked to demonstrate the proper technique. He received verbal reinforcement as a result of these demonstrations.

Subject D—She relied on a wheelchair for support. The target behavior for this subject was that she shift her center of gravity from the wheelchair to her feet and that she pick up her feet when she walked. The procedures to bring about these behaviors included a training program to educate her of the physical benefits of good walking posture and its relationship to her complaints. In addition, verbal reinforcement was contingent upon walking posture and not shuffling her feet.

The results indicated that the program was successful for subjects A, B, and C. Subject D only exhibited the target behavior in the presence of the staff, and it did not generalize into other situations. Nevertheless, the program did yield promising results and indicates the efficacy of active intervention reducing dependency in the institutionalized elderly.

The authors concluded: "The functional dependency of institutionalized elderly was effectively reduced in this study by: (1) reducing the staff's information deficits about the aged, (2) counteracting the staff's tendency to underestimate the role of environmental/situational factors in contributing to the functional dependency of elderly residents, and (3) teaching the staff principles and techniques of operant behavior management" (p. 274).

CONTACT WITH REALITY

A second goal of rehabilitative programs in long-term care facilities is to help individuals maintain contact with reality. Many programs have been designed to achieve this goal. One of the most common psychosocial approaches with elderly individuals with dementia is reality orientation (Zanetti, Frisoni, De Leo, Buono, Bianchetti & Trabucchi, 1995). Wilson and Moffat (1984) define reality orientation (RO) as being concerned with the maintenance or relearning of information related to time, place, names of others, and current events. The primary teaching methods are verbal repetition and the use of visual aids such as the RO board.

Reality orientation includes both structured classroom sessions and 24-hour RO in which all staff are involved. The purpose of reality orientation is to halt the confusion, social withdrawal, disorientation and apathy experienced by some elderly individual. The focus is on reorienting these individuals to reality (Gagnon, 1996; Wilson and Moffat, 1984). Weiner, Brok, and Snadowsky (1987) further describe RO as a simple technique that can be used by anybody, can be conducted along with other nursing care activities, and can be modified to fit a variety of settings.

The classroom RO consists of 30-minute sessions designed to accommodate small groups. Sessions should occur daily if possible. The class should be held in the same place and at the same time each session. Session schedules and names of participants should be prominently displayed. Participants are provided with information through multiple methods such as the use of clocks, calendars, and a reality orientation board. As the class advances, basic information of time, place, month, date, year, upcoming meals, weather, and holidays are introduced. Eventually, simple memory games requiring concentration and stimulating memory are introduced.

It is suggested that the basic RO class include three or four members. Once participants have learned the basic information, they should be moved to a more advanced class of 8 to 10 members. Taulbee also recommends discontinuing classes for individuals who are unable to retain basic reality information after participation in the program for a two-month period. In addition, she recommends training families in reality orientation so it may be continued when patients go home.

Twenty-four hour RO is the second aspect of the program. Everyone who comes into contact with residents in the program is involved in the program. Residents are reminded of who they are, where they are and why, as well as what is expected of them. A primary focus is reminding residents of their names. Residents are called by name and may be reminded of the time, the day, and the next meal. A total effort toward reality continues throughout the day.

According to Taulbee (1976), residents experience increased alertness and become more responsible for self-care. Taulbee provided the following eight guidelines for establishing RO programs:

1. Do not hurry elderly people.
2. Explain all procedures before asking people to do them. Face individuals when speaking to them and speak distinctly, but not too loudly.
3. Talk to them as though you expect them to understand, even if the individuals are confused or disoriented.
4. Treat the participants with dignity and respect. Do not talk to them or treat them like children. (Being treated like a child may hasten dependency and deterioration.)
5. Encourage them to care for themselves as much as possible.
6. Use social reinforcement; compliment success; and do not emphasize failure.
7. Use the positive approach by first looking for ability and then disability.
8. Establish a climate of caring and genuine concern.

Weiner et al. (1987) recommend the following:

1. Use repetition by beginning each session with a review of basic information and continue to use it throughout the class.
2. Establish attainable goals and do not expect too much.
3. Reinforce the correct answer immediately. Correct an inaccurate answer and ask the participant to repeat it.
4. Maintain coordination with others in the facility.

Their suggestions for 24-hour reality orientation techniques designed to keep individuals in touch with reality include:

1. All staff should address residents by their surname and title (e.g., Mr., Mrs.) and only use first names if given explicit permission.
2. Staff should know each patient, including their history, and use it in conversation.
3. A variety of clocks, bulletin boards and calendars should be located throughout the facility.
4. A diverse, interesting, and appropriate activity program, based on residents' needs, should be in place.
5. Daily reminders of time, place, and day should be announced on a public address system if possible.
6. Name cards should be placed in the dining hall and patients encouraged to behave appropriately while dining.
7. Special holiday meals should be provided.
8. Birthdays should be identified and celebrated appropriately.

9. Clearly written, up-to-date activity schedules should be given to all residents.
10. Liberal visiting hours should be in place, and visitors should be included in the RO program by being asked to reinforce reality as to time, place, and day.
11. Community contact should be maintained through volunteer opportunities.
12. Colors should be used to differentiate places throughout the facility.
13. Adequate lighting should be in place, with consideration given to intensity and glare.
14. Cheerful, appropriate decorations should be used throughout the facility.
15. Residents should be encouraged to retain photographs and other memorabilia of home and past achievements.
16. Independence should be encouraged as much as possible.
17. Sensory stimulation (see section on this below) should be used and should incorporate as many senses as possible.

Although the above lists were developed for RO programs, they are clearly useful in a variety of settings and facilities.

The props used in reality-based programs are limited only by the imagination of the program leader. Taulbee (1976) reports using clocks, calendars, scrapbooks, and discussions about the weather and upcoming holidays.

Data related to RO programs are mixed (Baldelli, Pirani, Motta, Abati, Mariani & Manzi, 1993; Scanland & Emershaw, 1993; Zanetti et al., 1995; Gagnon, 1996; Garinger, 1998). According to Smyer, Zarit, and Qualls (1990) "outcome research on RO has been equivocal . . . Although some have questioned its efficacy . . . a recent review concluded that RO is more effective than nonspecific treatments" (pp. 389–390).

The authors continue by citing Kastenbaum's (1987) belief that "'RO deserves more appropriate and capable research attention, and, probably, also has some continuing place in clinical gerontology'" (p. 390).

It appears that a carefully designed and conducted program, in conjunction with careful screening and selection of potential participants, increases the chances of a successful program.

Weiner et al. (1987) recommend incorporating attitude therapy in the RO program. In attitude therapy, each patient's behavioral style is identified and the staff decides on a corresponding staff behavior style, or attitude, toward the patient. This attitude is displayed in all interactions. There are five potential attitudes.

Active friendliness is used with apathetic and withdrawn patients. Staff need to seek out these individuals and focus on making positive, constructive statements, such as "I like that dress you are wearing" to them.

Passive friendliness is recommended for suspicious, frightened patients. It is typified by statements such as, "Let me know if I can help." The resident should make the first move toward friendliness and be permitted to take the initiative in interactions.

Matter-of-factness is useful when working with clients who need to take responsibility for their own behavior. This attitude is recommended with clients who are highly manipulative or exhibit poor social adjustment. Staff members indicate that they are not to be manipulated and will not reward manipulative behavior.

It is recommended that depressed patients be treated with *kind firmness* designed to help individuals shift the focus from themselves and toward interaction with others. An example of kind firmness would be insisting a patient get out of bed or get dressed.

The final attitude is labeled *no demand* and used with frightened, angry patients acting out their fears. These individuals may be panicked or aggressive. No demands removes pressure from the individual and puts him or her in control.

A different perspective on the need to assist older individuals in maintaining contact with reality is provided within the framework of validation therapy (Feil, 1993). According to Toseland, Diehl, Freeman, Manzanares, Naleppa, and McCallion (1997), validation therapy is based on the belief that the behavior of demented older adults, regardless of how bizarre or unusual, occurs for a reason. Individuals adapt to their illness by using whatever abilities remain intact. According to Toseland et al., "When short-term memory is impaired, older adults with dementia use memories and feelings from the distant past to help them continue to communicate with others. Similarly, when language abilities are lost, older adults rely on repetitive vocalizations and motions and on effective responses to communicate" (p. 32). These adaptations are survival techniques and explain what may appear to be unusual behaviors.

Validation therapy accepts the behavior of the individual as a starting point and does not attempt to impose the staff's reality on the older person with dementia. It de-emphasizes the relevance of orientation while exploring the meanings and motivations for the observed behaviors (Scanland & Emershaw, 1993). The approach is marked by respect for an older person's feeling in whatever time or place is real to him or her (Gagnon, 1996). The techniques used in validation therapy are based on empathy and unconditional regard for the individual and are designed to stimulate communication while tuning into and validating the communication of the older person (Toseland et al., 1997).

A validation therapy group typically consists of 5 to 10 individuals in a structured situation designed to stimulate energy, social interaction, and social roles. It includes music, talk, movement and food (Gagnon, 1996; Validation Training Institute, 1997). Toseland and his associates (1997) described a validation therapy group they ran as part of a study of its impact. Their program was divided into four segments of 5 to 10 minutes each. The session began with warm greetings, hand holding, and singing in order to stimulate participants. This was followed by bringing up a topic of interest and encouraging reminiscence about the topic. This was done to encourage interaction and communication. The third stage of the program focused on an activity such as singing or poetry reading. The session closed with refreshments and saying good-bye to each member individually and thanking them for coming. During the session, the leaders used the techniques common in validation therapy:

1. the use of nonthreatening, concrete, simple words;
2. using a low, clear, empathetic tone of voice;
3. rephrasing and paraphrasing unclear verbal communication;
4. responding to the explicit and implicit meaning in verbal and nonverbal communications;
5. mirroring nonverbal and verbal communication (Toseland et al., 1997).

Data examining the efficacy of validation therapy are limited, and the findings related to its efficacy are ambiguous. Toseland and his co-authors identified five studies in the literature and these were flawed in their methodology. Nevertheless, validation therapy is becoming more widespread and accepted as an effective technique to use with confused elderly.

INCREASED CONTROL

A third general goal of programs in long-term care facilities is to increase control (Martin & Smith, 1993; Bocksnick & Hall, 1994). According to Saul (1993) most residents of long-term care facilities experience loss of control. Indeed, institutionalization by definition requires giving up a degree of control over one's own life. Saul (1993) believes individuals should be given "active control" over their own lives. Allowing residents to plan, organize, and conduct activities as much as possible will restore some control to participants. A variety of programs have been used to do this. Two will be detailed in this section.

Langer and Rodin (1976; Rodin and Langer, 1976) studied the effects of enhanced personal responsibility and choice on residents of a long-term care facility. They believed most long-term care facilities to be decision-free environments and saw a need to return choice and control to the residents. They created a "responsibility-induced group" and a control group in order to assess the effect of choice on residents' lives.

The responsibility-induced group was told they were responsible for their own actions and then were asked to select a plant and were given responsibility to care for it. In addition, they were told that movies were shown several nights a week and were asked to choose the night they would like to attend. The other group was given a plant and was told the staff would care for it. In addition, individuals in this group were told what night they were to come to the movie.

It was found that the group given choice and control in their own lives was happier, more active, spent more time visiting with other residents, spent more time visiting with people from outside the institution, spent more time talking to staff, was rated as being less passive, and had higher movie attendance.

A similar study by Banziger and Roush (1983) used bird feeders to introduce personal responsibility and control into a long-term care facility. One group of residents received a verbal message that they were responsible for making their own decisions and for their own lives. They were also told that birds were having a difficult time surviving, and each person was requested to care for a bird feeder placed on their window. A second group of residents was told the staff was responsible for their care and was not given the opportunity to maintain a bird feeder. A third group received no verbal message and no bird feeder.

It was found that the residents given responsibility experienced an increase in life-satisfaction, an increase in self-reported control, increased happiness, and increased activity levels. More recent work (Vallerand, O'Connor, & Blais, 1989) has supported the crucial role choice and self-determination have in the quality of life for residents of long-term care facilities. The found the ability to make choices related to mealtime, personal care, room decoration, and encouragement of self-initiative by staff were related to life satisfaction.

A large degree of autonomy and control is guaranteed through the rights residents of nursing homes have. Fried, Van Booven, & MacQuarrie (1993) list 28 rights residents retain by law. These are listed below.

RESIDENT'S BILL OF RIGHTS

Each resident in a nursing home has a right to:

1. Be informed and have a written copy of the resident's rights and responsibilities.
2. Exercise rights as a resident of the facility and a citizen of the United States.
3. Be free from discrimination, interferences, and reprisal in the exercise of these rights.
4. Inspect his or her own medical records.
5. Be informed of his or her health status and medical condition.
6. Refuse treatment and refuse to participate in experimental research.
7. Be informed about services available and related charges, including information about coverage under the Medicare and Medicaid programs.
8. Have his or her family and physician notified promptly when there is a change in condition.
9. Be notified in a reasonable time frame of any changes in room assignment, roommate, transfer, and discharge.
10. Manage his or her own financial affairs.
11. Choose his or her attending physician.
12. Participate in his or her care and treatment.
13. Be granted privacy in accommodations; medical treatment; meetings with friends, family, and/or resident groups; written and telephone communications; and conjugal visits.

14. Have his or her personal and clinical records kept confidential.
15. Voice grievances and file complaints without discrimination, coercion, or reprisal.
16. Examine survey results.
17. Refuse to perform services for the facility.
18. Send and receive mail.
19. Receive visitors, including relatives, representatives from the state, and the area ombudsman.
20. Have regular access and private use of a telephone.
21. Retain and use personal possessions as space permits.
22. Share a room with his or her spouse.
23. Self-administer drugs, unless this is determined to be an unsafe procedure.
24. Be free from restraints.
25. Be free from abuse.
26. Choose activities, schedules, and health care consistent with his or her own interests and plan for cure.
27. Participate in social, religious, and community activities and interact with people of his or her own choosing.
28. Receive services and care with reasonable accommodation of individual preferences.

CONTINUED INVOLVEMENT IN LIFE

Research (Saul, 1993; Voelkl, 1993; Voelkl, Fries & Galecki, 1995) has supported the efficacy of activities in increased self-esteem, happiness, and self-concept. The ultimate result is improved quality of life in what has traditionally been viewed as a stagnant, penalizing environment. One of the benefits provided by activities is a sense of involvement and individuality within institutional settings.

The long-term care environment may make it more difficult to achieve continued growth and development, but it is not impossible. Increased efforts on the part of trained, professional staff are needed. Leisure service providers are a necessary part of this effort. Efforts at creating resident councils (Wells & Singer, 1988), encouraging independence and success in activities (Voelkl, 1986), taking activities to residents when needed, maximizing control, and addressing residents' needs are crucial.

Other programs effective in helping individuals remain interested and involved in their lives are remotivation therapy and sensory stimulation. Examples of both of these types of programs are provided below.

Remotivation is a group technique designed to stimulate and revitalize individuals who are no longer interested in the present or future (Weiner et al., 1987). It incorporates a structured program of discussion using materials and encouraging individuals to respond. The goals of remotivation are: (1) to stimulate patients into thinking about and discussing real world topics and (2) to assist patients in communicating with and relating to others.

Participants in the program should be capable of interacting, be willing to join the group, be able to hear and speak, and not be preoccupied with hallucinations. Patients in remotivation need its structure to assist in socialization. Participants are more advanced than those in reality orientation programs. The suggested maximum group size is 10 to 15, and sessions will typically be held once or twice a week for 30 minutes to an hour.

The first few minutes of a session should be devoted to establishing rapport and greeting the members. Each session is devoted to a different topic, and visual aids and objects are used to maintain interest and promote reactions.

Five structured steps should be employed at each remotivation session (Weiner et al., 1987; Ebersole & Hess, 1998; National Remotivation Therapy Organization, undated):

1. Creating a climate of acceptance. This is accomplished through greeting participants by name and making them feel welcome to the group.
2. Creating a bridge to reality. Interest-inducing questions are asked to lead the group into the subject of the day. The topic is then reinforced through poetry, music, visual aids, and other props, and participants are reinforced for appropriate responses.
3. Sharing the world of reality. Questions are used to lead participants through the topic. Questions such as "What is it?" and "How big is it?" may be used to stimulate conversation.
4. Appreciating the work of the world. The participants are encouraged to participate and reminisce by sharing experiences, ideas, and opinions about the relationship of the topic to work.
5. Creating a climate of appreciation. The focus at this stage is on enjoyment in having participated with the group and appreciation for participants' contributions. In addition, they are urged to bring poems, songs, stories, newspaper clippings, and other relevant items to the next session.

The topics in remotivation sessions are typically neither controversial nor emotionally laden. They are objective rather than subjective and center around everyday life.

Ebersole and Hess (1990) also list several steps to follow in a remotivation group. These include:

1. Use name tags for participants.
2. Explain the focus of the group in general terms.
3. Introduce the subject and, if possible, pass around a relevant object.
4. Ask for a description of the object as well as comments on it.

5. Talk about the origins and uses of the object.
6. Ask various people for their input. Use direct questions. Use names when addressing participants.
7. Urge nonrespondents to respond.
8. Acknowledge all contributions.
9. Do not let one member monopolize or stray from the topic.
10. Restate relevant comments of confused participants to refocus the group and ease anxiety.
11. Encourage interaction from the entire group.
12. Announce when the session is nearly over.
13. Express appreciation to participants.

The data related to the effectiveness of remotivation therapy is mixed. Nevertheless, it appears to be a useful technique to use with older individuals, providing the opportunity for at least some older individuals to enjoy a more fulfilling and focused life.

Sensory training is designed to bring disoriented patients back to reality (Weiner et al., 1987). It is designed to stimulate the senses of participants in order to improve their perceptions of the environment and is designed for individuals with sensory motor problems, poor sensory input discrimination, and depressed psychosocial performance. It is recommended that the group include five to seven members, all at approximately the same functioning level. Sessions are approximately one hour in length and can be conducted every day.

The leader brings everyday objects to class. The intent is to select objects that will activate the senses. Perfume, bells, rough cloth, a mirror, and spices might be used. The leader creates a friendly atmosphere built on acceptance. The focus is on participation rather than "right" or "wrong" responses. Information related to time, place, and day may be incorporated into the opening of each session.

Weiner et al. (1987) suggest the session be oriented around exercises for the mind and body. This would include identifying different body joints (shoulder, elbows, wrist, fingers, knee) and exercising those. For example, "We are now going to exercise our wrists. Here is my wrist and this is how it moves" (p. 75). This is done to introduce body awareness and movement to the participants.

This is followed by identification of the five senses and sensory organs. Materials are then used to stimulate each of the senses. Each sense should be stimulated every session. Weiner et al. (1987) give the following example for sight:

"The group members are told that they will exercise the sense of sight by using their eyes. The leader identifies her or his own eyes and helps the group members find theirs. The group may then be presented with something to see (a mirror) and asked to respond to, not identify, what they see. Questions such as 'Do you like what you see?' or 'How do you look today?' may be asked. The leader then repeats to the entire group what the individual member said, such as 'Sara said she looks nice today,' or 'Mr. J. says he sees his own face.' Not only does this stimulate sight, but it also heightens self-awareness" (p. 76). A similar process is followed with all the sensory props.

The final segment of the program identified by Weiner et al. (1987) is used to get feedback from participants. In addition, the time and place of the next session is announced.

Leadership suggestions for this technique are similar to those for most techniques. Repetition is important, as is calling participants by name. Sessions should be tightly structured, and the leader should move around. Touching participants to convey warmth is encouraged. Praise should be used copiously.

INCLUDING THE FAMILY

Another component in programming in long-term care facilities is the role of the resident's family. The move into a nursing home can be traumatic. It signals a major change in life, marked by a new environment filled with new people. Residents need to maintain as much continuity in life as possible, and this can be accomplished through continued contact with family and friends (Fried et al., 1993). Below is a sample of suggestions from the staff at Philadelphia Geriatric Center for relatives visiting family in the facility. Given the vital importance of visitation, anything that increases the likelihood of visitation is important.

1. Encourage reminiscing. Review your relative's life and achievements. Bring photographs, scrapbooks, or familiar objects from home to share.
2. Do not give advice unless asked, since residents may not want advice from their children. Instead, ask their advice or opinions about family matters.
3. Tell the resident what's happening in the family, community, and old neighborhood. Share problems as well as pleasant and exciting family events. Older people are not too fragile to deal with sadness and death. Protecting them may make them feel left out, and they have a right to know.
4. Include your relative's friends and roommate in your conversations. This encourages relationships and helps your relative see your interest in the present environment. However, some time should be set aside for private conversation.
5. Empathize with your relative's feelings of distress. Do not deny its existence or the resident's feelings. Even if your relative is upset about an event that did not occur (for example, if she thinks her roommate stole her dress when in fact it is in the laundry), it is not important to convince her that the dress is actually in the laundry. She needs your sympathy that sometimes things get lost and that it is hard living with a roommate. Listen to complaints. Don't feel your relative is angry with you. Often all that is needed is a sympathetic ear.

6. Talk to your relative's social worker. Every floor has a social worker, and she will discuss with you how to make your visit more pleasant.

WHAT TO DO TOGETHER

1. Bring newspaper or magazine articles you and your relative may look at together. Or you may read to a relative who is visually handicapped.
2. Play games your relative enjoys. Bring cards, dominoes, Scrabble, or other games you enjoy together.
3. Help decorate your relative's room. Bring photos, pictures, plants, wall hangings, and decide together where they will look best. This indicates your acceptance of your relative's present home and your interest in it.
4. Help your relative with personal grooming. You can file and polish nails, set hair, shave, and mend clothes. Looking better helps people feel better.
5. Assist your relative with correspondence. Encourage writing to friends and relatives. Those who cannot write may want to dictate a letter to you. Help with phone calls, sending greeting cards, and gifts. Let the older person do as much as possible, independently, even if only pointing to the card or gift to be sent.
6. Bring others to visit. Your relative will enjoy seeing other members of the family and friends. Try taking photos and sending them along as a remembrance of an enjoyable visit.
7. Bring grandchildren and great-grandchildren. Older people and children enjoy each other. It is meaningful to children to know their roots. Often they are fascinated, not frightened, by the attention of older people. If we have a positive and accepting attitude toward people who are physically or mentally impaired, children will accept them too.
8. Bring pets. But please, do so only if the older person likes animals and only when they visit out of doors.
9. Talk with the floor activities therapist. Your account of your relative's interests will help the therapist develop a program tailored to the older person's individual needs. Look at the activities schedules that are posted at the nursing station. There are floor activities and many activities for the whole center. What ideas do you have for programs? Tell the activities therapist about activities in which you can join your relative. This may also encourage him to participate when you are not there.
10. Visit other areas of the center. Taking your relative to visit a friend on another floor, or the cafeteria, gift shops, synagogue, patios, library, and outdoor grounds will give much pleasure. One way to become involved with your relative and his extended family here is to participate in some of the festivities and trips planned by the center. You will be welcome to come along on special trips to assist your relative and his friends with transportation or meals. And, for special events within the center, such as Family Fair

or Las Vegas night, it will be an enjoyable shared experience for you and your relative, if you manage a wheelchair (his own or his friend's) or offer a strong and willing arm.

11. Take your relative for an outing. An older person enjoys a drive in the car, dinner in your home, eating out, a visit to the old neighborhood, and attendance at family affairs. Wheelchairs and walkers can be taken in the car, and a physical therapist or nurse will be happy to teach you how to assist your relative.

12. Share your skills and talents. If you have skills or talents such as playing a musical instrument, singing, or art work that you could share with your relative or some of his friends, your accomplishments will give rise to feelings of pride.

Not only are the above suggested approaches helpful in encouraging friends and relatives to visit, they also provide several program ideas. Taking trips, use of pets, photographs of events for later reminiscing, and fostering intergenerational contact are all appropriate approaches for activity programs.

CONCLUSION

Weiner et al. (1987) indicate that programs in nursing homes serve one of three purposes: psychosocial stimulation, opportunities for social interaction, and opportunities for positive reinforcement related to achievements and growth. This chapter has provided a variety of applications of this triumvirate in the long-term care facility. The key is to be aware of residents' needs and be committed to the principle of Ulyssean living in this environment.

Although few would choose a long-term care facility as a desirable setting in which to live, it is the best environment for some older individuals. When family and community resources are not sufficient to meet the needs of an increasingly frail individual, the care available in the nursing home may be the optimum solution. However, the quality of life in a nursing home will vary greatly. An active program of activities and intervention, led by trained therapeutic recreation personnel, can help make this setting one where Ulyssean living can occur.

Chapter 12

◆

The Community Environment

The overwhelming number of older individuals live in age-integrated communities. They live in the places they have always lived: New York City; Dayton, Ohio; Central, South Carolina; Provo, Utah; and everywhere else. In most cases, they live without being noticed or labeled as a special group. At the same time, a continuum of care exists in many communities that allows people to remain in their homes with a little help from their friends, neighbors, and the social system. Many of these services and programs are provided by Area Agencies on Aging or county offices on aging and funded through the Older American's Act.

A STATISTICAL PROFILE OF COMMUNITY-RESIDING ELDERS

As was indicated in Chapter 1 most older individuals (67% of all noninstitutionalized elderly) lived in family settings in 1995. Nearly 75% of the 60 years of age and over population live in single-family homes, and about 10% of the population live in planned elderly housing. Seventy-seven percent of males and 48% of females aged 65 or over live with their spouse. However, many older individuals live alone. Indeed, 42% percent of older women and 17% of all older men lived alone in 1995. Most older people, whether living alone or with others, prefer to age in place (Pynoos and Galant, 1996) They do not want to give up their homes and live elsewhere. Many individuals' ties to the past are in their homes, and they do not want to surrender those ties. As one of the author's grandmother said, "I can still smell the popcorn from all the Christmases we spent in this house." In fact, 65% would secure assistance, such as help for household chores, in order to remain at home (Vierck, 1990).

Vierck (1990) provides insight into community life of the elderly. Sixty percent are either unaware of the services available to them or are not interested in age-segregated activities. Eleven percent use at least one community service, 15%

attend senior citizen centers, and 4% use transportation services. Fewer than 4% receive home-delivered meals, homemaker services, or home-based health services.

Ten percent are very active in their communities, 16% are fairly active, and 23% are somewhat active. Fifty-nine percent visit friends at least three times a week, and 57% regularly attend social gatherings. Fifty percent spend time in activities related to religion.

Seventy percent of older individuals view themselves as being in good health. Twenty-five percent of older women and 33% of men claim to exercise regularly. The vast majority (72%) of people 65 years of age or over are satisfied with life, and 82% do not experience frequent difficulties in life.

HOUSING OPTIONS

According to the National Association of Counties (undated a), "The vast majority of older persons' age in place in their own homes and communities" (p. 1). Therefore, it is necessary that the community living environment includes a variety of housing alternatives to meet the diverse needs of this population. These options increase the likelihood an older individual will not be placed in a nursing home inappropriately by providing resources needed to help maintain independence. Some of the options include (Heckheimer, 1989; Administration on Aging, undated):

1. Conventional home ownership—retaining one's own home and living independently.
2. Accessory apartment—a private unit built within a single-family house.
3. Boarding home—a private bedroom, private or shared bath, and a common dining area.
4. Congregate housing—a planned and designed multi-unit facility with private apartments for residents, and including services such as meals, transportation, housekeeping, and recreation.
5. Domiciliary care home—a group living arrangement with supervised meals, housekeeping, personal area, and private or shared sleeping rooms in a setting that is typically licensed and required to meet design and operating standards.
6. ECHO housing, also called a granny flat—a free-standing, removable unit adjacent to a single-family house and occupied by a relative on the same property.
7. Elderly housing project—a rental unit designed specifically to meet the needs of older residents with a variety of services designed to support independent living.
8. Foster care home—a single-family home including an older person living with a foster family, responsible for providing meals, housekeeping, and personal care.

9. Continuing care community—a planned housing development designed to provide a range of accommodations and services to older people, including independent living, congregate living, and medical care. An individual may move from one level to another as needs change.
10. Retirement community—a development designed for older individuals with home ownership and rental units available.
11. Assisted living facility—a facility where personal care assistance, such as help with medications as well as with bathing, grooming and dressing, is provided to residents.

The variety of housing options available to older individuals provides an opportunity to meet the needs for shelter. The nature of an individual's housing will shape the leisure services available to him or her. The next section will examine leisure in community settings.

LEISURE LIFE IN THE COMMUNITY

Altergott's (1988) work profiles daily life in later life. She examined involvement in leisure, obligatory activities, and social interaction among older people. Her findings provide a good starting point for examining the lives of community-dwelling elderly. On the average, the participants in Altergott's study spent approximately one hour per day in social leisure (visiting, conversing, parties, social gatherings). Approximately 2 ½ hours were spent in television watching each day. Passive leisure (radio, reading, writing letters) consumed approximately 1 ½ hours. None of the other activities examined—active leisure, religion, volunteerism, creative leisure, entertainment, education, or travel—averaged more than 30 minutes per day. Overall, older men averaged seven hours and 19 minutes leisure per day and older women averaged six hours and 31 minutes.

As can be seen in Table 12.1, there were age differences in leisure involvement. Leisure hours peaked between the ages of 65–74 for men and 75 or over for women.

Although the above provides some insight into how older individuals residing in the community spend their days, it focuses on activities. While knowledge of what people do is important to program development, it is also necessary to understand the paths they take in negotiating later life. This perspective provides understanding into the patterns of life.

Kelly (1987) provides a great deal of information on the community life of older residents of Peoria, Illinois. One thing that is clear from Kelly's work is that each individual takes a unique path through life. As Kelly wrote, "The journey of life is singular. No two life journeys are alike" (p. 1). However, some commonalities can be identified. In fact, Kelly identified several approaches to later life.

TABLE 12.1

GENDER AND AGE PATTERNS IN LEISURE ACTIVITIES:
DAILY AVERAGE HOURS AND MINUTES

	Men			Women		
	55-64	65-74	75+	55-64	65-74	75+
Active leisure	:32	:26	:09	:08	:08	:06
Passive leisure	1:13	2:06	1:26	1:02	1:24	1:52
Television	2:34	3:08	3:40	2:10	2:24	2:28
Social leisure	1:13	1:18	:59	1:23	1:20	1:22
Religious Practice	:14	:14	:18	:16	:20	:30
Volunteerism	:08	:10	:09	:12	:14	:04
Creative Leisure	:04	:06	:29	:24	:28	:38
Entertainment	:03	:06	:01	:03	:04	:07
Education	:07	:07	:01	:03	:02	:05
Travel for Leisure	:26	:26	:26	:17	:25	:13
Total Leisure	**6:34**	**8:05**	**7:35**	**5:49**	**6:49**	**7:23**

(ALTERGOTT, 1988)

1. *Balanced investors* remain invested in life. They are committed and invested in at least two of three life domains: family, work, and leisure. These individuals are likely to participate in community organizations, such as the church. These individuals follow the activity theory approach discussed in Chapter 2 on aging theories.

2. *Family-focused individuals* found most of their support in the family. Their investments and meanings revolve primarily around their family. The leisure focus is the family.

3. Individuals identified as *work-centered* were rare. Nevertheless, it appears some older individuals progress through life with a dominant work orientation.

4. In contrast to the work-centered individual is the *leisure-invested* person. This small group of individuals found meaning and importance in leisure. However, this was not a highly satisfied group.

5. *Faithful members* focused primarily on the church in later life.

6. Individuals labeled as *self-sufficient* relied on their own resources for dealing with changes in life. They were not engaged in work, leisure, or community groups.

7. An *accepting adaptor* reacted to change by accepting it and approaching life in a passive way. They are compliant individuals who react to change by changing. This approach to life is marked by low life satisfaction.

8. *Resistant rebels,* on the other hand, were angry individuals who tried to change their environments.

If you work in a community-based program, such as a senior center, leisure may play a role in the lives of older individuals. However, it is not a panacea. Not all the types of individuals described above will embrace leisure as a vehicle for dealing with change in later life. It would seem that balanced investors and leisure-invested individuals will be the most likely participants in organized programs. Most older individuals in the community will pursue their leisure interests outside the framework of organized programs such as centers or clubs.

COMMUNITY CONCERNS

Weiner, Brok, and Snadowsky (1987) identify five areas where older residents in the community may experience problems and state that "the goals of any comprehensive rehabilitation or service program could only be truly achieved by helping the elderly deal with all these problem source areas successfully" (p. 160). The problem areas and potential areas of stress included:

1. Economic—Income loss and retirement may result in less income in the later years. Some modifications in lifestyle may be needed.
2. Physical—As we indicated in an earlier chapter, old age is inarguably a time of physical loss and decline.
3. Social—Role losses, such as retirement, loss of friends, or other social roles, may result in need to find replacement roles. The role of leisure independent of work may need to be evaluated.
4. Psychological—Growing old may result in a reevaluation of the self. New developmental tasks emerge. Kelly (1987a), for example, identifies this as a time of culmination marked by attempts to pull life together and find meaning.
5. Philosophical—This issue revolves around "coming to grips with existential and/or religious issues" (p. 160). Questions about the meaning of life and the individual's place in the world become important issues.

Weiner et al. (1987) recommend life enrichment counseling as a technique for assisting in these five areas. The focus of life enrichment is congruent with the development of a Ulyssean approach to later life. Shared factors include:

1. The individual needs to take an active approach to life. The individual actively seeks and finds ways to construct the life she or he desires.
2. The older individual must function as an "open system" seeking new ideas and information rather than being a closed system unwilling to examine new ideas.

3. The importance of going outside the self and making an impact on others remains as a focus. Ulyssean lives are shared lives.
4. The individual should continue involvement in meaningful activities. What is meaningful is subjective and an individual choice.
5. Weiner et al. (1987) view the need to retain spontaneity and a sense of humor as being part of self-enrichment.

Clearly, leisure can be a major factor in achieving each of these components of enriched living. Assisting older individuals in identifying appropriate activities can be a function of community-based programs.

COMMUNITY PROGRAMS AND SERVICES

A variety of community-based services exist (see for example, Atchley, 1991; Gelfand, 1988; Harbert & Ginsberg, 1990) and include: (1) in-home services, (2) protective services and legal services, (3) volunteer and employment services, (4) information and referral services, (5) day care services, (6) transportation services; (7) friendly visiting and telephone reassurance, (8) escort services, (9) center services, and (10) educational services.

In-home services are provided to the person in his or her own home in order to maintain self-sufficiency and independence. They include chore services designed to assist in performing household repair and other light work needed to enable the person to remain at home. A chore service program might provide a person to replace window panes, install handrails, minor plumbing repair, and insect and rodent control.

A second type of in-home service is home-delivered meals. Many communities have a meals-on-wheels program to deliver at least one hot, nutritious meal per day to people in need. Homemaker services provide assistance in tasks of daily living, including housework chores such as laundry and cleaning and needed assistance in personal care. The fourth type of in-home services are home health services, including the provision of health services to the homebound. Part-time nursing care, occupational therapy, and physical therapy are examples of home health care.

Protective services include activities needed by individuals with a physical or mental dysfunction who are unable to carry out activities of daily living and unable to manage their own affairs. They may also be unable to protect themselves from abuse or neglect. A caseworker providing protective services might assist the individual in finding needed financial care, arrange legal services, find housing, and ultimately act as a court-appointed guardian if needed.

Volunteer services include the provision of formal volunteer opportunities with a variety of groups in the community. This may be done through local programs such as hospitals, delivering meals on wheels, or serving on committees or boards. There are also a variety of national volunteer programs such as Foster Grand-parents, the Retired Senior Volunteer program, and the Senior Corps of Retired Executives.

Approximately 40% of individuals between the ages of 65 and 75 had volunteered some hours and 26% of all people 75 and over had volunteered some hours in 1986. A 1991 report indicated approximately 17% of all individuals 65 and over were doing some kind of volunteer work. The most common setting for volunteering was with a religious organization (43.3%), followed by hospital and health organizations (17.8%), and social and welfare organizations (14.5%). The average time older people spent volunteering was 4.7 hour per week (Cutler & Danigelis, 1993).

Many older individuals would like to work, and efforts designed to assist in their search for employment should be part of a comprehensive community program. Employment services could range from vocational counseling and retraining to the initiation of a job referral or exchange service where older workers are matched with requests for workers from the community.

Information and referral services involve receiving calls in a central location from individuals needing assistance and providing referrals to these services. Usually the service will include a brief assessment followed by the provision of relevant information to the caller. Many agencies also publish a book of community programs and services, including recreation services available to the older individual.

Some older individuals cannot be left alone during the day, and day care programs for the elderly are becoming increasingly common. They provide a range of services within an organized setting for periods less than 24 hours. Prior to the initiation of day care, the only solution would have been placement in a long-term care facility. The origination of day care provided a sheltered location where the individuals could spend the day and return home at night.

Services at a day care program might include health services such as physical therapy, recreation therapy, and mental health services. The day care program will also include a planned program of recreational activities and a hot meal. The program allows the individual the opportunity to stay at home as a result of the provision of needed services while also providing relief to the caregiver who no longer needs to be available and involved 24 hours a day. As a result, both the individual and his or her family benefits.

Many people aged 65 and over are identified as "transportation disadvantaged" (see Chapter 10), meaning they lack adequate public transportation and do not, or cannot, drive an automobile. Such individuals require transportation services in order to get to needed services and activities. As a result, the provision of transportation is a major service of many agencies.

Atchley (1991) proposed an "ideal" transportation program. It includes fare reduction on all public transportation, public subsidies to ensure adequate scheduling and routing of public transportation, reduced taxi fares, and funds to senior citizen centers for the purchase of vehicles to be used in transportation programs.

Other transportation programs include the use of volunteer drivers, sharing of vehicles by senior centers with other groups, such as the Easter Seal Society, or corporations using vans for car pooling of employees, use of school buses, and contractual arrangements with transportation providers, such as taxi cab companies.

Regardless of the method used to provide transportation, it is an integral part of any program. No matter how good a program is, it will not be used unless people can get to it.

Telephone reassurance and friendly visitor programs are designed to provide daily contact between the older individual and the community. Telephone reassurance systems are built around a phone call to the individual on a preplanned basis. The call is a way to be sure the individual is doing well and does not need any assistance. If the individual does not answer the call and has not previously informed the caller this would be the case, a call is made to an emergency contact such as a neighbor or friend. This individual will then visit the older individual to determine why the call went unanswered. The impetus for telephone reassurance programs was the knowledge that older individuals can have accidents in the home, such as a fall and resulting broken hip, which would go unnoticed. The telephone call is a method of avoiding such a catastrophe. A friendly visitor program is similar, except a personal visit replaces the telephone call.

Escort services provide accompaniment for older individuals needing assistance in negotiating their environment. This may include trips to the doctor, shopping, or recreation activities.

The senior citizen center has become one of the mainstays of the organized system or services. The Older Americans Act provided the impetus for the development of many of these centers. They are crucial as a focal point for the delivery of services. Although relatively few older individuals actually participate in center programs, few communities do not have a center that serves as the focal point of aging services.

Centers today typically function as multi-purpose centers offering a variety of programs and services. The attempt to become locations allowing "one-stop shopping" has resulted in the placement of recreational programs, social services such as food stamp and social security information, meals counseling services, and information and referral in the center.

Ebersole and Hess (1998) provide the following list of opportunities typically available at multi-purpose centers:

* creative writing art appreciation;
* music appreciation;
* poetry;
* drama;
* self-awareness training;
* job training and placement;
* history and current events;

- educational opportunities;
- research participation;
- group activities;
- family counseling;
- intergenerational programs;
- community project participation;
- crisis counseling;
- glaucoma screening;
- audiometic evaluation;
- nutritional counseling;
- meal service;
- sexual counseling;
- homemaking service;
- housing assessment and referral;
- podiatry;
- hypertension screening;
- health monitoring (p. 929).

A variety of educational programs should be made available in the community. These could include programs developed and offered locally, such as classes at centers or community colleges, as well as national programs such as Elderhostel. The opportunity for continuing education is crucial to Ulyssean living.

Two groups may be in particular need of community services: widows and caregivers. Family and friends provide a network for reciprocal relationships which have been identified as a "crucial concomitant of an older person's well being and autonomy" (Hooyman & Kiyak, 1993; p. 266). This "convoy of social relations" (Antonucci, 1990) affecting health and well-being in later life may be more important in later life since the moving of children out of the house (although it is important to note that about one in five older individuals do not have children and death of a spouse may increase the need to develop strong bonds with others.

Widowhood can be a time of severe crisis for older men and women. According to Ebersole and Hess (1998), "Losing a partner, when there has been a long, close and satisfying relationship is essentially losing one's self and one's core" (p. 729). A lifelong relationship with a spouse usually provides bonds of intimacy, independence, and belonging. The involuntary breaking of such bonds may have serious emotional and social implications for the older person. Feelings of grief, loneliness, and depression may result. The loss of companionship may be difficult to overcome, especially if social support from other sources is not readily available. As a result of widowhood, the role of spouse is lost, leaving some individuals with an identity problem. Opportunities for social interaction may also diminish once a partner is gone, creating a sense of isolation.

A role that may be assumed by spouses as they age is that of caregiver. The National Survey of Caregivers, conducted by the American Association of Retired

Persons in 1988, estimated that there are approximately 1.5 to 7 million caregivers nationwide. Of all the primary caregivers contacted, 51% were 50 years or older, and 77% were female (daughter or wife). The time dedicated to caregiving varies, but 10% of those contacted reported constant care, providing help in activities of daily living such as walking, dressing, bathing, toileting and feeding. As the disability or illness progresses, caregiving becomes more demanding, causing increased levels of stress.

Although the role of caring for a loved one may be fulfilling to an individual, it is impossible to ignore the potential problems associated with it. Such problems range from issues directly related to the illness or disability to emotional reactions displayed by care-receivers. Many studies report "burnout," a behavioral manifestation of stress. In a manual for caregivers developed by the Pennsylvania Department of Aging (undated), burnout is described as having three components. The first is emotional exhaustion, which results from a sense of energy depletion. The second, depersonalization, is associated with negative feelings toward the care-receiver. Lastly, reduced personal accomplishments stem from the feeling of total immersion in the caregiving role, leaving no time or energy to invest in anything else. Burnout may be hazardous to mental and physical health, and it may eventually have a negative impact on the caregiver/care-receiver relationship.

A conceptual model developed by Pearlin, Mullan, Semple, and Skaff (1990) offers a comprehensive picture of the stress process involved in caregiving. It is composed of four parts: (a) the background and context of stress, (b) primary and secondary stressors, (c) the mediators of stress, and (d) the outcomes or manifestations of stress. Factors under the background or context dimension are:

1. Socio-economic status characteristics, which may explain access to resources or additional sources of stress in one's life.
2. Caregiving history, which includes issues such as history of the problem requiring caregiving, length of caregiving, caregiver/care-receiver past relationship.
3. Family and network composition, which will determine amount of social, emotional and instrumental support available to the caregiver.
4. Program availability, which determines what types of resources, such as information or program, can be accessed by the caregiver.

The types of stressors identified by Pearlin and his associates are grouped into three subgroups: (a) primary stressors, (b) secondary role stressors, and (c) secondary intrapsychic strains. Primary stressors are related to objective indicators (such as behavioral characteristics and dependency level) and subjective indicators (such as overload and relational deprivation). Secondary role strains are conflicts that arise from the time and energy demands placed on the caregiver. They range from family conflicts, to job conflict, to economic problems and reduction of social life. Secondary intrapsychic strains relate to emotional factors such as self-esteem, competence, and identity. Also associated with intrapsychic stressors is role captivity, an interesting concept which refers to a sense of being captive, seeing no alternative, no choice but to engage in such role, a feeling which may result in depression (Pearlin, 1975).

The principal mediators of stress include coping skills and social support. These mediators are believed to limit the proliferation of secondary stressors described earlier, thus buffering outcomes.

According to Pearlin and associates (1990), coping has three functions: (a) management of situation causing stress, (b) management of the meaning of the situation, and (c) management of stress symptoms that result from the situation. Social support is an important resource that may mediate the negative consequences of stressing situations. Caregivers need to vent their feelings, and they also need respite from the demands of their role. Oftentimes, friends and relatives become more distant when the situation leading to caregiving intensifies; this reaction may leave the caregiver with an enormous sense of isolation and abandonment.

The outcomes listed in Pearlin's model are: (a) depression, (b) anxiety, (c) irascibility, (d) cognitive disturbance, (e) physical health, and (f) yielding of role. Another emotional outcome found in the literature is a sense of guilt. The constant stress may take its toll, caregivers may become impatient and resent the care-receiver. Self-blame may follow, and with it a sense of personal failure, which is associated with depression and helplessness.

The role of caregiving is depicted as rather problematic above. Once again, it is necessary to stress that feelings of self-worth and identity may also be attached to this relationship. Some caregivers may derive pleasure from knowing that they are providing a meaningful service to a loved one and see their role almost as a mission. In order to facilitate the adjustment to this role, there are several services that need to be provided to older adults.

In the American Association of Retired Persons' survey of caregivers (1988), the three most important types of assistance indicated were: (a) information about developments in medicine and health care, (b) help in dealing with bureaucracies to obtain services, and (c) updates on federal and state legislation affecting their situation. Secondary needs were (a) someone to talk to when overburdened, (b) someone with whom to share coping strategies, and (c) free time for vacation.

From these responses, we may conclude that three major sources of help are needed. The first relates to information regarding what services are available and how to access them. Many individuals are not aware of their rights as senior citizens. Information and referral is available through the local Area Agency on Aging. Another good provider of free information is the American Association of Retired Persons. Publications and audiovisuals may be obtained from these sources. Also, experts on specific topics such as Medicare benefits or in-home services may be asked to deliver informative workshops for those interested in the topics.

The second area of need is that of social support. In this area, the formation of support groups, in which caregivers get together to share their experiences and exchange knowledge, may be very effective in diminishing the feeling of isolation.

Finally the need for respite seems to be clear. Time away from the stresses of caregiving is important not only for the mental health of the caregiver, but also for the quality of the relationship. Placing the care-receiver temporarily in a respite program to give the caregiver the opportunity to take a vacation or simply relax for a while is an option. Another option is to seek a day program, such as adult day care, which keeps the person in need of care for part of the day, allowing the caregiver time to enjoy some normalcy.

As the American population grows older, and caregiving needs increase, so will the need for creative community agencies to assume part of the care for seniors with more severe functional impairments. Such programs may also be called to provide supportive services to caregivers, such as seminar and discussion groups. Recreation professionals may be responsible not only for providing meaningful activities to the care recipient, but also for engaging in leisure education for the caregiver, who oftentimes complains of a "leisureless" life.

The variety of community-based services for the elderly can be confusing and overwhelming. However, they are needed if people are to remain in the community for as long as possible. The leisure service provider has an important role in the range of services. If older individuals are to continue to grow and prosper, it is important they are aware of and use all available programs. At the least, individuals in the leisure field need to be aware of the multitude of programs and services and be able to function in an information and referral role. They must be able to identify needed services and refer their participants to them. In some cases it may be necessary to directly provide some of the services listed above.

For example, it may be appropriate to function as an employment clearinghouse or become involved in the recreation component of a day care program. In many cases it will be necessary to develop a transportation program to provide access to programs. Leisure service providers can best serve their constituents by adopting a broad perspective on service delivery. The leisure service provider working in the age-integrated community should be concerned with the whole person and not solely with the provision of recreation activities. Such a perspective will increase the likelihood of involvement in the entire network of aging services and not only with one small part of it.

Survival Skills

The development of programs to provide older individuals with survival skills needed to function in the community is a role leisure service providers may take. Such programs might include a section on defensive driving, negotiating the government bureaucracy in order to receive benefits to which one is entitled, cooking classes for individuals who either never cooked before or who need tips on cooking for one or two, banking skills such as manipulating a checking account, use of computers, driving classes for individuals who have never driven, accident prevention classes, and classes in recognizing and dealing with con artists. Other programs needed to assist individuals to not only survive, but to actually thrive in their community are needed. Such a broad perspective on programming is needed if people are to continue on the path to Ulyssean lifestyles in the later years.

Harbert and Ginsberg (1990) support the need for supportive services. They stated, "Agencies must sometimes provide supportive services to guarantee that older adults are able to use their programs. The primary service provided by an agency must often be supplemented with support services in order for the agency to respond effectively to the needs of older clients" (p. 203). Personnel involved in leisure services must be involved in this provision of supportive services.

THE COMMUNITY NEEDS ASSESSMENT

One way to determine whether a community has the supports necessary to assist in helping older individuals lead lives marked by growth is to complete a community audit. The National Association of Counties (undated b) indicated that "in order for older persons to 'age in place' communities must be responsive to the safety, physical accessibility, and quality of life concerns of older residents" (p. 1). They recommend the following guidelines be used to determine whether a community is a good place to grow old:

I. Community safety
    a. Are residents encouraged to develop a sense of ownership in their community through programs such as "neighborhood watches" to monitor the community and watch for questionable behavior? (Older individuals are at home more often than other people and may be ideal candidates for block captains.)
    b. Is a "gatekeeper" program in place in which mail carriers and meter readers identify older individuals who appear to be in need of assistance?
    c. Are police, fire, and emergency medical personnel provided instruction in identifying and meeting the needs of the elderly?
    d. Are parking lots, walkways, and bike trails well lit?
    e. Do homebound elderly have an emergency response system available to notify them in case of community emergency?

II. Improving mobility

    a. Are public buildings and other facilities accessible by use of elevators or ramps, as required by the Americans with Disabilities Act?
    b. Are buildings, streets, and signage marked with visible letters and symbols?
    c. Are there pedestrian pathways to connect parks, transportation, shops,

and buildings?

d. Do traffic lights provide sufficient time for crossing?

e. Are sidewalks kept free of debris, such as ice, snow, and leaves, and smooth of bumps and cracks?

f. Are the slower reflexes and poorer eyesight of older drivers taken into account when signs and signals are replaced and roadway repairs made?

g. Has consideration been given to increasing the number of left turn lanes and traffic signals with left turn indicators to reduce accidents?

h. Are older drivers provided safe driver classes?

i. Are public transportation services available, and do they provide a variety of routes to accommodate the needs of older users?

j. Are car pool programs, volunteer services, and home-delivery programs available to those needing hem?

III. Housing

a. Are home-sharing programs, in which two or more unrelated individuals (such as a college student and an older individual) can live together and share responsibility and costs, available?

b. Do zoning laws permit secondary units, such as ECHO cottages?

c. Are home repair and modification programs, allowing older people to stay safely in their homes, available? Do they include approved contractors and workers?

d. Do local lenders offer programs, such as home equity conversion programs, to allow the elderly to use the equity that is tied up in their homes?

IV. Services

a. Is there a clearly identified agency or organization in the community where the elderly can receive information, help, or a referral on aging issues?

b. Do the aging-related agencies and services exhibit coordination in referrals and services?

c. Are the needs of the elderly taken into account when programs, including transportation, recreation, and public safety, are developed?

d. Is a collaborative decision-making approach used by the public, voluntary, religious, private, civic, and business organizations, and older individuals in the community?

e. Are there special programs targeted at the frail, minority, and isolated elderly?

V. Sense of community

a. Are older individuals' talents used as part of volunteer programs giving opportunities to contribute to the community?
b. Do intergenerational programs provide opportunities for young and old residents to donate their time and talents to the community?
c. Are employment opportunities, including part-time and flexible-hour positions, available?
d. Do community centers and shopping malls offer outreach and community information to residents?
e. Is the development of small home-based businesses, allowing individuals to be employed at home, encouraged by local zoning practices?
f. Are there water fountains, benches, and restrooms that offer rest and rejuvenation in parks, shops, public buildings and supermarkets?

The results of the community audit can be used to target areas for improvement. Trained recreation professionals can take the lead in this process. The National Association of Counties recommends the following steps be taken:

1. Form a broad-based community coalition to solve identified problems.
2. Define a few high priority problems to work on.
3. Identify strategies and options for addressing the problems.
4. Negotiate agreements among key players in the community, including the government, businesses, churches, and voluntary organizations.
5. Implement and monitor the agreements.

The result of this process will be a community designed for Ulyssean living.

However, some elderly people are not able to find the quality of life they desire in their local communities. As a result, they may seek out special communities more amenable to their lifestyle. The next section of this chapter will examine this living option in greater detail.

AGE-SEGREGATED COMMUNITIES

According to Atchley (1991), retirement may be an opportunity to change living environment. In fact, 35% of older individuals stated they plan to move to another home after retirement (Vierck, 1990), and others choose to move into retirement communities with other individuals of their age. The selection of an age-segregated community is not a choice made by many older individuals. According to Streib (1993), individuals choosing retirement communities generally have higher levels of health, educational attainment, and economic status.

Regnier (1975) noted that the older individual's ability to control his or her own destiny in the open neighborhood is less than in the self-contained housing environment. With the losses of aging experienced by many individuals, movement into some type of congregate housing setting may help in retaining independence and control. Such housing units are often designed with older individuals in mind and incorporate many design features, such as handrails and grab bars, which foster independence and control. The move into a more supportive environment may be effective in alleviating many of the losses of old age.

Regardless of personal attitudes toward the appropriateness of retirement communities—old-age ghettos to some and Shangri-La to others—they are a housing alternative that merits consideration. This is especially so for individuals involved in the delivery of leisure services, since retirement communities are often viewed, and sold, as leisure villages.

Data related to retirement communities present a mixed picture. Jacobs (1974) described one he called Fun City. He paints a bleak picture of residents isolated from the rest of society, who felt trapped in a place providing few amenities and little hope for change. On the other hand, Hochschild presented Merrill Court, an apartment for older people, as an effective solution to a bad situation. This congregate living situation assisted in the formation of an effective social group. It is interesting to note that Hochschild observed that a major precipitator of group formation was the presence of a communal coffee pot and, thus, a leisure situation.

Gelfand (1988) provided an example of a successful retirement community, Leisure World in Laguna Hills, California. The community was developed "to provide security, quick accessibility to good health care, good nearby shopping, good transportation, excellent facilities for recreation, and adult education and additional activities to ensure freedom from boredom" (p. 183).

Clearly, recreation is a major factor for immigration to a retirement community. In fact, Gelfand stated, "Retirement communities appear to be growing in popularity, particularly because they offer security, recreation, good housing, and social opportunities with neighborhoods of a similar age" (p. 184).

The opportunities that retirement communities provide to participate in familiar activities and also develop new skills is important (Streib, 1993). Activities are close by and require limited effort to participate. Streib describes the "staggering" number of activity offerings in a community of 2,000 residents:

- social—potlucks, dance, movies, bridge, singles club;
- sports—golf, tennis, swimming, boating, shuffleboard;
- crafts and hobbies—ceramics, lapidary, quilting, stamp collecting;
- arts, music, and dramatics—art classes, concerts, choral groups;
- education—foreign language classes, investment groups, book review club;
- health and fitness—exercise groups, yoga, hiking clubs, Weight Watchers;
- self-governance—committees and groups related to running the community;
- religious—Bible study, religious groups, hymn singing;

- service and philanthropic—money-raising groups for various charities, good neighbor groups.

Clearly, this is a leisure-rich environment for individuals seeking an active lifestyle.

The age-segregated program is inherently neither good nor bad. It is what its residents and the staff make it. This is illustrated in an article by Mary Louise Williams (1972), a retired school teacher who moved into an age-segregated apartment building she calls "the center." Her first reactions to the center are best described by her calling it "Seniliput" where the residents "unlike the diminutive inhabitants of Gulliver's Isle . . . were senile, most of them seemed in their eighties or nineties" (p. 38).

She was unhappy living in an environment one of the other residents described as a snake pit, and the main activities appeared to be bingo and bridge. This was in contrast to the center brochure, which talked about meeting interesting people while participating in numerous activities, discussion groups, and enjoying the advantages of a nearby university and the cultural opportunities of a big city.

She envisioned herself attending plays, symphonies, and operas while growing spiritually, socially, and intellectually. She felt deceived and trapped without the finances to go elsewhere. Rather than giving in and giving up, Williams developed a philosophy of looking for ideas and beauty in her surroundings. She was able to find them, not only in nature, but also in her neighbors. She tells of one woman who started a poetry hour and another who was an author.

She also found salvation in the church, which sponsored the home, and interaction with individuals as part of a research group examining work such as Paul Tournier's "The Strong and The Weak," Carl Jung's "Modern Man in Search of a Soul," and "Becoming" by Gordon Allport. Later they read plays, with assistance from younger church members, such as "Our Town."

The center had changed for the author. The reasons for the change are complex, but she summed them up by stating, "If there is ever to be an ideal retirement center, the leadership, the people, and the program would of course need to be ideal." She goes on to state that a great deal of time and insight are needed to plan and direct activities, people need to be taught how to use their leisure time, and our image of older people must change.

These three components, trained leadership, an educated population, and a more positive image of aging and the elderly can turn any environment into one that is as conducive to Ulyssean living as the one described by Williams in the thought-provoking piece.

CONCLUSION

The vast majority of older individuals live in the community, and the variety of housing and service opportunities available in an increasing number of communities allows the elderly to remain active, contributing members who make contributions to these environments. As a result, they experience many opportunities for Ulyssean living.

Examination of the community in which an individual lives will make it possible to alter the environment in order to facilitate Ulyssean living. Just as earlier chapters discussed designing the micro environment to be prosthetic rather than penalizing, this chapter provided a method of making the macroenvironment more amenable to growth and development by removing obstacles to independence and freedom.

Individuals whose needs are not being met in their local communities may decide to leave and migrate to a retirement community. These facilities are often leisure-rich environments where individuals can select from an array of opportunities for engagement. In some ways, these communities may be models for Ulyssean living. However, they may also be stagnant environments without the tensions and dynamics in age-integrated communities. The option of living solely with other older individuals will therefore be attractive to some and abhorrent to others.

Although there is a clear need to assist in developing prosthetic communities, we must be cautious and not overestimate the need for special services. This may be especially true in the leisure domain. Kelly and Godbey (1992) discussed the concept of leisure in ordinary life. This concept provides an excellent description of leisure in the lives of most older people. They wrote, "Most leisure in ordinary life is woven in the process of the daily round, neither special nor clearly differentiated . . . it is 'ordinary leisure' that consumes the most time for most people (p. 195).

The implication of ordinary leisure is that many older individuals are able to negotiate their own path to Ulyssean living and need little or no assistance. Our role is to know whether help is needed and how to give it when it is.

References

Abra, J. (1989). Changes in creativity with age: Data, explanations and further predictions. *International Journal of Aging & Human Development,* 28,105–126.

Administration on Aging (undated). *Decisions about retirement living.* Washington, DC: Department of Health and Human Services.

Administration on Aging (1997). *Profiles of older Americans: 1997.* Washington, DC: Administration on Aging.

Administration on Aging (1997b). Projected health conditions among the elderly. Washington DC: Department of Health and Human Services. *www.aoa.dhha.gov/aoa/stats/aging21/health.htm* (March 1999).

Aldana, S. & Stone, W. (1991). Changing physical activity preferences of American adults. *Journal of Physical Education, Recreation and Dance,* April, 67–71, 76.

Allen, K. & Chin-Sang, V. (1990). A lifetime of work: The context and meanings of leisure for aging black women. *The Gerontologist, 30,* 734–740.

Allison, M. (1988). Breaking boundaries and barriers: Future directions in cross-cultural research. *Leisure Sciences, 10,* 247–259.

Allison, M. T. & Geiger, G. W. (1993). Nature of leisure activities among the Chinese American elderly. *Leisure Sciences, 15,* 309–319.

Allport, G. W. (1961). *Pattern and growth in personality.* New York: Holt, Reinhart & Winston.

Altergott, K. (1988). Social action and interaction in later life: Aging in the United States. In K. Altergott (ed.), *Daily life in later life: Comparative perspectives.* Newbury Park: Sage, 117-146.

Alzheimer's Association (1995). Comparison of general characteristics of Alzheimer's disease and vascular dementia. Chicago, IL: The Alzheimer's Association.

Alzheimer's Association (1998a). Statistics/prevalence. Chicago, IL: The Alzheimer's Association. *www.alz.org/facts/rtstats.htm* (March 1999).

Alzheimer's Association (1998b). What are the warning signs? Chicago, IL: The Alzheimer's Association. *www.alz.org/facts/rtwrngsns.htm* (March 1999).

Alzheimer's.com (1998). Alzheimer's disease terminology. *www.alzheimers.com/L3TABLES/L3T101.32.HTM* (March 1999).

American Association of Retired Persons (1985). *Aging and vision: Making the most of impaired vision.* Washington, DC: American Association of Retired Persons.

American Association of Retired Persons (1986). *Coping and caring: Living with Alzheimer's disease.* Washington, DC: American Association of Retired Persons.

American Association of Retired Persons (1988). *National survey of caregivers.* Washington, DC: American Association of Refired Persons.

American Association of Retired Persons (1990). *Programming techniques: A guide for community crime prevention program planning.* Washington, DC: American Association of Retired Persons.

American Museum of Natural History (1998). Human aging: Genetic factors. *www.amnh.org/enews/aging/a5.html* (March 1999).

American Psychiatric Association (1994) *Diagnostic and statistical manual of mental disorders, fourth edition.* Washington, DC: American Psychiatric Association.

Antonucci, T. C. (1990). Social supports and social relationships. In R. H. Binstock & L. K. George (eds.), *Handbook of aging and the social sciences.* San Diego: Academic Press.

Aronson, M. (1988). *Understanding Alzheimer's disease.* New York: Charles Scribner's Sons.

Atchley, R. C. (1977). *Social forces in later life* (2nd ed.). Belmont, CA: Wadsworth.

Atchley, R. C. (1991). *Social forces in later life* (6th ed.). Belmont, CA: Wadsworth.

Baas, J. M., Ewert, A., & Chavez, D. J. (1993). Influence of ethnicity on recreation and natural environment use patterns: Managing recreation sites for ethnic and social diversity. *Environmental Management, 17,* 523–526.

Backman, K., Backman, S., & Silverberg, K. (1999) An investigation into the psychographics of senior nature-based travelers. In press. *Tourism Recreation Research Journal.*

Backman, L., Mantayla, T., & Herlitz, A. (1990). The optimization of episodic remembering in old age. In P. B. Baltes & M. M. Baltes (eds.), *Successful aging: Perspectives from the behavioral sciences.* New York: Cambridge University Press, 118–163.

Baldelli, M. V., Pirani, A., Motta, M., Abati, E., Mariani, E., & Manzi, V. (1993). Effects of reality orientation therapy on elderly patients in the community. *Archives in Gerontology and Geriatrics, 17,* 211–218.

Baltes, M. M., Wahl, H., & Reichart, M. (1991). Successful aging in long-term care institutions. In K. W. Schaie & M. P. Lawton (eds.), *Annual review of gerontology and geriatrics,* Vol. 11. New York: Springer, 311–337.

Baltes, P. B. & Baltes, M. M. (1990). Selective optimization with compensation. In P. B. Baltes & M. M. Baltes (eds.), *Successful aging: Perspectives from the behavioral sciences.* New York: Cambridge University Press, 1–34.

Baltes, P. B., Smith, J., & Staudinger, U. M. (1991) Women and successful aging. In *Nebraska Symposium on Motivation, Vol. 39,* 123–162. University of Nebraska, Lincoln NE.

Bandura, A. (1982). Self-efficacy: Toward a unifying theory of behavioral change. *Psychological Review,* 84, 191–215.

Banzinger, G. & Roush, S. (1983). Nursing homes for the birds: A control relevant intervention with bird feeders. *The Gerontologist, 23,* 527–531.

Barbara Krueger & Associates (1996). Aging in place. Delmar CA: Barbara Krueger & Associates. *www.seniorresource.com/ageinpl.htm* (March 1999).

Barrett, C. (1989). The concept of leisure: Idea and ideal. Int. Winnifrith & C. Barrett (eds.), *Philosophy of leisure.* New York: St. Martin's Press.

Bartol, M. (1979). Dialogue with dementia: Nonverbal communication in patients with Alzheimer's disease. *Journal of Gerontological Nursing, 5,* 21.

Beard, B. B. (1991). In B. B. Beard, N. Wilson, & A. Wilson (eds.), *Centenarians, the new generation.* New York: Greenwood Press.

Beard, G. (1974). *Legal responsibility in old age.* New York: Russell Sage Foundation.

Beck, S. H., & Pagej, W. (1988). Involvement in activities and the psychological well-being of retired men. *Activities, Adaptation & Aging, 11,* 31–47.

Becker, M. & Yost, B. (1991). *1990 recreation participation survey: Final report.* Harrisburg, PA: Center for Survey Research, Penn State Harrisburg.

Bengston, V.L., Burgess, E.O., & Parrott, T.M. (1997). Theory, explanation, and a third generation of theoretical development in social gerontology. *Journal of Gerontology: Social Sciences, 52B,* S72-S88.

Bialeschki, D. & Henderson, K. (1991). The provision of leisure services from a feminist perspective. *World Leisure and Recreation, 33* (3), 30–33.

Bialeschki, D. & Walbert, K. (1998). "You have to have some fun to go along with your work": The interplay of race, class, gender and leisure in the industrial new South. *Journal of Leisure Research,* 30(1). 79-100.

Bickson, T. A. & Goodchilds, J. D. (1989). Experiencing the retirement transition: Managerial and professional men before and after. In S. Spacapan and S. Oskamp (eds.), *The social psychology of aging.* Newbury Park: Sage, 81–108.

Birchenall, J. M. & Streight, M. E. (1993). *Care of the older adult* (3rd ed.). Philadelphia: J. B. Lippincott.

Birren, J. E. & Fisher, L. M. (1991). Aging and slowing of behavior: Consequences for cognition and survival. *Nebraska Symposium on Motivation Vol. 39,* 1–37. University of Nebraska, Lincoln, NE.

Blazey, M. (1987). The differences between participants and nonparticipants in a senior travel program. *Journal of Travel Research, 26,* 7–12.

Bocksnick, J. G. & Hall, B. L. (1994). Recreation activity programming for the institutionalized older adult. *Activities, Adaptation & Aging, 19* (1), 1–25.

Botwinick, J. (1967). *Cognitive processes in maturity and old age.* New York: Springer.

Bowlby, G. (1993). *Therapeutic activities with persons disabled by Alzheimer's disease and related disorders.* Gaithersburg, MD: Aspen Publishers.

Bowles, J. T. (1998). The evolution of aging: A new approach to an old problem of biology. *Medical Hypotheses, 51,* 179–221.

Boyd, R. & Tedrick, T. (1994). Leisure in the lives of older African American females. Unpublished manuscript.

Braus, P. (1995). Vision in an aging America. *American Demographics Magazine,* June.

Breystpraak, L. M. (1984). The development of self in later life. Boston: Little Brown.

Brock, D. B., Guralink, J. M., & Brody, J. A. (1990). Demography and epiden-dology of aging in the United States. In E. L. Schneider & J. W. Rowe (eds.), *Handbook of the biology of aging.* San Diego: Academic Press, 3–23.

Brooks-Lambing, M. C. (1972). Leisure time pursuits among retired blacks by social status. *The Gerontologist, 12,* 363–367.

Brown, M. & Tedrick, T. (1993). Outdoor leisure involvements of older black Americans: An exploration of ethnicity and marginality. *Activities, Adaptation & Aging, 17* (3), 55–65.

Burch, W. R. & Hamilton-Smith, E. (1991). Mapping a new frontier: Identifying, measuring, and valuing social cohesion benefits related to nonwork opportunities and activities. In B. L. Driver, P. J. Brown. & G. L. Peterson (eds.), *Benefits of leisure.* State College, PA: Venture, 369–382.

Burdge, R. (1969). Levels of occupational prestige and leisure activity. *Journal of Leisure Research, 1,* 262–274.

Burdman, G. M. (1986). *Healthful aging.* Englewood Cliffs, NJ: Prentice Hall.

burlingame, j., & Skalko, T. K. (1997). *Glossary for therapists.* Ravensdale, WA: Idyll Arbor.

Campanelli, L. C. (1990). Theories of aging. In C. B. Lewis (ed.), *Aging: The health care challenge* (2nd ed.). Philadelphia: F. A. Davis, 7–21.

Carr, D. & Williams, D. (1993). Understanding the role of ethnicity in outdoor recreation experiences. *Journal of Leisure Research, 25,* 22–38.

Carruthers, C., Sneegas, J. J., & Ashton-Shaeffer, C. (1986). *Therapeutic recreation: Guidelines for activity services in long-term care.* Champaign, IL: Office of Recreation and Park Resources, University of Illinois.

Caudron, S. (1997) Boomers rock the system. *Workforce, 76* (12),42.

Chambre, S. M. (1993). Volunteerism by elders: Past trends and future prospects. *The Gerontologist, 33,* 221–228.

Charness, N. & Bosman, E. A. (1990). Human factors and design for older adults. In J. E. Birren & K. W. Schaie (eds.), *The handbook of the psychology of aging* (3rd ed.). San Diego: Academic Press, 446–463.

Cheek, N., Field, D., & Burdge, R. (1976). *Leisure and recreation places.* Ann Arbor: Science Publishers.

Cheng, E. (1978). *The elder Chinese.* San Diego: Center for Aging, San Diego University.

CIGNA HealthCare of Colorado (1995). Aging, exercise, and depression: Separating myths from realities. Article provided by The Medical Reporter. *www.ihr.com/medrept/articles/agingexr.html* (March 1999).

Clarke, N. (1956). The use of leisure and its relation to level of occupational prestige. *American Sociological Review, 21,* 301–307.

Cohen, G. D. (1990). Psychopathology and mental health in the mature and elderly adult. In J. E. Birren & K. W. Schaie (eds.), *Handbook of the psychology of aging.* San Diego: Academic Press, 359–371.

Cole, N. (1981). Bias in testing. *American Psychologist, 36,* 1067–1077.

Columbia/HCA (undated). Exploring the "aging process." *www.columbia.net/consumer/datafile/boomexpl.html* (March 1999).

Comfort, A. (1976). *A good age.* New York: Crown.

Cook, A. (1983). *Contemporary perspectives on adult development and aging.* New York: MacMillan.

Cowgill. D. O. (1974). Aging and modernization: A revision of the theory. In J. F. Gubrium (ed.), *Later life: Communities and environmental policy.* Springfield, IL: C. C. Thomas, 123-246.

Cox, H. G. (1993). Later life: *The realities of aging.* Englewood Cliffs, NJ: Prentice Hall.

Cox, H. G. (1998) Roles for the aged individual in post-industrial societies. In H. Cox (ed.), *Aging (12th ed.)* Guilford, CT: Dushkin/McGraw Hill

Crandall, R. C. (1980). *Gerontology: A behavioral science approach.* Reading, MA: Addison-Wesley.

Crohan, S. & Antonucci, T. (1989). Friends as a source of social support in old age. In R. Adams & R. Blieszner (eds.), *Older adult friendship: Structure and process.* Newbury Park: Sage, 129–146.

Csikszentimihalyi, M. (1975). *Beyond boredom and anxiety.* San Francisco: Jossey Bass.

Csikszentmihalyi, M. (1990). *Flow: The psychology of optimal experience.* New York: Harper and Row.

Csikszentmihalyi, M. & Kleiber, D. (1991). Leisure and self-actualization. In B. L. Driver, P. J. Brown, & G. L. Peterson (eds.), *Benefits of leisure.* State College, PA: Venture, 91-102.

Cumming, E. & Henry, W. E. (1961). *Growing old: The process of disengagement.* New York: Basic Books.

Cutler, S. J. & Danigelis, N. L. (1993). Organized contexts of activity. In J. R. Kelly (ed.), *Activity and aging: Staying involved in later life.* Newbury Park: Sage, 146–163.

Dangott, L. R. & Kalish, R. A. (1979). *A time to enjoy: The pleasures of aging.* Englewood Cliffs, NJ: Prentice Hall.

Dannifer, D. (1988). What's in a name? An account of the neglect of variability in the study of aging. In J.E. Birren, and V.L. Bengston (Eds.) *Emergent theories of aging,* (pp. 356-384). New York: Springer.

Davison, G. & Neale, J. (1986). *Abnormal psychology: An experimental clinical approach.* New York: John Wiley.

Deem, R. (1986). *All work and no play? The sociology of women and leisure.* Milton Keynes, England: Open University Press.

deGrazia, S. (1962). *Of time, work and leisure.* New York: Twentieth Century Fund.

Dennis, W. (1966). Creative productivity between the ages of 20 and 80 years. *Journal of Gerontology, 21,* 1–8.

Dinsmoor, R. (1993). Strength training after sixty. *Harvard Health Letter,* July, 68.

Dorsey, V. L. (1993). Games show positive side to growing old, athletes say. *USA Today,* June 11, 12C.

Driver, B. L., Tinsley, H. E. A., & Manfredo, M. J. (1991). The Paragraphs about Leisure and Recreation Experiences Preference Scales: Results from two inventories designed to assess the breadth of the perceived psychological benefits of leisure. In B. L. Driver, P. J. Brown, & G. L. Peterson (eds.), *Benefits of leisure.* State College, PA: Venture Press, 263–286.

Dunkle, R. E. & Kart, C. S. (1990). Long-term care. In K. F. Ferraro (ed.), *Gerontology: Perspectives and issues.* New York: Springer, 225–243.

Dwyer, J. & Gobster, P. (1992). Recreation opportunity and cultural diversity. *Parks and Recreation,* September, 22, 24, 25, 27, 28, 30, 33, 128.

Dwyer, J. & Hutchinson, R. (1990). Outdoor recreation participation and preferences for black and white Chicago households. In J. Vining (ed.), *Social science and natural resource recreation management.* Boulder, CO: Westview Press, 49–67.

Dychtwald, K. & Flower, J. (1989). *Age Wave: The challenges and opportunities of an aging America.* Los Angeles: Jeremy P. Tarcher.

Ebersole, P. & Hess, P. (1990). *Toward healthy aging: Human needs and nursing response.* 3rd Edition. St. Louis: C. V. Mosby.

Ebersole, P. & Hess, P. (1998). *Toward healthy aging: Human needs and nursing response.* 5th Edition. St. Louis: C. V. Mosby.

Eden Alternative (1999) Ten principles: The heart of the Eden Alternative. Sherburne, NY: The Eden Alternative. *www.edenalt.com/about_eden/tenprinciples.htm* (March 1999).

Elder, G.H., Jr. (1985). *Life course dynamics: Trajectories and transitions, 1968-1980.* New York: Siminar Press.

Ellis, M. (1973). *Why people play.* Englewood Cliffs, NJ: Prentice Hall.

Erikson, E. H. (1950). *Childhood and society.* New York: Norton.

Ewert, A., Chavez, D. J., & Magill, A. W. (1993). *Culture, conflict, and the wildlifeurban interface.* Boulder, CO: Westview Press.

Facts of Life (1998) Getting old: A lot of it is in your head. Washington, DC: Center for the Advancement of Health.

Feil, N. (1993). *The validation breakthrough.* Baltimore: Health Professions Press.

Fergunson, K. (1989). Qualitative research with older adults. In E. Thomas (ed.), *Adulthood and aging: The human science approach.* Albany, NY: State University of New York.

Ferri, F. F. & Fretwell, M. D. (1992). *Practical guide to the care of the geriatric patient.* St. Louis: Mosby.

Floyd, M. & Gramann, J. (1993). Effects of acculturation and structural assimilation in resource-based recreation: The case of Mexican Americans. *Journal of Leisure Research, 25.* 6-21.

Floyd, M., Shinew, K., McGuire, F., & Noe, F. (1994). Race, class and leisure activity preferences: Marginality and ethnicity revisited. *Journal of Leisure Research, 26,* 158–173.

Floyd, M. (1998). Getting beyond marginality and ethnicity: The challenge for race and ethnic studies in leisure research. *Journal of Leisure Research.* 30(1), 3-22.

Fried, L. P., Freedman, M., Endres, T. E., & Wasik, B. (1997). Building communities that promote successful aging. *Western Journal of Medicine, 167,* 216–219.

Fried, S., Van Booven, D., & MacQuarrie, C. (1993). *Older adulthood: Learning activities for understanding aging.* Baltimore: Health Professions Press.

Froelicher, V. F. & Froelicher, E. S. (1991). Cardiovascular benefits of physical activity. In B. L. Driver, P. J. Brown, & G. L. Peterson (eds.), *Benefits of leisure.* State College, PA: Venture Press, 59–72.

Gagnon, D. (1996) A review of reality orientation (RO), validation therapy (VT), and reminiscence therapy (RT) with the Alzheimer's client. *Physical and Occupational Therapy in Geriatrics, 14* (2), 61–77.

Gallup, G. (1986). T.V. remains our favorite pastime, but other diversions grow. *The Gallup Report,* May (248), 7–9.

Garinger, K. (1998). Reality orientation in institutions for the elderly: The perspective from interactional linguistics. *Journal of Aging Studies, 12,* 39–56.

Gatz, M., Kasl-Godley, J. E. & Karel, M. J. (1996). Aging and mental disorders. In J. E. Birren & K. W. Schaie (eds.), *Handbook of the psychology of aging* (4th ed.) San Diego: Academic Press.

Gelfand, D. E. (1988). *The aging network: Programs and services* (3rd ed.). New York: Springer.

George, L. K. (1996). Missing links: The case for a social psychology of the life course. *The Gerontologist, 36,* 248-255.

George, L. K. (1990). Social structure, social processes, and social-psychological states. In R. H. Binstock & L. K. George (eds.), *Handbook of aging and the social sciences.* San Diego: Academic Press, 186–204.

Goldberg, A. & Hagberg, J. M. (1990). Physical exercise in the elderly. In E. L. Schneider & J. W. Rowe (eds.), *Handbook of the biology of aging.* San Diego: Academic Press.

Gordon, C. & Gaitz, C. (1976). Leisure and lives: Expressivity across the life span. In R. Binstock & E. Shanas (eds.), *Handbook of aging and the social sciences.* New York: Van Nostrand Reinhold.

Gottlieb, D. (1957). The neighborhood tavern and the cocktail lounge: A study of class differences. *American Journal of Sociology, 62,* 559–562.

Gramann, J., Floyd, M., & Saenz, R. (1993). Outdoor recreation and Mexican American ethnicity: A benefits perspective. In A. Ewert, D. Chavez, & A. Magill (eds.), *Culture conflict and communication: The wildland-urban interface.* Boulder, CO: Westview Press, 69–84.

Greenblatt, F. S. (1988). *Therapeutic recreation for long-term care facilities.* New York: Human Sciences Press.

Haberkost, M., Dellman-Jenkins, M., & Bennett, J. M. (1996). Importance of quality recreation activities for older adults residing in nursing homes: Considerations for gerontologists. *Educational Gerontology, 22,* 735–745.

Haggard, L. M. & Williams, D. R. (1991). Self-identity benefits of leisure activities. In B. L. Driver, P. J. Brown, & G. L. Peterson (eds.), *Benefits of leisure.* State College, PA: Venture Press, 103–119.

Haight, B. K. (1991). Psychological illness in aging. In E. M. Baines (ed.), *Perspectives on gerontological nursing.* Newbury Park: Sage, 296–322.

Harbert, A. S. & Ginsberg, L. H. (1990). *Human services for older adults: Concepts and skills* (2nd ed.). Columbia, SC: University of South Carolina Press.

Harris, C. (1978). *Fact book on aging.* Washington, DC: National Council on Aging.

Harris, J. (1984). Methods of improving memory. In B. A. Wilson & N. Moffat (eds.), *Clinical management of memory problems.* Rockville, Maryland: Aspen, 46–62.

Havighurst, R. J. (1961). The nature and value of meaningful free time activities. In R. W. Kleemier (ed.), *Aging and leisure.* New York: Oxford University Press, 309–344.

Havighurst, R. J. & Albrecht, R. (1953). *Older people.* New York: Longmans Green.

Hawes, D. (1988). Travel-related lifestyle profiles of older women. *Journal of Travel Research, 27,* 22–32.

Hayflick, L. (1985). *The aging process: Current theories.* New York: A. R. Liss.

HealthAnswers (1997a). Aging changes in the bones, muscles, and joints. Applied Medical Infomatics Inc. and Orbis-AHCN, L.L.C. *www.healthanswers.com/database/ami/converted/004015.html* (March 1999).

HealthAnswers (1997b). Aging changes in the heart and blood vessels. Applied Medical Infomatics Inc. and Orbis-AHCN, L.L.C. *www.healthanswers.com/database/ami/converted/004006.html* (March 1999).

HealthAnswers (1997c). Aging changes in the senses. Applied Medical Infomatics Inc. and Orbis-AHCN, L.L.C. *www.healthanswers.com/database/ami/converted/004013.html* (March 1999)

Heckheimer, E. F. (1989). *Health promotion of the elderly in the community.* Philadelphia: W. B. Saunders.

Helender, J. (1978). The richness and poorness of being old in Sweden. Paper presented at a seminar on facing an aging society.

Hellen, C. (1993). Alzheimer's disease: Finding purposeful activities. The Council Close-up: Illinois Council on long-term care. *www.nursinghome.org/closeup/cupdocument/cu023.htm* (March 1999).

Henderson, K. (1990a). An oral history perspective on the containers in which American farm women experience leisure. *Leisure Studies, 9* (2), 27–38.

Henderson, K. (1990b). The meaning of leisure for women: An integrative review of the research. *Journal of Leisure Research, 22,* 228–243.

Henderson, K. (1991). The contribution of feminism to an understanding of leisure constraints. *Journal of Leisure Research, 23,* 363–377.

Henderson, K. (1992). Broadening an understanding of the gendered meanings of leisure for women. Paper presented at the NRPA Leisure Research Symposium, Cincinnati, Ohio.

Henderson, K., Bialeschki, D., Shaw, S., & Freysinger, V. (1989). *A leisure of one's own: A feminist perspective on women's leisure.* State College, PA: Venture Publishing.

Henderson, K. & Rannells, J. (1988). Farm women and the meaning of work and leisure: An oral history perspective. *Leisure Sciences, 10,* 41–50.

Hess, B. (1974). Stereotypes of the aged. *Journal of Communications, 24,* 76–85.

Hochschild, A. R. (1973). *The unexpected community.* Englewood Cliffs, NJ: Prentice Hall.

Hochschild, A. R. (1989). *The second shift: Working parents and the revolution at home.* New York: Viking.

Hooyman, N. R. & Kiyak, N. R. (1993). *Social gerontology: A multidisciplinary perspective* (3rd ed.) Boston: Allyn and Bacon.

Horna, J. (1991). The family and leisure domains: Women's involvement and perceptions. *World Leisure and Recreation, 33* (3), 11–14.

Howard, D. V. (1992). Implicit memory: An expanding picture of cognitive aging. In K. W. Schaie & M. P. Lawton (eds.). *Annual review of gerontology and geriatrics,* Vol. 11. New York: Springer, 1–22.

Howe, D. A. (1992). Creating vital communities: Planning for our aging society. *Planning Commissioners Journal,* 7 (Nov/Dec), 1.

Hultsch, D. F. & Dixon, R. A. (1990). Learning and memory in aging. In J. E. Birren & K. W. Schaie (eds.), *Handbook of the psychology of aging.* San Diego: Academic Press, 258–274.

Iso-Ahola, S. (1980). *Social psychological perspectives on leisure and recreation.* Springfield, IL: Charles C. Thomas.

Iso-Ahola, S. E. (1989). Motivation for leisure. In E. L. Jackson & T. L. Burton (eds.), *Understanding leisure and recreation: Mapping the past, charting the future.* State College, PA: Venture, 247–279.

Jackson, J. J. (1972). Black women in a racist society. In C. Willie, B. Krouer, & B. Brown (eds.), *Racism and mental health.* Pittsburgh, PA: University of Pittsburgh Press, 185–268.

Jackson, M., Kolody, B., & Wood, J. (1982). To be old and black: The case for double jeopardy on income and health. In R. Manuel (ed.), *Minority aging: Social and social psychological issues.* Westport, CT: Greenwood Press, 77–82.

Jacobs, J. (1974). *Older persons and retirement communities.* Springfield, IL: C. C. Thomas.

Johnson, C., Bowker, J., English, D., & Worthen, D. (1998). Wildland recreation in the rural South: An examination of marginality and ethnicity theory. *Journal of Leisure Research 30(1).* 101-120.

Johnson, F. B., Marciniak, R., & Guarente, L. (1998). Telomeres, the nucleolus and aging. *Current Opinion in Cell Biology, 10,* 332–338.

Juniu, S. (1997). *Effects of ethnicity on leisure behavior and its meaning in the life of a selected group of South American immigrants.* Unpublished doctoral dissertation, Temple University, Philadelphia, PA.

Kalish, R. A. (1975). *Late adulthood: Perspectives on human development.* Monterey, CA: Brooks Cole.

Kalish, R. A. (1979). The new ageism and the failure model: A new polemic. *The Gerontologist, 19,* 398–402.

Kalish, R. A. (1982). *Late adulthood: Perspectives on human development* (2nd ed.). Monterey, CA: Brooks Cole.

Kamptner, N. L. (1989). Personal possessions and their meaning in old age. In S. Spacapan & S. Oskamp (eds.), *The social psychology of aging.* Newbury Park: Sage, 165–196.

Kaplan, M. (1975). *Leisure: Theory and policy.* New York: John Wiley.

Kaplan, M. (1979). *Leisure: Lifestyle and lifespan perspectives for gerontology.* Philadelphia: W. B. Saunders.

Kastenbaum, R. (1987). Prevention of age-related problems. In L. L. Carstensen & B. A. Edelstein (eds.), *Handbook of clinical gerontology.* New York: Pergammon, 322–334.

Kausler, D. H. (1990). Motivation, human aging, and cognitive performance. In J. E. Birren & K. W. Schaie (eds.), *Handbook of the psychology of aging* (3rd ed.). San Diego: Academic Press, 171–182.

Kelly, J. R. (undated). Life-in-between: Continuity and construction. Unpublished paper.

Kelly, J. R. (1982). *Leisure.* Englewood Cliffs, NJ: Prentice Hall.

Kelly, J. R. (1987a). *Freedom to be: A new sociology of leisure.* New York: MacMillan.

Kelly, J. R. (1987). *Peoria winter.* Lexington, MA: Lexington Books.

Kelly, J. R. (1991). Sociological perspectives on recreation benefits. In B. L. Driver, P. J. Brown, & G. L. Peterson (eds.), *Benefits of leisure.* State College, PA: Venture, 419–422.

Kelly, J. R. (1996). *Leisure.* Englewood Cliffs, NJ: Prentice Hall.

Kelly, J. R. & Godbey, G. (1992). *The sociology of leisure.* State College, PA: Venture.

Kelly, J. R. & Westcott, G. (1991). Ordinary retirement: Commonalities and continuity. *International Journal of Aging and Human Development, 32,* 81–89.

Kliegl, R. & Baltes, P. (1987). Theory-guided analysis of mechanisms of development and aging through testing the limits and research on expertise. In C. Schooler & K. W. Schaie (eds.), *Cognitive functioning and social structure over the life course.* Norwood, NJ: Ablex.

Kogan, N. (1990). Personality and aging. In J. E. Birren & K. W. Schaie (eds.), *Handbook of the psychology of aging.* San Diego: Academic Press, 330–346.

Lakatta, E. G. (1990). Heart and circulation. In E. L. Schneider & J. W. Rowe (eds.), *Handbook of the biology of aging.* San Diego: Academic Press, 181–216.

Langer, E. & Rodin, J. (1976). The effects of choice and enhanced personal responsibility for aged: A field experiment in an institutional setting. *Journal of Personality and Social Psychology, 34,* 191–198.

Lawton, M. P. (1989). Environmental proactivity and affect in older people. In S. Spacapan & S. Oskamp (eds.), *The social psychology of aging.* Newbury Park: Sage.

Lawton, M. P. (1993). Meanings of activity. In J. R. Kelly (ed.), *Activity and aging: Staying involved in later life.* Newbury Park: Sage, 25–41.

Lehman, H. C. (1953). *Age and achievement.* Princeton: Princeton University Press.

Leitner, M. & Leitner, S. (1985). *Leisure in later years: A source book for the provision of recreational services for elders.* New York: Haworth.

Lemon, B. W., Bengston, V. L., & Peterson, J. A. (1972). An exploration of the activity theory of aging: Activity types and life satisfaction among inmovers to a retirement community. *Journal of Gerontology, 27*, 511–523.

Levinson, D. J. (1986). A conception of adult development. *American Psychologist, 41*, 3–13.

Lewis, C. B. (1990). *Aging: The health care challenge.* Philadelphia: F. A. Davis.

Lieberman, S. (1991). *Sports poll 1991: A national survey commissioned by Sports Illustrated.* New York: Lieberman Research.

Lindeman, L. (1991). *Beating time. Modern Maturity,* June–July, 27–35.

Loevinger, J. (1976). *Ego development: Conception and theory.* San Francisco: Jossey Bass.

Lomranz, J., Bergman, S., Eyal, N., & Shmotkin, D. (1988). Indoor and outdoor activities of aged women and men as related to depression and well being. *International Journal of Aging and Human Development, 26*, 303–314.

Longino, C. F. & Kart, C. S. (1982). Explicating activity theory: A formal replication. *Journal of Gerontology, 37*, 713–722.

Losier, G. F., Bourque, P. E., Vallerand, R. J. (1993) A motivational model of leisure participation in the elderly. *Journal of Psychology, 127*, 153–170.

MacKenzie, S. (1980). *Aging and old age.* Glenview, IL: Scott, Foresman and Co.

MacNeil, R., Teague, M., McGuire, F., & O'Leary, J. (1987). Aging and leisure. In L. B. Szwak (ed.), *A literature review: The President's Commission on Americans Outdoors.* Washington, DC: U.S. Government Printing Office, S103–SS111.

MacNeil, R. D. & Teague, M. L. (1992). *Leisure and aging: Vitality in later life* (2nd ed.) Dubuque, IA: Brown and Benchmark.

MacNeil, R. D. & Teague, M. L. (1987). *Leisure and aging: Vitality in later life.* Englewood Cliffs, NJ: Prentice-Hall.

Mannell, R. C. (1993). High-investment activity and life satisfaction among older adults: Committed, serious leisure, and flow. In J. R. Kelly (ed.), *Activity and aging: Staying involved in later life.* Newbury Park: Sage, 125–145.

Mannell, R. & Kleiber, D. (1997). *A social psychology of leisure.* State College, PA: Venture Publishing Inc.

Marshall, V. W. (1986). Dominant and emerging paradigms in the social psychology of aging. In V. W. Marshall (ed.), *Later life: The social psychology of aging.* Beverly Hills: Sage, 9–31.

Marshall, V.W. (1979). No Exit: A symbolic interactionist perspective on aging. *International Journal of Aging and Human Development, 80*, 1124-1144.

Marshall, V.W. (1995). Social models of aging. *Canadian Journal on Aging, 14*, 12-34.

Martin, S. & Smith, R. W. (1993) OBRA legislation and recreational activities: Enhancing personal control in nursing homes. *Activities, Adaptation & Aging, 17* (3), 1–13.

Mayo Clinic Health Letter (1998) Sexuality and aging: What it means to be sixty or seventy or eighty in the '90s. In H. Cox (ed.), *Aging,* (12th ed.) Guilford, CT: Dushkin/McGraw Hill.

McAndrew, F. T. (1993). *Environmental psychology.* Pacific Grove, CA: Brooks Cole.

McCall, G. J. & Simmons, J. L. (1966). *Identities and interactions.* New York: Free Press.

McCormick, B. (1993). Same place, different worlds: Leisure styles and community life of older residents of rural retirement and village communities. Doctoral Dissertation. Clemson University.

McDowell, C. F. (1978). *So you think you know how to leisure? . . . A guide to leisure well-being in your lifestyle.* Eugene, OR: Leisure Lifestyle Consultants.

McGuire, F. A. & Dottavio, F. D. (1986–87). Outdoor recreation participation across the lifespan: Abandonment, continuity or liberation? *International Journal of Aging and Human Development, 24,* 87-100.

McGuire, F. A., and Hawkins, M. O. (1999) Introduction to intergenerational programs. In M. O. Hawkins, F. A. McGuire, and K. E. Backman (eds.). *Preparing participants for intergenerational interaction: Training for success.* New York: Haworth Press.

McGuire, F. A., O'Leary, J., Alexander, P., & Dottavio, D. (1987). A comparison of outdoor recreation preferences and constraints of black and white elderly. *Activities, Adaptation & Aging, 9* (4), 95–104.

McLeish, J. (1976). *The Ulyssean adult: Creativity in middle and later years.* Toronto: McGraw-Hill Ryerson.

McPherson, B. D. (1991). Aging and leisure benefits: A life cycle perspective. In B. L. Driver, P. J. Brown, & G. L. Peterson (eds.), *Benefits of leisure.* State College, PA: Venture, 423–430.

Melamed, L. (1991). Leisure, what leisure? Questioning old theories. *World Leisure and Recreation, 33* (3), 34–36.

Miller, S. J. (1965). The social dilemma of the aging leisure participant. In A. M. Rose & W. A. Peterson (eds.), *Older people and their social world.* Philadelphia: Davis.

Millett, M. (1984). *Voices of experience: 1,500 retired people talk about retirement.* New York: TIAA–CREF.

Mobily, K. E., Lemke, J. H. and Gisin, G. J. (1991). The idea of leisure repertoire. *The Journal of Applied Gerontology,* 10, 208–223.

Mullins, L. & Mushel, M. (1992). The existence and emotional closeness of relationships with children, friends and spouses: The effect on loneliness among older persons. *Research on Aging, 14,* 448–470.

Myers, G. C. (1990). Demography of aging. In R. H. Binstock & L. K. George (eds.), *Handbook of aging and the social sciences* (3rd. ed.). San Diego: Academic Press, 1944.

National Association of Counties (undated a). *Aging in place: Options for home and community-based care.* Washington, DC: National Association of Counties.

National Association of Counties (undated b). *Is your community a good place to grow old: A community needs assessment.* Washington, DC: National Association of Counties.

National Institute of Mental Health (1994). Alzheimer's disease. Washington, DC: National Institutes of Health.

National Institute on Aging Age Page (1991). Dealing with diabetes. Washington DC: U.S. Department of Health and Human Services.

National Institute on Aging Age Page (1995a). Hearing and older people. Washington DC: U.S. Department of Health and Human Services.

National Institute on Aging Age Page (1995b). Don't take it easy exercise. Washington DC: U.S. Department of Health and Human Services.

National Institute on Aging Age Page (1995c). Aging and your eyes. Washington DC: U.S. Department of Health and Human Services.

National Institute on Aging Age Page (1995d). Sexuality in later life. Washington DC: U.S. Department of Health and Human Services.

National Institute on Aging Age Page (1996a) Urinary incontinence. Washington DC: U.S. Department of Health and Human Services.

National Institute on Aging Age Page (1996b). Arthritis advice. Washington DC: U.S. Department of Health and Human Services

National Institute on Aging Age Page (1996c). Osteoporosis: The silent bone thinner. Washington DC: U.S. Department of Health and Human Services.

National Institutes on Health (1997). Disability rates among older Americans decline dramatically. Washington, DC: National Institutes on Health.

National Mental Health Association (1996). Depression and later life. Alexandria, VA: National Mental Health Association. *www.nmha.org/infoctr/factsheets/22.cfm* (March 1999).

National Remotivation Therapy Organization (undated). Basic remotivation. Andover, MA: National Remotivation Therapy organization. *www.miseri.edu/conted/basic.htm* (March 1999).

Neugarten, B. L. (1964). *Personality in middle and later life.* New York: Atherton Press.

Neugarten, B. (1968). Adult personality: Toward a psychology of the life cycle. In B. Neugarten (ed.), *Middle age and aging: A reader in social psychology.* Chicago: University of Chicago Press.

Neugarten, B. L. (1977). Personality and aging. In J. E. Birren & K. W. Schaie (eds.), *Handbook of the psychology of aging.* New York: Van Nostrand Reinhold, 626–649.

Neugarten, B. L., Havighurst, R. J., & Tobin, S. S. (1961). The measurement of life satisfaction. *The Gerontologist, 16,* 134–143.

Neugarten, B. L., Havighurst, R. J., & Tobin, S. S. (1968). Personality and patterns of aging. In B. L. Neugarten (ed.), *Middle age and aging.* Chicago: University of Chicago, 77–102.

Neulinger, J. (1981). *To leisure: An introduction.* Boston: Allyn and Bacon.

Newman, S., Ward, C. R., Smith, T. B., Wilsson, J. O., McCrea, J. M., Calhoun, G., & Kingson, E. (1997). *Intergenerational programs: Past, present, and future.* Washington, DC: Taylor & Francis.

New York Hospital Cornell Medical Center (1996). Fact sheet: Dementia. White Plains, NY: New York Hospital—Cornell Medical Center. *noah.cuny.edu/illness/mentalhealth/cornell/conditions/dementia.html* (March, 1999).

O'Brien, M. E. (1989). *Anatomy of a nursing home: A new view of resident life.* Owings Mill, MD: National Health Publishing.

O'Neill, W. (1991). Women: The unleisured majority. *World Leisure and Recreation, 33* (3), 6–10.

Ostroff, J. (1989). An aging market. *American Demographics,* May, 26–28, 33, 58–59.

Paffenberg, R. S., Hyde, R. T., & Dow, A. (1991). Health benefits of physical activity. In B. L. Driver, P. J. Brown & G. L. Peterson (eds.), *Benefits of leisure.* State College, PA: Venture Publishing, 49–57.

Palmore, E. (1990). *Ageism: Negative and positive.* New York: Springer.

Parmelee, L. S. & Lawton, M. P. (1990). The design of special environments for the aged. In J. E. Birren & K. W. Schaie (eds.), *Handbook of the psychology of aging* (3rd ed.). San Diego: Academic Press, 465–488.

Pasuth, P. M. & Bengston, V. L. (1988). Sociological theories of aging: Current perspectives and future directions. In J. E. Birren & V. L. Bengston (eds.), *Emergent theories of aging.* New York: Springer, 333–355.

Patterson, I. (1996). Participation in leisure activities by older adults after a stressful life event: The loss of a spouse. *International Journal of Aging and Human Development, 42,* 123–142.

Patterson, I. & Carpenter, G. (1994). Participation in leisure activities after the death of a spouse. *Leisure Sciences, 16,* 105–117.

Pearlin, L. (1975) Sex roles and depression. In N. Patan & L. Gensburg (eds) *Life-span Development Psychology: Normative Life Crises.* New York: Academic Press.

Pearlin, L. I., Mullan, J. T., Semple, S., & Skaff, M. M. (1990). Caregiving and the stress process: An overview of concepts and their measures. *The Gerontologist, 30,* 583–594.

Pennsylvania Department on Aging (undated). *Caregivers: Practical health.*

Peterson, C. A. & Gunn, S. L. (1984). *Therapeutic recreation program design: Principles and procedures.* Englewood Cliffs, NJ: Prentice Hall.

Pfister, R. E. (1993). Ethnic identity: A new avenue for understanding leisure and recreation preferences. In A. Ewert, D. Chavez, & A. Magill (eds.), *Culture, conflict and the wildland-urban interface.* Boulder, CO: Westview Press, 53–65.

Prado, C. G. (1986). *Rethinking how we age: A new view of the aging mind.* Westport, CT: Greenwood Press.

Pynoos, J. & Golant, S. (1996). Housing and living arrangements for the elderly. In R. H. Binstock and L. K. George (eds.), *Handbook of aging and the social sciences.* San Diego: Academic Press, pp. 303–324.

Quinn, J. F. & Burkhauser, R. V. (1990). Work and retirement. In R. H. Binstock & L. K. George (eds.), *Handbook of aging and the social sciences.* San Diego: Academic Press.

Ragheb, M. G. & Griffith, C. A. (1982). The contribution of leisure participation and leisure satisfaction to the life satisfaction of older persons. *Journal of Leisure Research, 14,* 295–306.

Regnier, V. (1975). Neighborhood planning for the urban elderly. In D. Woodruff & J. E. Birren (eds.), *Aging: Scientific perspectives and social issues.* New York: D. Van Nostrand, 295–312.

Reker, G. T., & Wong, P.T. (1988). Aging as an individual process: Toward a theory of personal meaning. In J. E. Birren & V. L. Bengston (eds.), *Emergent theories of aging.* New York: Springer, 214–216.

Resnick, H. E., Fries, B. E., & Verbrugge, L.M. (1997). Windows to their world: The effect of sensory impairments on social engagement and activity time in nursing home residents. *Journal of Gerontology 52, 135-144.*

Riley, M. W. (1971). Social gerontology and the age stratification of society. *The Gerontologist, 11,* 19–87.

Riley, M. W. (1985). Age strata in social systems. In R. H. Binstock & E. Shanas (eds.), *Handbook of aging the social sciences* (2nd ed.). New York: Van Nostrand Reinhold, 369–411.

Robertson, C. & Welcher, D. (1978). Light shed on lives of visually impaired. *Perspectives on Aging, 7,* 17–21.

Robinson, J. (1989a). Time's up. *American Demographics,* July, 33–35.

Robinson, J. (1989b). Who's doing the housework? *American Demographics.* December, 24–28.

Robinson, J. (1991). Quitting time. *American Demographics,* May, 34–36.

Robinson, J. & Godbey, G. (1997). *Time for life: The surprising way Americans use their time.* University Park, PA: Penn State Press.

Rockstein, M. & Sussman, M. (1979). *Biology of aging.* Belmont, CA: Wadsworth.

Rodin, J. & Langer, E. J. (1976). Long-term effects of control-relevant intervention with the institutionalized ages. *Journal of Personality and Social Psychology, 35,* 897–902.

Rosenberg, J. H. (1993). As you age: 10 keys to a longer, healthier, more vital life. *Nestle Worldview, 5* (2), 2–3.

Rosow, J. (1975). *Socialization to old age.* Berkeley: University of California Press.

Rowe, J. W. & Kahn, R. L. (1998). *Successful aging.* New York: Random House.

Ruth, J. & Coleman, P. (1996) Personality and aging: Coping and management of the self in later life. In J. E. Birren, & K. W. Schaie (eds.), *Handbook of the psychology of aging,* (4th ed.) San Diego: Academic Press

Ryan, J. E. (1993). Building theory for gerontological nursing. In E. M Baines (ed.), *Perspectives on gerontological nursing.* Newbury Park, CA: Sage, 29–40.

Sabin, E. (1993). Social relationships and mortality among the elderly. *Journal of Applied Gerontology, 12* (1), 44–60.

Samdahl, D. (1987). A symbolic interactionist model of leisure: Theory and empirical support. *Leisure Sciences, 10,* 27–39.

Saul, S. (1993). Meaningful life activities for elderly residents of residential health care facilities. *Activities, Adaptation and Aging,* ??, 79–86.

Saxon, S. & Ettel, M. (1987). *Physical change and aging.* New York: The Theresias Press.

Scanland, S. G. & Emershaw, L. E. (1993). Reality orientation and validation therapy: Dementia, depression, and functional status. *Journal of Gerontological Nursing, 19* (6), 7–11.

Scannell, T., & Roberts, A. (1994). *Young and old serving together: Meeting community needs through intergenerational partnerships.* Washington, DC: Generations United.

Schaie (1990). Intellectual development in adulthood. In J. E. Birren & K. W. Schaie (eds.), *Handbook of the psychology of aging, 3rd Ed.* San Diego: Academic Press, 291–309.

Schaie, K. W. (1996). Intellectual development in adulthood. In J. E. Birren & K. W. Schaie (eds.). *Handbook of the psychology of aging, 4th Ed.* San Diego: Academic Press, 266-286.

Schaie, K. W. & Hertzog, C. C. (1986). Toward a comprehensive model of adult intellectual development: Contributions of the Seattle Longitudinal study. In R. J. Sternberg (ed.), *Advances in human intelligence* (Vol. 3). Hillsdale, NJ: Erlbaum.

Schneider, E. L. & Rowe, J. W. (1990). *Handbook of the biology of aging* (3rd ed.). San Diego: Academic Press.

Schonfield, D. (1982). Who is stereotyping whom and why? *The Gerontologist, 2,* 267–272.

Schooler, C. (1990). Psychosocial factors and effective cognitive functioning in adulthood. In J. E. Birren & K. W. Schaie (eds.). *Handbook of the psychology of aging.* San Diego: Academic, 347–358.

Schroots, J.J.F. (1995a). Gerodynamics: Toward a branching theory of aging. *Canadian Journal on Aging, 14* (1), 74-81.

Schroots, J.J.F. (1995b). Psychological models of aging. *Canadian Journal on Aging, 14,* 46-66

Schroots, J. J. F. (1996) Theoretical developments in the psychology of aging. *The Gerontologist, 36,* 742–748.

Schultz, R. & Ewen, R. (1993). *Adult development and aging myths and emerging realities.* New York: Macmillan.

Schwartz, A. N. (1975). Planning macro-environments for the aged. In D. Woodruff and J. E. Birren (eds.), *Aging: Scientific perspectives and social issues.* New York: D. Van Nostrand, 279–294.

Searle, M. S., Mahon, M. J., Iso-Ahola, S. E., Sdrolia, H. A., & van Dyck, J. (1995). Enhancing a sense of independence and psychological well-being among the elderly: A field experiment. *Journal of Leisure Research, 27,* 107–124.

Shaull, S. & Gramann, J. (1998). The effect of cultural assimilation on the importance of family-related and nature-related recreation among Hispanic Americans. *Journal of Leisure Research, 30 (1),* 47-63.

Shoemaker, S. (1989). Segmentation of the senior pleasure travel market. *Journal of Travel Research, 27,* 14–21.

Shore, H. (1976). Designing a training program for understanding sensory losses in aging. *The Gerontologist, 16,* 157–165.

Simoneau, G. G. & Leibowitz, H. W. (1996). Posture, gait, and falls. In J. E. Birren & K. W. Schaie (eds.), *Handbook of the psychology of aging.* San Diego: Academic Press.

Simonton, D. K. (1988). Age and outstanding achievement: What do we know after a century of research? *Psychological Bulletin, 104,* 251–267.

Simonton, D. K. (1990). Creativity and wisdom in aging. In J. E. Birren & K. W. Schaie (eds.), *Handbook of the psychology of aging.* San Diego: Academic Press, 320–329.

Small, G. W., LaRue, A., Komo, S., & Kaplan, A. (1997). Mnemonics usage and cognitive decline in age-associated memory impairment. *International Psychogeriatrics, 9*(1), 47–56.

Smyer, M. A., Zarit, S. H. & Qualls, S. H. (1990). Psychological intervention with the aging individual. In J. E. Birren & K. W. Schaie (eds.), *Handbook of the psychology of aging.* San Diego: Academic Press, 375–403.

Spacapan S., & Oskamp, S. (1989). Introduction to the social psychology of aging. In S. Spacapan & S. Oskamp (eds.), *The social psychology of aging.* Newbury Park, CA: Sage, 9–24.

Sperbeck, D. J. & Whitbourne, S. K. (1981). Dependency in the institutional setting: A behavioral training program. *The Gerontologist, 21,* 268–275.

Stamps, S. & Stamps, M. (1985). Race, class, and leisure activities of urban residents. *Journal of Leisure Research, 17,* 40–56.

Steinfeld, E. & Shea, S. M. (undated) Enabling home environments: Strategies for aging in place. Buffalo, NY: IDEA—Center for Inclusive Design & Environmental Access, SUNY Buffalo.

Stemberg, R. & Wagner R. (1986). *Practical intelligence.* Cambridge: Cambridge University Press.

Stodolska, M. & Jackson, E. (1998). Discrimation in leisure and work esperienced by a white ethnic minority group. *Journal of Leisure Research, 30(1)*, 23-46.

Streib, G. F. (1985). Social stratification and aging. In R. H. Binstock & E. Shanas (eds.), *Handbook of aging and the social sciences* (2nd ed.). New York: Van Nostrand Reinhold, 339–368.

Streib, G. F. (1993). The life course of activities and retirement communities. In J. R. Kelly (ed.), *Activity and aging: Staying involved in later life.* Newbury Park: Sage, 246–263.

Sturnbo, N. & Thompson, S. (1988). *Leisure education: A manual of activities and resources.* Peoria: Center for Independent Living and Easter Seals Center.

Taulbee, L. (1976). Reality orientation and the aged. In I. M. Burnside (ed.). *Nursing and the Aged.* New York: McGraw Hill.

Taylor, D. (1992). *Identity in ethnic leisure pursuits.* San Francisco: Meders Research University Press.

Taylor, R. & Chatters, L. (1986). Church based informal support among elderly blacks. *The Gerontologist, 26,* 637–642.

Teaff, J. (1991). Leisure and life satisfaction of older Catholic women religious. *World Leisure and Recreation, 33* (3), 27–29. 9

Teague, M. L. (1987). *Health promotion: Achieving high-level wellness in the later years.* Indianapolis: Benchmark Press.

Tedrick, T. (1982). Leisure competency: A goal for aging Americans in the 1980s. In N. Osgood (ed.), *Life after work: Retirement, leisure, recreation and the elderly.* New York: Praeger, 315–318.

Tedrick, T. (1989). Images of aging through leisure: From pluralistic ignorance to master status trait? *Journal of Leisurability, 16* (3), 15–19.

Tedrick, T. & Boyd, R. (1992). Leisure in the lives of older Black women. Leisure Research Symposium, National Recreation and Parks Association Annual Conference, Cincinnati, OH.

Tedrick, T. & Boyd, R. (1999, October). Older African American men and leisure. Proceedings of the Leisure Research Symposium, National Recreation and Park Association Congress, Nashville, TN.

Tedrick, R. & Green, E. R. (1995). Activity experiences and programming within long-term care facilities. State College, PA: Venture.

Tedrick, T. & MacNeil, R. (1991). Sociodemographics of older adults: Implications for leisure programming. *Activities, Adaptation & Aging, 15* (3), 73–91.

Texas Agricultural Extension Service (1995a). Fact sheet on aging: Changes in taste. College Station, TX: Texas Agricultural Extension Service, Texas A & M University.

Texas Agricultural Extension Service (1995b). Fact sheet on aging: Changes in hearing. College Station, TX: Texas Agricultural Extension Service, Texas A&M University.

Texas Agricultural Extension Service (1995c). Fact sheet on aging: Changes in vision. College Station, TX: Texas Agricultural Extension Service, Texas A&M University.

Timiras, P. S. & Hudson, D. B. (1993). Physiology of aging: Current and future. In B. Vellas, J. L. Albarede, & P. J. Garry (eds.), *Facts and research in gerontology.* New York: Springer Publishing, 31–39.

Tinsley, H. E. A. & Teaff, J. D. (1983). *The psychological benefits of leisure activities for the elderly: A manual and final report of an investigation.* Carbondale, IL: Southern Illinois University Department of Psychology.

Tinsley, H. E. A., Teaff, J. D., Colbs, S. L., & Kaufman, N. (1985). A system of classifying leisure activities in terms of the psychological benefits of participation reported by older persons. *Journal of Gerontology, 49,* 172–178.

Toseland, R. W., Diehl, M., Freeman, K., Manzanares, T., Naleppa, M., & McCallion, P. (1997) The impact of validation group therapy on nursing home residents with dementia. *Journal of Applied Gerontology, 16*(1), 31–50.

Troll, L. (1982). *Continuations: Adult development.* Philadelphia: W. B. Saunders.

United Media Enterprises (1983). *Where does time go?* New York: Newspaper Enterprise Association.

U.S. Census Bureau (1997). *Sixty-five plus in the United States.* Washington, DC: U.S. Census Bureau. *www.census.gov/socdemo/www/agebrief.html* (March, 1999).

U.S. Senate Special Committee on Aging (1987). *Developments in aging: Volume 3.* Washington, DC: U.S. Government Printing Office.

U.S. Senate Special Committee on Aging, American Association of Retired Persons, Federal Council on Aging, U.S. Administration on Aging (1991). *Aging America: Trends and predictions.* Washington, DC: U.S. Department of Health and Human Services.

Validation Training Institute (1997). What is validation? Cleveland, OH: The Validation Training Institute. *www.vfvalidation.org/whatis.html* (March 1999).

Vallerand, R., O'Connor, B., & Blais, M. (1989). Life satisfaction of elderly individuals in regular community housing, and high and low selfdetermination nursing homes. *International Journal of Aging and Human Development, 28,* 277–283.

Vierck, E. (1990). *Fact book on aging.* Santa Barbara: ABC-Clio.

Voelkl, J. (1986). Effects of institutionalization upon residents of extended care facilities. *Activities, Adaptation & Aging, 8* (3/4), 37–46.

Voelkl, J. E. (1993). Activity among older adults in institutional settings. In J. R. Kelly (ed), *Activity and aging: Staying involved in later life.* Newbury Park: Sage, 231–245.

Voelkl, J. E., Fries, B. T., & Galecki, A. T. (1995). Predictors of nursing home residents' participation in activity programs. *The Gerontologist, 35,* 44–51.

Wall, G. (1989). Perspectives on recreation and the environment. In E. L. Jackson & T. L. Burton (eds.), *Understanding leisure and recreation: Mapping the past, charting the future.* State College, PA: Venture, 453–480.

Ward, R. (1984). *The aging experience: An introduction to social gerontology.* New York: Harper and Row.

Washburne, R. (1978). Black underparticipation in wildland recreation: Alternative explanations. *Leisure Sciences, 1,* 175–189.

Weaverdyck, S. E. (1991). Developing an encouraging environment for residents with dementia. *Long-term Care, 1* (2), 19–20.

Weiner, M. B., Brok, A. J. & Snadowsky, A. M. (1987). *Working with the aged: Practical approaches in the institution and community* (2nd ed.). Norwalk: Appleton-Century-Crofts.

Wells, L. & Singer, C. (1988). Quality of life in institutions for the elderly: Maximizing well-being. *The Gerontologist, 28,* 266–269.

West, M. & Grafman, J. (1998). Cognitive neuroscience section: Memory exercises. Washington DC: National Institutes of Health. *www.intra.ninds.nih.gov/mnb/cns/memory.html* (March 1999).

West, R., Wincour, G., Ergis, A, & Saint-Cyr, J. (1998) The contribution of impaired working memory monitoring to performance of the self-ordered pointing task in normal aging and Parkinson's disease. *Neuropsychology, 12,* 546-554.

White J. (1975). The relative importance of education and income as predictors in outdoor recreation. *Journal of Leisure Research, 7,* 191–199.

Williams, M. L. (1972). One of the best retirement centers as seen by one of the residents. *The Gerontologist, 12,* 39–42.

Willis, S. L. (1987). Cognitive training and everyday performance. In K. W. Schaie (ed.), *Annual review of gerontology and geriatrics* (Vol. 7). New York: Springer, 159–188.

Willis, S. L. (1992). Cognition and everyday competence. In K. W. Schaie & M. P. Lawton (eds.), *Annual review of gerontology and geriatrics,* Vol. 11. New York: Springer, 80–109.

Willis, S. L. (1996). Everyday problem solving. In J. E. Birren & K. W. Schaie (eds.), *Handbook of the psychology of aging.* San Diego: Academic Press.

Willis, S. L. & Schaie, K. W. (1986). Training the elderly on the ability factors of spatial orientation and inductive reasoning. *Psychology and Aging, 1,* 239–247.

Wilson, B. & Moffat, N. (1984). Running a memory group. In B. A. Wilson & N. Moffat (eds.), *Clinical management of memory problems.* Rockville, MD: Aspen, 171–196.

Wold, G. (1993). *Basic geriatric nursing.* St. Louis: Mosby.

Women and Aging Newsletter (1996). Memory loss: Is it inevitable? Waltham, MA: The National Policy and Resource Center on Women and Aging, Brandeis University.

Woodard, M. D. (1988). Class, regionality, and leisure among urban black Americans. *Journal of Leisure Research, 20,* 87–105.

Zanetti, O., Frisoni, G. B., De Leo, D., Buono, M. D., Bianchetti, A., & Trabucchi, M. (1995). Reality orientation therapy in Alzheimer's disease: Useful or not? A controlled study. *Alzheimer's Disease and Related Disorders, 9,* 132–138.

Index